Practical Virtualization Solutions

NEGUS SOFTWARE SOLUTIONS SERIES

Practical Virtualization Solutions

Virtualization from the Trenches

Kenneth Hess and Amy Newman

An Imprint of Pearson Education

Upper Saddle River, NJ ■ Boston ■ Indianapolis ■ San Francisco

New York ■ Toronto ■ Montreal ■ London ■ Munich ■ Paris ■ Madrid

Cape Town ■ Sydney ■ Tokyo ■ Singapore ■ Mexico City

Many of the designations used by manufacturers and sellers to distinguish their products are claimed as trademarks. Where those designations appear in this book, and the publisher was aware of a trademark claim, the designations have been printed with initial capital letters or in all capitals.

The authors and publisher have taken care in the preparation of this book, but make no expressed or implied warranty of any kind and assume no responsibility for errors or omissions. No liability is assumed for incidental or consequential damages in connection with or arising out of the use of the information or programs contained herein.

The publisher offers excellent discounts on this book when ordered in quantity for bulk purchases or special sales, which may include electronic versions and/or custom covers and content particular to your business, training goals, marketing focus, and branding interests. For more information, please contact

U.S. Corporate and Government Sales
(800) 382-3419
corpsales@pearsontechgroup.com

For sales outside the United States, please contact

International Sales
international@pearson.com

Visit us on the Web: informit.com/ph

Library of Congress Cataloging-in-Publication Data:

Hess, Kenneth, 1961-

Practical virtualization solutions : virtualization from the trenches / Kenneth Hess, Amy Newman. — 1st ed.

p. cm.

ISBN 978-0-13-714297-2 (pbk. : alk. paper) 1. Virtual computer systems. 2. Virtual computer systems—Management. I. Newman, Amy, 1971- II. Title.

QA76.9.V5H47 2009

005.4'3—dc22

2009029966

ISBN-13: 978-0-137-14297-2
ISBN-10: 0-137-14297-8

Text printed in the United States on recycled paper at R.R. Donnelley in Crawfordsville, Indiana.
First printing October 2009

Editor-in-Chief
Mark Taub

Executive Editor
Debra Williams Cauley

Development Editor
Songlin Qiu

Managing Editor
Kristy Hart

Project Editor
Jovana San Nicolas-Shirley

Copy Editor
Barbara Hacha

Indexer
Cheryl Lenser

Proofreader
Leslie Joseph

Technical Reviewers
Jesse Keating
Joe Brockmeier

Publishing Coordinator
Kim Boedigheimer

Cover Designer
Alan Clements

Compositor
Jake McFarland

For Melissa, Connor, Walker, and Maria

and

For Eric, Jakob, and Rebecca

Contents

Foreword

A few years ago, the idea of running multiple operating systems concurrently on the same computer captured the imagination of the computing industry. Virtualization became the hot buzzword and projects were launched to fulfill the dream.

With virtualization, you don't need an extra computer every time you want to bring up a new server. Extra demand on your infrastructure can be handled by simply launching new guest operating systems. An entire guest can be dedicated to a single application, and that guest can be different than the host operating system. Using features like storage virtualization, guests can be moved around on-the-fly to make the best use of your computing hardware.

Now you have been asked to pick the right virtualization solution for your business. Ahead of you is the daunting task of sorting through competing technologies, finding what best suits your situation, and getting it all to work within your IT infrastructure. What you need is a guide to virtualization choices that clearly describes how to implement those choices. *Practical Virtualization Solutions* is that guide.

All sorts of questions might be in your mind right now. What new computer hardware demands must I meet? Should I use Windows or Linux as my host operating system? How do I secure and maintain my guest operating systems? Should I use local or networked storage? What are the differences between server and desktop virtualization?

Besides helping you answer those questions, *Practical Virtualization Solutions* also answers some questions you probably haven't even thought of yet. Where can I find prepackaged server appliances to quickly configure specialized Web, file, or CMS servers? How can I migrate an existing physical system to a virtual system?

To write this book, we were fortunate to enlist the excellent skills of Kenneth Hess and Amy Newman. Besides bringing years of expertise to this project, they have spent many hours providing step-by-step procedures for configuring virtual systems using many different technologies. I think you will find that their hard work will save you many hours of research as you go about setting up your own virtualization infrastructure.

—*Christopher Negus*
  Series Editor

Acknowledgments

My thanks go out to Jason Perlow for the use of his basement data center. He spent many long hours setting up infrastructure so that I would have access to VMware ESXi and Microsoft's Hyper-V. Without Jason's help, this book wouldn't exist.

Thank you to Amy Newman who graciously agreed to coauthor this book. She made it better with her fresh perspective and many years of experience in the virtualization space. She was a major force in making it a reality and taking it to completion.

To my mom, whose passing ten years ago makes me wish I hadn't been such a late bloomer.

I wish to thank my children for putting up with me during the stresses and strains of another book. I'm sorry for the endless hours and loss of quality time that accompanied this project. But now that it's over, Daddy's back.

Thanks to my wife for her patience when I didn't have any, her honesty when I needed it, and her prodding when I didn't want it. Hi, honey, I'm home—finally.

—*Kenneth Hess*

Many thanks to:

Kenneth Hess, for believing in me enough to take an unknown entity on board. It's been quite a ride, and I'm grateful for every bump in the road this opportunity has hit. In this case, what happened in Vegas certainly didn't stay there!

Dan Muse, who nudged me to step up on the soapbox five years ago and allowed me to stay there when I finally started enjoying it.

Wesley Baker, Ryan Makamson, Buddy Newton, Jameel Syeed, and the companies they represent, for agreeing to be part of the book and sharing with me their experiences with virtualization.

Cirba, Emulex, and VMware, for allowing us to use their figures to better illustrate our prose.

Michael Hall and Paul Shread, who allowed me to pick their brains about network and storage—both virtual and otherwise.

Richard Panchyk and Diane Merians, for being mentors and friends who were always there with sage advice when needed and an ear to lend at other times.

My dad, who talked telecom at the dinner table all those years and tried to spark my interest in routers and LANs. I was (half) listening back then, really.

My mom, who insisted I stick it out in the after-school computer science class, even though I was the only girl fighting for a seat in front of one of three Commodore PETs and claimed to have little interest in being there.

Jakob and Rebecca, it's been a long year. I love you both. I am grateful for your patience and impatience during this time. Looking forward to watching more soccer games, hosting more playdates, and more leisurely evenings and weekends together.

Eric, who still makes me laugh like no one else can and who almost always knows just what to say when everything seems wrong. Without your patience, support, understanding, and most of all confidence in me and my abilities, this undertaking would not have been possible.

—*Amy Newman*

There are also several people whom Kenneth and Amy would like to jointly thank:

Thank you Joe Brockmeier, Eli Dow, Jesse Keating, John Kennedy, Jeanna Matthews, and Jim Owens for your peer review of the manuscript, and Songlin Qiu, for making sure everything flowed properly and logically within the correct format. All of you challenged us, frustrated us, and at times even irritated us, but it was all for a good cause and in the end, we came away with a better book.

Thanks go out to Michael Hall for reading the manuscript in close to one swoop to ensure there were no inadvertent contradictions or inconsistencies.

Finally, our thanks go out to our editor, Debra Williams Cauley, for always being two steps ahead with what we needed, whether it was space, prodding, or encouragement, and keeping us moving forward all the while.

About the Authors

Kenneth Hess is the virtualization columnist at *Linux Magazine*. His column covers all aspects and types of virtualization from desktop to server to cloud. Kenneth has used just about every type of virtualization product available since 1999 and was a beta tester of the original VMware product line. He also writes the Linux blog on DaniWeb and the *Cover Your Assets* column on Internet.com's ServerWatch. You'll also find Kenneth on the air weekly at *The Frugal Tech Show's Frugal Friday*. His day job with HP involves virtualization and web hosting at an enterprise level.

Amy Newman has been following the virtualization space since 2001. She has been blogging about it since 2006 in her weekly column, *Virtually Speaking*. *Virtually Speaking* provides analysis of news and trends on everything virtual from hypervisors to hardware. The column appears weekly on Internet.com's Server-Watch. Amy has been managing editor of ServerWatch since 1999 and Enterprise IT Planet since 2009. Prior to that, she was a research editor at Gartner, where she edited and managed the workflow of four monthly research deliverables related to software infrastructure.

Preface

If you've picked up this book, chances are that you're thinking about virtualizing at least some part of your IT infrastructure. The odds are probably also good that you've been tasked with doing it in a way that will ultimately save your company money. Or maybe you're curious about this technology that has gotten so much press, and you would like to get your feet wet in a way that won't cost a fortune, either at home or in the office.

If any of these scenarios sounds at all familiar, *Practical Virtualization Solutions* has the answers you're looking for. We offer, first and foremost, a practical look at how to fit virtualization into your organization.

Reasons for virtualizing are as varied as the companies choosing them, and in Chapter 1, "To Virtualize or Not to Virtualize?" we look at the more popular reasons, offering explanations about each one. We provide a general explanation of virtualization and a look back at virtualization's roots. We also look at recommended virtualization workload candidates.

Chapter 2, "Comparing Virtualization Technologies," steps through the different kinds of virtualization and the environments that support them. We look at the guest OS or host OS virtualization and hypervisor-, emulation-, kernel-level-, and shared-kernel-based virtualization.

Then we're off to the heart of virtualization. Chapters 3 through 8 dive into six x86 virtualization environments, all of which are free of charge and each of which takes a different approach. We look closely at VMware Server, VMware ESXi, Citrix XenServer, Microsoft Virtual PC, Microsoft Hyper-V, and VirtualBox. For each environment we look at the client console, stepping through how to create a virtual machine (VM) setup and secure VM files and folders. We do not discuss in these chapters how to install an operating system on the VM. For that you will be referred to the Appendix, "Virtual Machine Installation," because it is consistent across environments.

In keeping with the "practical" nature of this book, most of these chapters conclude with a case study that demonstrates how the technology is being used in a production environment.

In Part II we look at ways to apply virtualization. First, in Chapter 9, "Server Virtualization in Action," we step through how to configure a server with virtualization, from preparing the VM to dedicating the server. We also look at virtual appliances, adjusting and tuning virtual servers, and securing and backing up virtual servers. The chapter also covers migration, both from VMs to new servers and from physical to virtual servers.

In Chapter 10, "Desktop Virtualization in Action," we look at terminal services, both smart and dumb, along with hosted desktops. We dissect two types of web-based solutions on the market: hosted web applications and hosted web-based pseudo-desktop systems. Finally, we explore the three methods of localized virtual desktops: live CD, live operating system distribution on a USB drive, and desktop virtualization software running a VM.

Chapter 11, "Network and Storage Virtualization in Action," concludes Part II with an explanation of virtual private networks, differentiating between a hardware VPN and a software VPN, and stepping through how to set up the latter for both server and client. We then look at VLANs, both standard and combination, and conclude with a discussion of SANs, VSANs, and NAS.

With Part III, our focus shifts somewhat from looking at virtualization itself to looking at virtual infrastructure—specifically, hardware's role in virtualization. Chapter 12, "Form-Factor Choices and Their Implications," discusses how hardware impacts performance and reliability in virtualized environments. We begin with an assessment of racks, towers, and blades, and then look at the options available for filling these footprints. The chapter concludes with a look at how to mitigate I/O and memory issues, two key pain points for virtualized environments.

In Chapter 13, "Choosing a Vendor," we apply the general principles discussed in Chapter 12 in the context of what the major OEMs—IBM, HP, Sun, and Dell—are offering. We also evaluate how compatible each vendor's hardware is with the various virtualization software options. The chapter concludes with a look at white box and cloud computing options.

With Chapter 14, "Beyond the Box," we delve into the virtual infrastructure. We return to network and storage virtualization, this time in the context of an ecosystem perspective, and discuss the various available options for pulling together a virtual infrastructure.

Part IV moves into the virtual infrastructure realm with a look at the deployment process. We begin with the ever-important planning phase in Chapter 15, "Laying the Foundation: The Planning Stage." We cover everything from selling senior management on virtualization, to choosing an autodiscovery tool, to testing.

In Chapter 16, "Deployment," we focus on the nitty-gritty that comes with the actual rollout and flipping the virtual switch. We look at how to choose which applications to virtualize, incorporating automation and autodiscovery, and securing VMs.

We conclude Part IV with a look at a fully virtualized infrastructure in Chapter 17, "Postproduction: Wrapping It Up." We discuss monitoring tools, which become a necessity to keep systems running efficiently; disaster recovery planning; and budgeting.

Part I

Virtualization Basics and Technology Choices

## CHAPTER 1

To Virtualize or Not to Virtualize?

That's the first question you'll have to answer for yourself before investing any significant amount of time or money in a virtualization project. Your first step into virtualization should be to try out some virtualization products for yourself: Demos and screencasts just aren't the same as experiencing it firsthand.

This chapter is for those who haven't quite decided to make the virtualization commitment yet. This chapter explores reasons to use virtualization products and reasons not to. After you have read this chapter, you can make a more informed decision about whether virtualization will work for you.

A VIRTUAL HISTORY

Virtualization, despite what many believe, did not begin in 1999 with the release of VMware's first product. It began about 40 years ago on the mainframe platform at IBM. At that time, virtual machines (VMs) were called pseudo machines. Originally, the mainframe used the control program to allocate resources to and isolate the various instances of these pseudo machines from one another.

The contemporary version of the control program is called a hypervisor, which is a VM monitor that's installed directly on what's known as bare metal. Bare metal is a new term for a computer, typically a server system, with no operating system installed on it. It is hardware only. The hypervisor is not directly accessible but employs what's known as a Domain0 VM that is an operating system that feels as if it's installed on the bare metal as the primary operating system. Through this primary VM the user interacts indirectly with the hypervisor.

Hypervisor technology is one of several types of VM host technology that will be discussed further in Chapter 9, "Server Virtualization in Action."

VIRTUALIZATION EXPLAINED

The "formal" definition of virtualization refers to physical abstraction of computing resources. In other words, the physical resources allocated to a VM are abstracted from their physical equivalents. Virtual disks, virtual network interface cards, virtual LANs, virtual switches, virtual CPUs, and virtual memory all map to physical resources on a physical computer system. The host computer "sees" its guest VMs as applications to which its resources are dedicated or shared.

There are many types of virtualization: application, platform, network, and storage. Typically, when someone mentions virtualization, that reference is to platform virtualization. Platform virtualization is the use of server hardware to host multiple VMs as guests. Each VM is a consistent virtual hardware environment onto which an operating system is installed. Each guest VM operates independently of all other guests.

A host computer is equipped with sufficient hardware resources to donate computing power and disk space to its guests. A typical host system consists of multiple multicore processors, several gigabytes (GB) of RAM, several terabytes (TB) of disk space, and network attached storage (NAS) or a storage area network (SAN).

VIRTUALIZATION WORKLOAD CANDIDATES

A common question among those considering virtualization is, "What can and cannot be virtualized?" Any underutilized hardware workloads can be successfully virtualized. Prime virtualization candidates are web servers, mail servers, other network servers (DNS, DHCP, NTP), application servers (WebSphere, Weblogic, Tomcat), and database servers. There's also no limitation or restriction based on which operating system you use. Windows systems are equally good candidates for virtualization as Linux, Solaris, and others.

Load-balanced services work well in virtualized environments because their workloads can be spread out among multiple server systems.

CONSOLIDATING WEB SERVICES WITH VMS

Web services are particularly well suited for consolidation into VMs. Services such as web databases, static websites, and dynamic sites, including those that use Java,

.NET, PHP, Python, and other dynamic languages, are easily migrated to virtual infrastructure.

Following are the top five reasons to consolidate web services:

- Mean time to restore is too long.
- Infrastructure is suffering from aging hardware.
- Infrastructure is out of capacity.
- Systems are underutilized.
- The economy of virtualization.

Mean Time to Restore

Mean time to restore (MTTR) is the average amount of time it takes to restore a service to customers after the service goes offline. Virtualization shortens this time by having snapshots or backups of entire VMs available for restoration of failed services. A direct file copy restoration is a far quicker method for restoring services than installing a new system and then fumbling through differential backups to bring a system up to date and back online.

Aging Infrastructure

Hardware life is short. Life expectancy for hardware infrastructure is about three to four years. The reason for the short life expectancy of hardware is that failure rates increase dramatically after four years. A good general rule on the true life expectancy of hardware is the length of the manufacturer's warranty on the product.

Virtualization is a clear winner in the aging infrastructure dilemma. Sure, your VM host system will get old, die, become obsolete, or go off lease, but your VMs never do any of those things. You can keep adding RAM, CPUs, disk space, virtual NICs, and other peripherals regardless of the physical hardware sitting under your VMs. You can even upgrade the OS after upgrading your virtual hardware to support it.

Infrastructure That Is Out of Capacity

A physical system has capacity limits that can't be changed. A single CPU system will always be a single CPU system. If your system has a maximum RAM capacity of 4GB, you can't add more. These limitations don't affect VMs. As long as your host has available capacity and your virtualization software supports it, you can add capacity to your VMs.

Underutilization

As noted earlier, underutilized systems are perfect for virtualization and consolidation—not because the VM will be any more utilized than the physical one, but you won't have the physical machine sucking power, requiring cooling, and taking up space.

Economy of Virtualization

In addition to being an economic solution, virtualization also provides an economy of scale. You can easily convert two or more physical servers, which were set up in a high availability (HA) configuration, to virtual ones. You can also add to that HA solution with virtual systems while keeping your physical ones intact. No added hardware expense is associated with the added HA capacity.

PRACTICAL ASPECTS OF VIRTUALIZATION

There's a lot of buzz surrounding virtualization and you might be asking yourself, "Why do I need to virtualize anything?" This is a legitimate question and the answer is easy. First, it is a money-saving technology. By using virtualized computing resources, you'll save significant money on hardware, power, cooling, and possibly IT staff.

Beyond the excitement and the obvious *cool* factor of virtualization, practical aspects exist, too. The following list summarizes those aspects.

- Minimize hardware costs
- Provide disaster recovery
- Consolidate idle workloads
- Balance loads
- Test software
- Centralize server management
- Conserve power
- Deploy servers faster

Minimizing Hardware Costs

It's easy to see that virtualization eases the burden of purchasing more hardware each time a new system is put in place. The question is, how cost-effective is it to do so? Consider the following scenario:

The server is a typical system used for File/Print services, mail, DNS, and web serving—a dual-core CPU, 2GB RAM, 80GB disk, rack-mountable system. It is priced starting at about $2,000 USD, for a standard system. If you need RAID configuration plus drives, you can expect to add another $300–$500 USD. In the end, this "basic" system costs between $2,000 and $2,500 USD.

NOTE

These calculations do not include the operating system and other software because any costs relating to software will be the same whether the machines are physical or virtual.

Our enterprise-class server system is a rack-mountable, 2x quad-core CPU, 32GB RAM, three 400GB disk drives in a RAID 5 configuration. This system cost is approximately $18,000. This does not factor any NICs into the equation, but be aware that most standard systems ship with (or should ship with) two NICs. Typically, one is configured for the LAN and the other for backups. The Enterprise server should be configured with one for its own LAN connection, one for backups, and at least four others for VM use. Our system ships with four NICs, and an additional four would add about $400 more to the price tag. The additional cost is relatively insignificant compared to the total price of the system at about $100 per NIC.

Table 1-1 offers a simple analysis and cost breakdown using system cost, rack units used, power consumption, and number of network connections.

TABLE 1-1 Physical Versus Virtual Machine Cost Comparison

SPECIFICATION	PHYSICAL ENTERPRISE	PHYSICAL STANDARD	VIRTUAL
Cost	$18,000	$2,000-$2,500	$0
Rack Units	4U	1U	0
Power (Watts)	1570	670	0
Network Connections	2*	2	0**

*Minimum for any single server.

**Using shared network connections on the host machine.

Now look at the same data (Table 1-2) but with eight servers (eight physical standard versus eight virtual).

TABLE 1-2   Physical Versus Virtual Machine Cost Comparison

SPECIFICATION	PHYSICAL ENTERPRISE	PHYSICAL STANDARD	VIRTUAL
Cost	$18,000	$16,000-$20,000	$0
Rack Units	4U	8U	0
Power (Watts)	1570	5360	0
Network Connections	2 + 8*	16	8**

*Two for the host server and one for each virtual.

**The same physical eight on the host server.

These two tables clearly illustrate how virtualization pays off in many ways—not just financially. The lower power requirement is perhaps the most significant savings, followed closely by the number of used network connections, and finally by rack space units.

The tables might at first appear misleading, because the value shown for power consumption for VMs is $0. It is set at zero because a VM has no power supply from which to directly draw power. However, as VMs are powered on, they raise the power consumption on the VM host. Power consumption by individual VMs is difficult, if not impossible, to isolate from the VM host's overall power consumption.

To further lower network connection cost, you can configure your VMs to share network connections. Shared connectivity works quite well in situations where network traffic is relatively low for individual servers. If you find network utilization for a particular interface is edging toward the 80% level, you should split a VM off to its own network interface.

Although breaking down cost to a per-VM basis is close to impossible, it is possible to parse out a rough estimate. Continuing with the current example, consider how many VMs you can run simultaneously on this enterprise server. Realistically, with 32GB of RAM total, 1GB of which is reserved for the host system, 31GB remains to allocate to VMs. Each individual VM may have from 64MB up to 4GB of RAM. You have a wide range of possibilities. If you take our standard server number of 2GB and allocate that amount for each VM, you can theoretically have 15 VMs running. Divide the total cost of the server by 15, and there is a rough number to attribute to each VM.

Note, however, that 15 is probably not a practical number unless there is very little disk I/O for more than just one or two of the VMs. Disk I/O significantly degrades performance for all of the VMs unless paravirtualization is employed.

Providing Disaster Recovery

Virtualization provides the least expensive and shortest MTTR (mean time to recovery) that we can think of. An old saying in the disaster recovery business goes something like, "You can have any two of the following for your disaster recovery solution: Fast, cheap, reliable." With virtualization, you can dash this old adage against the rocks.

Recovery is as fast as starting up the VM. You may have to restore some data from backup, but in the meantime you have a functional server that didn't require downtime because of hardware failure or a reinstall of any software.

You saw in the previous section that using VMs could be very inexpensive. The software cost is the same for a physical or VM. Moreover, the hardware already exists and is waiting to be utilized.

VMs themselves are very reliable because they have no physical hardware that is susceptible to failure. Each VM has its own set of adapters, RAM, disk space, and peripherals that map to their physical counterparts. You'll never replace a motherboard, NIC, or CD drive in a VM, and the integrated video card can't go bad. A backup of a VM will always be a stable and reliable recovery point for your hardware.

Taking disaster recovery to a new level are products like PlateSpin, Xen, and VMware Converter, which grab copies of physical machines and convert them to virtual ones. In the case of PlateSpin and VMware Converter, this conversion takes place without rebooting the physical machine before or after conversion. The VMware Converter is simple, elegant, and often used as a regular P2V backup method. Should your physical machine fail in some way, you would have to boot up only the VM in its place. Fast, cheap, and reliable—you really *can* have all three.

Consolidating Idle Workloads

One of the primary reasons most CIOs and IT professionals consider virtualization is to consolidate idle workloads. Server consolidation either takes the form of reducing the number of physical systems by combining workloads onto newer and more reliable hardware or by using virtualization software to create VMs to handle those workloads. The effect is essentially the same: to use hardware more efficiently, decrease power usage, and increase manageability of services. Consolidation may also have the effect of lowering vendor support costs by having fewer physical machines to support.

Consolidation efforts may cause in-house support staff reductions or reallocations to different tasks. New systems created via VM templates, provisioned with a few mouse clicks and keystrokes, and fired up no longer require extra staff to perform those physical functions. There is no need to order, deliver, rack, stack, and provision a piece of hardware or to calculate any new power or cooling requirements.

You know that it's possible to consolidate idle workloads, and you know that it can reduce costs associated with support contracts, power, cooling, and possibly even labor, but how do you know that a system is eligible for consolidation? What constitutes an idle system?

There can be many answers to this question, depending largely on whom you ask. For projects that I have been directly or indirectly involved with, I generally look for systems with an average utilization of under 50%. Systems that are under 50% utilized come under significant scrutiny for redeployment, consolidation, repurposing, or decommissioning. They also make prime candidates for virtualization.

Balancing Loads

VMs set up in load-balanced configurations is an effective and inexpensive method of spreading network traffic among multiple systems. Network traffic is easily dispersed to multiple systems, virtual or physical, using a network load-balancer appliance. These appliances have special software that allows you to configure a single TCP/IP port's traffic to multiple systems.

For example, suppose you want to virtualize your web services, removing reliance on physical systems. Currently, all your web traffic (port 80) is directed to a single dot com address that is served by three physical systems, as shown in Figure 1-1.

Figure 1-2 shows the same scenario but using VMs instead of physical ones. Notice that the number of physical servers hasn't changed, because balancing loads in this fashion requires some degree of separation. All three VMs *can* exist on a single physical system because each VM has its own IP address. Each VM can also have its own separate NIC mapped to its virtual NIC.

The disadvantage to the single host scenario is that because your web service is load balanced, there must be a reason—lots of web traffic and a single host's performance may suffer. The best way to mitigate performance issues related to the disk I/O on a shared host is to use network-attached storage that all three VMs connect to for content. Utilizing a single network-attached source (SAN or NAS) is a very common solution even when using physical machines.

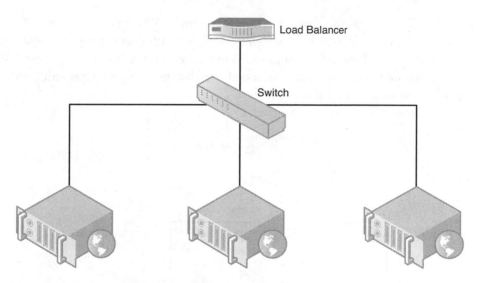

FIGURE 1-1   Standard load-balanced scenario with three web servers.

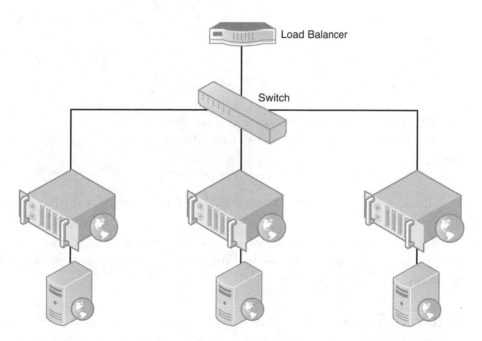

FIGURE 1-2   Load-balanced scenario with three virtual web servers.

In Figure 1-3, the scenario shows a single VM host with three VMs and network-attached storage from which to serve content. This is an example of a poorly planned load-balanced environment. Why? After all, the three web server VMs are load balanced. They are load balanced, but not in a way that provides maximum throughput or safety for the VMs.

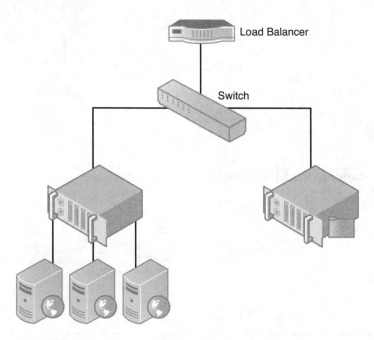

Load Balancer

Switch

FIGURE 1-3 Incorrectly load-balanced systems scenario with three virtual web servers and shared storage.

Figure 1-4 shows a correctly load-balanced web service with shared network attached storage.

Realize that this scenario shows a single VM guest per VM host as an example only. In an actual data center, each VM host would have several guest VMs performing various functions.

Software Tests

The use of VMs for software testing is one of the early applications of x86 virtualization. A VM is created, started, patched, given an IP address and a name, and then a backup of this pristine VM is made. The working copy is used to install, modify, and uninstall software packages.

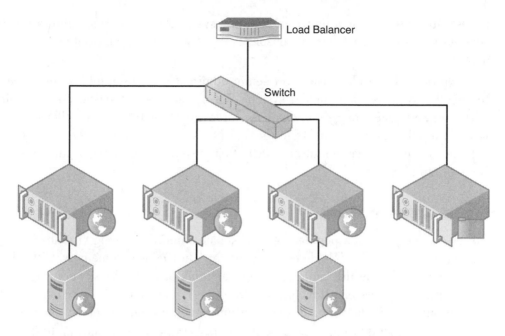

FIGURE 1-4   Correctly load-balanced systems scenario with three virtual web servers and shared storage.

Using a VM in this way gives you the opportunity to troubleshoot any conflicts or potential problems before deploying software to server or desktop systems. Should problems arise out of a conflict or poorly constructed application that result in crashes, reboots, blue screens, core dumps, or other faults, you can continue to troubleshoot or remove the crashed VM, make a working copy of your pristine image, and begin anew. This type of software testing gives you the ability to rigorously test and retest applications without reinstalling the operating system, base applications, and patches each time the system crashes.

After you have a working system, move the working VM into production by copying the VM image to a production VM host system. Virtualization makes testing, problem resolution, and deployment a streamlined process.

Centralized Server Management

All the major virtualization products have a console or centralized viewer to view and manage VMs from a single interface. This centralized management interface makes virtualization a palatable solution to server sprawl, KVM (keyboard, video, and mouse) interfaces, and managing various operating system types.

A management console gives system administrators a single, operating–system-independent interface to manage any number of VMs; no special methods of access are required for interaction with any system. This interface allows you to interact with the system's actual console as if you were sitting in front of a physical system.

Centralized consoles also allow senior administrators to grant console access to specific systems, or groups of systems, on a case-by-case basis. For example, you can grant access to a set of database servers to the DBA group. When a member of the DBA group connects to the VM host server, he sees only his group of servers to which he has permission. All other systems, regardless of function, are invisible to him.

Power Conservation

Power consumption is a popular topic of debate when discussing virtualization or blade servers, or both. VMs do consume power. They consume memory, CPU, disk space, network bandwidth, and power. You can think of a VM like any other application that runs on a system. If it consumes resources, it consumes a piece of all available resources. An idle server doesn't consume much power, but a busy one does.

As shown in Table 1-3, even a small number of physical systems multiply consumption far beyond that of a single large system. Although those numbers are for maximum output, it gives us a concrete number with which to operate.

TABLE 1-3 Physical Machine Power Consumption

Server Type	Power Output (Max)
Enterprise	1570
Standard	670

The rated output for five standard servers is 3,350 watts (max), which is more than twice the amount of the single Enterprise server power rating. You can see from this simple table that power consumption decreases dramatically through virtualization.

Closely tied with power consumption is cooling and air circulation. Virtualization reduces the number of power supplies, CPUs, and disk drives—all of which generate and give off a significant amount of heat. By lowering the number of heat-producing pieces of hardware, you also decrease amount of power needed to cool a server room effectively.

Faster Server Deployment

In a recent consulting job, our task was to create four new Microsoft SQL Servers using Microsoft Windows Server 2003 (32 bit). With few differences among the VMs, we cloned the original VM into the four that we needed. The original VM took about 3 hours to install, update, reboot, update again, name, and test. The four clones took 30 minutes or so to copy to new VMs. Each VM had to be started individually to rename, create a new SID, and reboot. Two of the VMs required additional hard disk space, which took an extra 15 minutes each. Within 6 hours of arriving on site, our client had four new SQL Server systems that were production ready for that evening's testing and deployment.

This process was so fast because there was no need for inventory check-in, racking, cabling, plugging into power, or having to worry about cooling capacity for four new systems. We also have the original VM in case something goes wrong with any of the other VMs.

This was an exceptional project, but it illustrates how quickly you can set up new systems and provide services to users, developers, or other administrators.

When you use VM templates, system creation is even more streamlined. At the same client site, we had to set up a new server for some application development testing. We used a template that we had set up a few days earlier. When we began installing the new system via the template, we thought the system had hung and we would have to start again from scratch. We waited for the next screen in the creation wizard when we saw our new system booting up for the first time. We created three more systems using our template before we realized how our system could have been created so quickly with hardly any interaction from us.

What we didn't realize was that the Debian Linux VM template we installed was a complete preconfigured operating system installation. Using a VM as the source for a template gives you a ready-made, and quick to install, operating system built to your exact specifications. Templating your operating systems is a great way to extend and streamline your server provisioning.

Service Commoditization

When you deploy a new service on your network or on the Internet, you may have neither the budget nor the desire to spend a lot of money on a solution—especially if that service is something like DNS, NTP, LDAP, FTP, or HTTP. Database services are also becoming victims of commoditization. The introduction of Linux and FreeBSD has commoditized these and other services. Virtualization has further commoditized services for companies on a tight budget because now you don't have to use a physical machine to provide the service.

Physical hardware, operating system costs, licensing fees, the costs of a never-ending hardware and software upgrade cycle, and ongoing support has led companies to seek out ways to control their IT budgets.

SUMMARY

The focus of this chapter is figuring out whether virtualization is right for you, as well as educating you on some basic terminologies and concepts. You can save significant money by going virtual in your data center or server room. The other benefits to virtualization are more than just icing on the cake—they are the reality facing all who dare enter the realm of server support. Power and cooling are going to increase in importance in the future because of rising costs, shrinking space, and the perennial requirement to do more with and for less.

You'll find that virtualization is a feasible alternative to traditional hardware, and with the proliferation of Linux, you might find yourself spending no money for hardware or software. Just think of how much money that will free up as the company profits. Virtualization is the way of the future, and those who embrace it early will be ahead of the pack.

The next chapter, "Comparing Virtualization Technologies," is an overview of the different types of virtualization, their application to specific problems, product examples, and the vendors who provide them.

## CHAPTER 2

Comparing Virtualization Technologies

With this chapter, we begin our exploration of several popular virtualization strategies and explain how each works. The aim is to bring you the operational information you need to make informed choices for your strategy. Each vendor's software has its own interface (console), its own methods of building, importing, and altering virtual machines (VM), and its own idiosyncrasies, tweaks, and tools.

This chapter gives you a vendor-neutral but technical overview of the types of virtualization available. We approach the various types of virtualization from an application and performance perspective—in other words, a practical look at each technology and its implication for you. Each section also includes at least two representative examples of that technology.

GUEST OS/HOST OS

Virtualization aficionados perhaps know Guest OS/Host OS as *classic* or hosted virtualization. This type of virtualization relies on an existing operating system (the host operating system), a third-party virtualization software solution, and creation of various guest operating systems. Each guest runs on the host using shared resources donated to it by the host.

Guests usually consist of one or more virtual disk files and a VM definition file. VMs are centrally managed by a host application that sees and manages each VM as a separate application.

Guest systems are fully virtualized in this scenario and have no knowledge of their virtual status. Guests assume they are standalone systems with their own hardware. They are also not aware of other guests on the system unless it's via another guest's network services.

The greatest advantage of this kind of virtualization is that there are a limited number of devices and drivers to contend with. Each VM (guest) possesses a consistent set of hardware. The major disadvantage is that disk I/O suffers greatly in this particular technology. Nondisk operation speed, however, is near native. Therefore, we tell those who use hosted virtualization to interact with their VMs over the network using Windows Terminal Services (RDP) for Windows VMs or SSH for UNIX and Linux systems.

VMware Server

VMware Server is used throughout this book to illustrate virtualization techniques and technologies. It is a free offering from VMware and is considered an introductory package for use in small environments, testing, or for individuals. It has limited usefulness in large environments because of its memory limitations for VMs and sluggish disk performance. VMware Server supports 64-bit machines as hosts and guests.

Sun xVM (VirtualBox)

VirtualBox, which is now Sun xVM VirtualBox, is one of my favorite virtualization packages. Like VMware Server, it is free and cross-platform, but unlike VMware Server, it is open source. With adjustable video memory, remote device connectivity, RDP connectivity, and snappy performance, it may well be the best hosted virtualization package in your arsenal.

VirtualBox is best suited for small networks and individuals for the same reasons as VMware Server.

HYPERVISOR

A hypervisor is a bare metal approach to virtualization. Bare metal refers to the server system hardware without any OS or other software installed on it. The best way to describe hypervisor technology is to draw a comparison between it and hosted virtualization. At first glance, the hypervisor seems similar to hosted virtualization, but it is significantly different.

A hypervisor is virtualization software that runs an operating system. Conversely, hosted virtualization utilizes an operating system and runs virtualization software as an application. The hypervisor software is installed to the bare metal; then the operating system is installed, which is itself, a paravirtualized VM. The host operating system, if you can call it that, is designated as VM zero.

A new product, VMware ESXi, implements a bare metal hypervisor without a traditional operating system interface. It installs directly to the hardware in an almost impossibly small 32MB footprint. ESXi must be installed onto hardware that is virtualization optimized. VM management is performed via Direct Console User Interface (DCUI), which is the low-level configuration and management interface performed at the physical console of the server system. The VMkernel allows for remote management via a set of APIs and agents.

Citrix Xen

Xen versions 3.0 and earlier weren't particularly interesting to me because they were somewhat difficult to use and didn't seem to perform all that well for my specific applications. Xen 4.x products, however, have converted me heart and soul. The graphical interface is intuitive, fast, and extremely well thought out. The template engine in the new product is a pleasure to use, and provisioning a new VM with it is fast, fast, fast. If you have a need for high-end virtualization, you must check it out.

VMware ESX/VMware ESXi

Enterprise virtualization at its finest is brought to you by the people who breathed life into PC-based virtualization. ESX is a mature product that is rivaled only by Xen at this level of virtualization. Both products require 64-bit architecture, but ESXi has very special hardware requirements beyond those of ESX. ESXi is now a free product.

Microsoft Hyper-V

Microsoft steps up to the plate with its Windows 2008 Server family and Hyper-V virtualization solution where Citrix and VMware fall short: a Windows-based Enterprise virtualization product. Both Citrix Xen and VMware are Linux-based, which means that if you aren't familiar with Linux or UNIX commands, you may be better off using the Microsoft product.

This product, when more mature, promises to be a formidable challenge to VMware's and Xen's dominance in the Enterprise virtualization world

EMULATION

Emulation refers to the capability to mimic a particular type of hardware for an operating system regardless of the underlying host operating system. For example, using an emulation virtualization solution, you can install a Sparc version of the Solaris operating system on a non-Sparc host computer. The emulation software runs as an application on the host system, but emulates an entire computer of another platform. The guest operating system has no awareness of its status as a guest operating system or that it is running in a foreign environment.

In some cases, hardware emulation can be painfully slow, but newer technology, updated emulation software and drivers, and faster 64-bit host processors make emulation a viable virtualization option—especially for those who need to develop drivers or technologies for other platforms without a large investment in support staff or hardware for them.

The best examples of hardware emulation software are Bochs (http://bochs. sourceforge.net) and QEMU (http://bellard.org/qemu).

Bochs

Bochs is a free, open source, Intel architecture x86 (32-bit) emulator that runs on UNIX and Linux, Windows, and Mac OS X, but only supports x86-based operating systems. Bochs is a very sophisticated piece of software and supports a wide range of hardware for emulating all x86 processors and x86_64 processor architecture. It also supports multiple processors but doesn't take full advantage of SMP at this time.

QEMU

QEMU is another free, open source emulation program that runs on a limited number of host architectures (x86, x86_64, and PowerPC) but offers emulation for x86, x86_64, ARM, Sparc, PowerPC, MIPS, and m68k guest operating systems.

Microsoft Virtual PC and Virtual Server

Virtual PC is a free virtualization software package from Microsoft. Virtual PC uses emulation to provide its VM environment. These are good solutions for hosting a few VMs on a Windows XP Workstation or Windows 2003 Server. It isn't a large environment solution by any stretch of the imagination, but it can get some VMs up and running cheaply and in very short order.

VM performance on these products is surprisingly good for Windows VMs. It is difficult, if not impossible, to tell that you are using a VM when connecting over the network. Console performance tends to be a little sluggish at times—so whenever possible, minimize the console and use RDP to connect to your virtualized Windows systems.

KERNEL-LEVEL

Kernel-level virtualization is kind of an oddball in the virtualization world in that each VM uses its own unique kernel to boot the guest VM (called a root file system) regardless of the host's running kernel.

KVM

Linux KVM (Kernel Virtual Machine) is a modified QEMU, but unlike QEMU, KVM uses virtualization processor extensions (Intel-VT and AMD-V). KVM supports a large number of x86 and x86_64 architecture guest operating systems, including Windows, Linux, and FreeBSD. It uses the Linux kernel as a hypervisor and runs as a kernel loadable module.

User-Mode Linux

User-mode Linux (UML) uses an executable kernel and a root file system to create a VM. To create a VM, you need a user-space executable kernel (guest kernel) and a UML-created root file system. These two components together make up a UML VM. The command-line terminal session you use to connect to the remote host system becomes your VM console. UML is included with all 2.6.x kernels.

SHARED KERNEL

Shared kernel virtualization, also called operating system virtualization or system level virtualization, takes advantage of the unique ability of UNIX and Linux to share their kernels with other processes on the system. This shared kernel virtualization is achieved by using a feature called change root (chroot). The chroot feature changes the root file system of a process to isolate it in such a way as to provide some security. It (chroot) is often called a chroot jail or container-based virtualization. A chrooted program, set of programs, or entire system in the case of shared kernel virtualization is protected by setting up the chrooted system to *believe* that it is a standalone machine with its own root file system.

The chroot mechanism has been enhanced to mimic an entire file system so that an entire system can be chrooted, hence creating a VM. The technical advantages and disadvantages of shared kernel virtualization are listed next:

- Advantages
  Enhanced Security and Isolation
  Native Performance

Higher Density of Virtualized Systems
- Disadvantages
Host Kernel and Guest Compatibility

The chroot system offers much in the way of enhanced security features and isolation; however, the greatest advantages of shared kernel virtualization are not in its security, although that's certainly important to consider, but in its performance. With this kind of virtualization, you'll get native performance for each individual system. Not only does each system perform at native speeds, but you can also have more than the standard number of VMs on a host system. By standard number, we mean the number that you could logically have on a host system if you used memory as the limiting factor—leaving 1GB for the host and taking the rest of the RAM for VMs.

The limit of the number of chrooted systems you can have on a host system more closely resembles a standalone system supporting multiple applications. If you think of each chroot system as an application instead of a VM, you'll more accurately allocate resources and enjoy performance that surpasses many other types of virtualization.

The disadvantage of shared kernel virtualization is a big one: All VMs have to be compatible with your running kernel. In other words, you can't run Windows operating systems, Solaris, Mac OS X, or any other operating system that couldn't run your system's kernel on its own. Major web hosting providers have run this scenario for years so that customers get their own virtual server for their hosting needs. They don't know that the system is virtual, nor can they contact the host system through their VM.

Solaris Containers (Zones)

Solaris 10 comes with built-in virtualization. The Solaris 10 operating system, itself, is known as the Global Zone. Solaris Zones are actually BSD jails, each with its own virtual root that mimics a complete operating system and file system. When you create a new zone, a full file system is copied to the new zone directory. Each zone sees only its own processes and file systems. The zone believes that it is a full, independent operating system; only the Global Zone has any knowledge of virtualization.

Each zone essentially creates a clean sandbox in which you may install applications, provide services, or test patches. Solaris zones are a scalable, enterprise-level virtualization solution providing ease of use and native performance.

OpenVZ

We use the OpenVZ kernel on my personal Linux server system. The OpenVZ kernel is optimized for virtualization and proves to be extremely efficient at handling VM performance for other virtualization products as well.

On my personal Linux server system, we run VMware Server, Sun's xVM, and QEMU. Before we installed the OpenVZ kernel, we had many CPU-related performance problems with some of my VMs. OpenVZ is similar to Solaris Zones except that you can run different Linux distributions under the same kernel. Various distribution templates are available on the OpenVZ website at www.openvz.org.

In the Virtual Trenches

As someone who works with virtualization software on a daily basis, we can give you some pointers, opinions, and suggestions for your environment. These are from my experiences; they may be biased, and, as always, your mileage may vary.

For true Enterprise-ready virtualization, you can't beat Xen or VMware ESX. They are robust, easy to use, well supported, well documented, and ready to go to work for you. Hypervisor technology is absolutely the right decision if you need to virtualize multiple operating systems on one host system. They are both costly solutions but well worth the price you pay for the performance you receive. You should use this technology in situations where disk I/O is of major concern.

As to which one of the hypervisor technologies we prefer, we're afraid that we can't answer that for you. Either one you choose will serve you well.

Solaris Zones (containers), and any jail-type virtualization, works extremely well for UNIX host systems where you want a consistent and secure environment with native performance. Kernel-level virtualization is extremely well suited for isolating applications from each other and the global zone (host operating system). This type of virtualization is an excellent choice for anyone who wants to get acquainted with virtualization for no money, little hassle, and ease of use. We highly recommend this virtualization method for your Solaris 10 systems.

Microsoft Virtual PC and VMware Server are great choices for testing new applications, services, patches, service packs, and much more. We use Virtual PC and VMware Server on a daily basis and can't live without them. We wouldn't recommend either for heavy production or Enterprise use, but for smaller environments, desktops, or IT laboratories, you can't go wrong with these. They're free, easy to use, durable, and can host a wide range of guest operating systems. In this same arena, Sun's xVM is also very good.

VMware Server and Sun xVM are both available on multiple platforms, whereas Virtual PC is available only for Windows.

We deliberately left out several other virtualization products from this dialog. Either we've had less experience with them or less good experience with them than the others mentioned previously, and we don't want to keep you from investigating them on your own. We are not diminishing their value or importance for viable virtualization solutions, but we just don't feel qualified to speak for or against them in this context.

Summary

This chapter was an overview of virtualization technology from a vendor-neutral perspective. There is always the question of which virtualization software is best. There is no single correct answer to this question unless it is either emotionally based or prejudicial in some way.

All virtualization software does the same thing: virtualize physical machines and the services that they provide. You'll have to decide what you need from virtualization and then choose the best technology that fits that need—and worry about vendor specifics later. You may also use more than one virtualization solution to solve the various needs within your network.

If you're going to invest thousands, perhaps hundreds of thousands, in virtualization, you need to experience the software for yourself. Vendors know this and are willing to work with you. Many offer full versions for a trial period. If a trial version won't work for you, get in touch with the vendor and get the actual licensed software for evaluation.

## CHAPTER 3

VMware Server

When VMware first arrived on the scene in 1998, it had only one product: VMware, which enabled desktop computers to run more than one operating system at a time. At the time this was considered revolutionary. Sure, mainframes had been able to do this for decades, but now it was an option for organizations with a shoestring hardware budget. A few years later, VMware shifted its focus to the server with the release of VMware GSX and VMware ESX, and that was when things began to really take off. Since then, VMware has created myriad products for all levels of virtualization experimentation and implementation as well as the infrastructure and management tools around them. As the competition has heated up, it has become increasingly clear that this is where the real battle is being fought; in response, VMware has made VMware Server and VMware ESXi, two of its primary hypervisor offerings, available free of charge. The third, VMware ESX, is sold as part of VMware Infrastructure. This chapter looks at VMware Server, which is positioned as an introductory product for those who are new to virtualization and wanting to get their feet wet. The plan is for users to outgrow VMware Server and graduate to the larger commercial versions of their software, either ESXi (which is the subject of Chapter 4, "VMware ESXi") and VMware ESX, which at one point was VMware's flagship offering, but its status has since been usurped by ESXi. Chapter 4 spotlights the differences more in depth, but for now, note that the chief differentiator between them is that ESXi lacks the service console, which means a smaller hypervisor, and thus increased security and reliability due to the smaller "attack surface."

Unlike ESX and ESXi, which install over bare metal and thus do not require an operating system, VMware Server is an application that requires an operating system (Windows, Linux, or Solaris) to run beneath it. In addition, unlike ESX or ESXi, it does not require a dedicated server; nor does it offer a centralized management option. In terms of usability, although VMware Server can be used in production, it is far more suitable for testing and development environments.

This chapter focuses on VMware Server and its inner workings, features, configurations, and idiosyncrasies.

THE VMWARE SERVER CONSOLE

The VMware Server Console (Console) is the main method of interaction with your virtual machines (VM) when creating, removing, editing, starting, and stopping them. You can interact with VMs via the Console as if you are directly on the machine's console. For those systems using a graphical interface, as is the case for Windows or Linux, you should use a remote connectivity client just as you would for a physical machine. Even if you install VMware Tools, the response is still sluggish over a network. For a more enjoyable experience when interacting with a virtual system, use the system's remote connectivity capability.

The Windows version of VMware Server Console has a different look than its Linux counterpart, although the functionality is the same. The Windows VMware Server Console is shown in Figure 3-1.

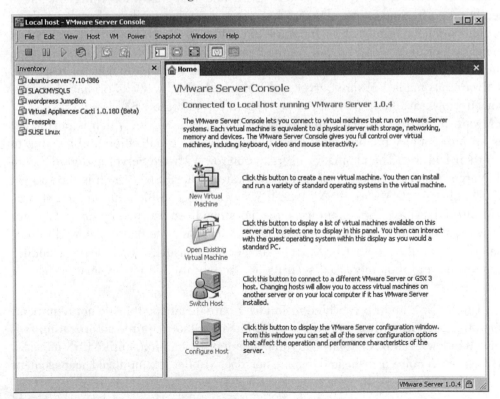

FIGURE 3-1 The Windows VMware Server Console.

The Linux VMware Server Console is shown in Figure 3-2.

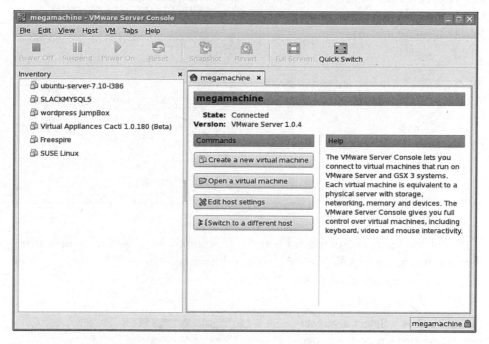

FIGURE 3-2 The Linux VMware Server Console.

Creating Virtual Machines

VM creation is a primary function of the Console. You can use three ways to create a new VM using the Console:

- **New**—Creates a new VM from scratch via the Virtual Machine Wizard
- **Open**—Opens an existing VM not in inventory
- **Import**—Creates a new VM using the VMware Virtual Machine Importer

Virtual Machine Wizard

You use the Virtual Machine Wizard to create new VMs completely from scratch. The wizard provides the most control over all aspects of the VM you create.

1. To invoke the New Virtual Machine Wizard, as shown in Figure 3-3, select File, New, Virtual Machine from the VMware Server Console menu or use the keyboard shortcut Ctrl+N. Then click Next.

2. The next screen prompts you to choose between Typical or Custom configuration for your new VM. Custom offers maximum control and flexibility, and we have chosen that for demonstration purposes here.

FIGURE 3-3 The Select the Appropriate Configuration screen in the Virtual Machine Wizard.

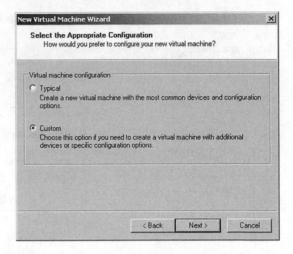

The next screen, shown in Figure 3-4, prompts you to select an operating system for your VM. We have chosen Linux (specifically, Debian 4) as the operating system for this VM.

FIGURE 3-4 Select a guest operating system and version.

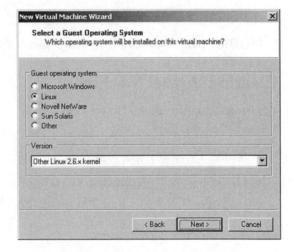

3. Select Linux, Other Linux 2.6.x kernel, and then click Next to continue.

4. Now it's time to name your VM. Figure 3-5 shows the Name the Virtual Machine screen. Enter the name, and you'll notice that the name in the Location field changes accordingly. It is best to use a descriptive name that includes the operating system and version number, unless you have another way to describe the VM, such as a corporate naming convention (DNS01, for example). Click Next to continue.

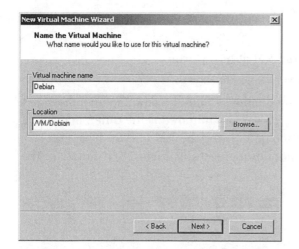

FIGURE 3-5 Name the VM and location.

5. In the next screen, shown in Figure 3-6, you set access rights to the VM you're creating. If you want everyone to have access to the VM, deselect the Make This Virtual Machine Private check box. If you want to keep the VM private, and thus accessible only to the user logged in to the VMware Server Console, click Next to continue.

FIGURE 3-6 The Set Access Rights screen.

NOTE

For purposes of this chapter, we will assume that the VM will remain private. Therefore, keep the check box selected and click Next.

The next screen prompts for Startup and Shutdown behavior for the VM. The options are

- Power on/Don't power on the VM at host startup.
- Power off/Shutdown the VM at host shutdown.

Some VMs, especially those in production, should be powered on at host startup; others should not. Power off versus shutdown is the difference between pressing the power button or allowing the VM to shut down gracefully. Always allow the VM to shut down gracefully. Figure 3-7 illustrates the selections.

FIGURE 3-7 VM startup and shutdown options.

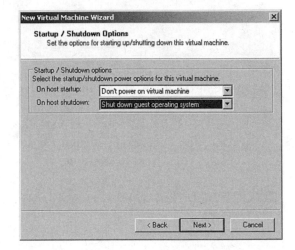

6. Select Don't Power on Virtual Machine and Shut Down Guest Operating System; then click Next to continue.

Figure 3-8 allows you to allocate either one or two virtual processors to your VM.

FIGURE 3-8 Select the number of processors for the VM.

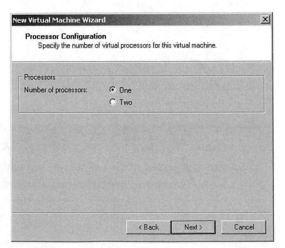

7. Select One and click Next.

Next, you'll allocate RAM to the new VM, as shown in Figure 3-9.

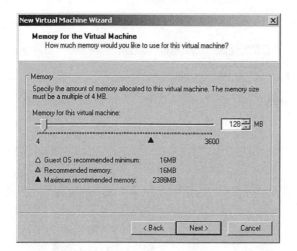

FIGURE 3-9   Allocate RAM to the VM.

8. Adjust the RAM to 128MB and click Next.

Select the network type on the screen shown in Figure 3-10. We recommend a bridged connection so that the VM behaves like all other computers on the network and receives an IP address from the network DHCP server.

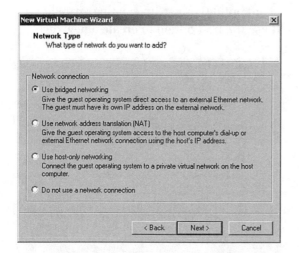

FIGURE 3-10   Select the network type.

9. Select Use Bridged Networking and click Next.

On the next screen, shown in Figure 3-11, you'll select the type of SCSI I/O adapter to use for your new VM. The LSI Logic adapter works well, except when working with older operating systems. The default adapter for your operating system is already selected for you. You should select LSI Logic for all modern OS types because the LSI adapter type has better performance. If you mix BusLogic and LSI Logic adapters, your VM will try to boot from the BusLogic adapter.

FIGURE 3-11   Select the SCSI I/O adapter type.

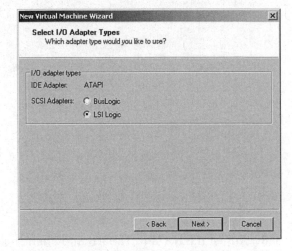

10. Select LSI Logic and click Next.

   The next few steps in the wizard assist you in creating a new virtual disk on which your VM will reside. The first screen, shown in Figure 3-12, allows you to create a new virtual disk (the default option) or use an existing virtual or a physical disk. In most cases, you'll use the first option to create a new disk.

FIGURE 3-12   Disk options for the new VM.

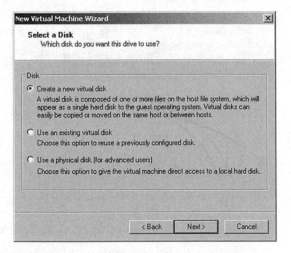

11. Keep the default selection (Create a New Virtual Disk) and click Next to continue.

Figure 3-13 shows the next screen in the steps to create your new virtual disk. Here you select from IDE or SCSI. Depending on the operating system choice, your recommended choice is selected for you. For modern operating systems (newer Windows or Linux), you should select SCSI for performance reasons unless you have a compelling reason not to do so.

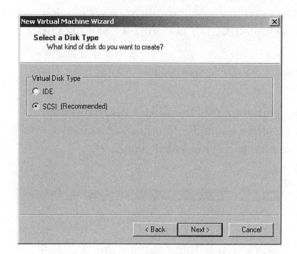

FIGURE 3-13 Select the Disk Type (IDE or SCSI) for the VM.

12. Accept the default (SCSI) and click Next.

On the next screen, Figure 3-14, configure your virtual disk. Allocate space, decide whether the disk will have a static size or be configured as dynamically expanding, and whether to create one large file or split your disk into 2GB-sized chunks.

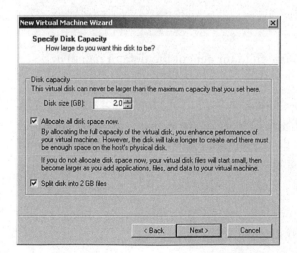

FIGURE 3-14 Specify disk capacity and configuration.

Disk size depends mostly on the type of system and its use. It can be any size you need and is limited only by the amount of free space on your system. The decision to create a static or dynamic disk is one that is debatable. The advantage of static disks is that they increase performance and more closely emulate physical disks. You can resize static disks with tools like GParted, so there isn't much need to take the performance hit for a dynamically resizing disk. Finally, this screen allows you to choose to split your virtual disk into chunks or leave it intact as a single file. For performance and backup, choose to use 2GB chunks.

13. Enter 2.0 for 2.0GB, accept Allocate All Disk Space Now, accept Split Disk into 2GB Files, and click Next.

The final step in the virtual disk creation part of the wizard is to name your virtual disk. Give your disk a descriptive name that uniquely identifies it with the operating system to which it is attached. This VM is named Debian4.vmdk. See Figure 3-15.

FIGURE 3-15   Name the virtual disk file.

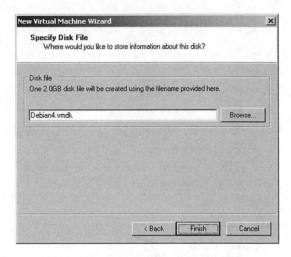

14. Enter Debian4.vmdk into the name field (or accept the default name) and click Finish.

After you click Finish, a progress indicator tracks the creation of your new VM.

After the virtual disk is created, your VM is ready to use. Your next step is to install an operating system. Refer to the Appendix, "Virtual Machine Installation," for instructions in how to install the generic VM operating system.

Opening a Virtual Machine

Opening a VM adds it to your inventory. Adding a VM in this way is common when you are copying VMs between host systems or restoring a VM.

1. On the VMware Server Console menu, click File, Open or use the keyboard shortcut Ctrl+O to open the VM browse window.

   The default location is the directory specified during VMware Server installation.

2. Click the Browse button to locate and select the VM you want to open.

3. Select the .vmx file for the VM and click Open.

   The VM will appear in your inventory and is ready to use.

Importing a Virtual Machine

To import a VM, you must have the VMware Server Console open locally on the VMware host system. You can't import using a remote connection. For the example in this section, a Microsoft Virtual PC VM serves as the VM to be imported.

1. Click File, Import on the VMware Server Console menu.

   The VMware Virtual Machine Importer Wizard launches with information about the types of VMs that can be imported using this tool.

   You can import images created with VMware Workstation, VMware Server, Microsoft Virtual PC, Microsoft Virtual Server, Symantec LiveState Recovery, or Norton Ghost 9 or later.

 NOTE

Your original VM image remains unchanged during the import process. The VMware Import Wizard makes a copy of the original VM.

2. Click Next to continue.

   The next screen prompts you to decide between using a Typical or Custom import process for the new VM. Here, Typical is preferable because the Custom options are used when you need to specify a particular version of VMware software or link directly to the original VM disk images.

3. Accept the default (Typical) and click Next.

4. Browse to the .vmc or .sv2i file that describes the VM you want to import, select the file, click Open, and then click Next to continue.

 WARNING

If you're importing a Microsoft Virtual PC image, you can import only Windows images with this tool. Additionally, the VM you're importing must be powered off.

On the next screen, shown in Figure 3-16, you must name your new VM and specify a location. Defaults are given but you can change the name and path here.

FIGURE 3-16 Specify the name and location for the new VM.

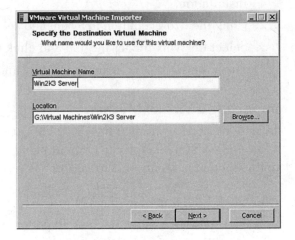

5. Change the name or accept the defaults and click Next.

    The next screen is informational only and describes the process about to take place.

6. Click Next to import the VM.

    Figure 3-17 is a progress indicator shown during the import process.

    When the import process is complete, you'll see the screen shown in Figure 3-18, informing you that the import process is complete.

FIGURE 3-17 VM import progress.

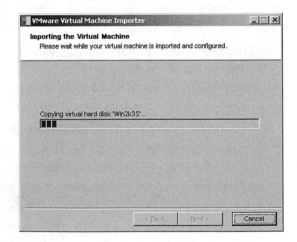

7. Click Finish to complete.

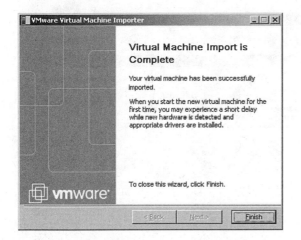

FIGURE 3-18   Successful VM import screen.

Your new VM is added to inventory and is ready for use. As Figure 3-18 indicates, when you first start a newly imported VM, some hesitation occurs at startup. The application isn't frozen; it is preparing for successful startup by detecting new hardware and installing drivers.

Customizing Virtual Machines

VMware offers a flexible array of options for customizing VMs. If you correct a mistake made during the creation stage or need to enhance an existing or imported VM, this section explains how to do it. With a VM powered off, you may add, remove, or reconfigure its hardware.

Removing Hardware from a Virtual Machine

Part of the beauty of VMs is their flexibility. By design, it is easy to remove hardware associated with a VM that is no longer needed or applicable. The following steps explain how to do that for VMware Server.

1. Power off the VM or confirm it is powered off.
2. On the main VMware Server Console screen, select the VM you want to work with, and click Edit Virtual Machine Settings, as shown in Figure 3-19.

   The screen shown in Figure 3-20 lists the VM's hardware details.
3. Select the floppy drive and click the Remove button to remove it from your system.

   The floppy drive isn't just disconnected but removed from the VM just as if you had removed a physical device from a standard hardware system.

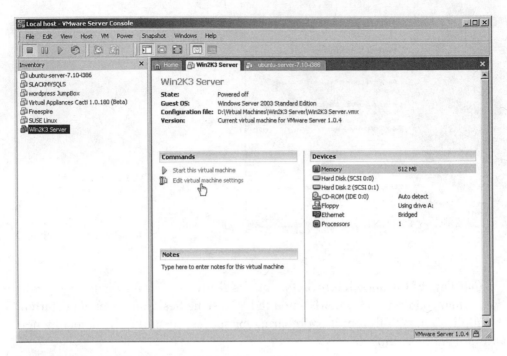

FIGURE 3-19   The VMware Console main screen.

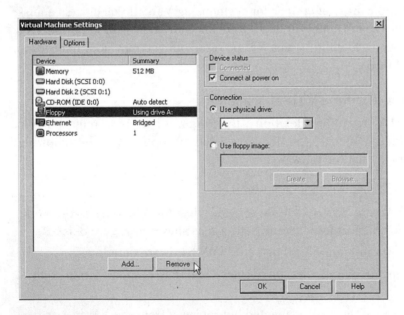

FIGURE 3-20   The Virtual Machine Settings screen showing hardware details.

Adding Hardware to a Virtual Machine

Adding hardware to your VMs isn't as easy as removing it but is made simpler with the use of the Add Hardware Wizard.

1. To add a new device to your VM, click the Add button on the Hardware details screen.

   The Add Hardware Wizard launches and prompts you to click Next.

2. Click Next to continue.

   The Hardware Type screen lists the various devices that you can add to your system, as shown in Figure 3-21.

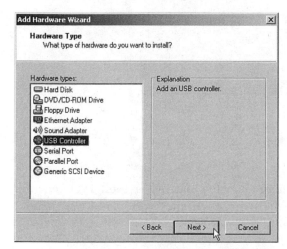

FIGURE 3-21 The hardware device list.

3. Select USB Controller, click Next, and then click OK on the message screen.

   The message screen you saw after you added the USB controller describes how to power on the controller and use a USB device in your VM. The message appears in the Hardware details window as well when you select USB controller. See Figure 3-22.

   The VM, when fully operational, will discover and install the detected USB device the same as if it were on a local physical machine. You can add multiple hard drives, Ethernet adapters, parallel ports, and serial ports, but you are allowed only one USB controller. A single USB controller can handle multiple devices.

Reconfiguring Virtual Machine Hardware

VMs, even more so than their physical counterparts, are dynamic entities. Rarely will you create or import a VM and not change any aspect of its hardware configuration. VMware Server allows you to change some hardware settings and attributes to match your needs.

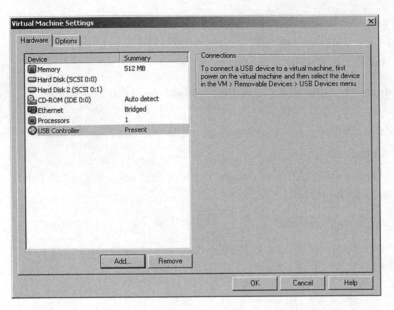

FIGURE 3-22 The Hardware details screen and USB controller information.

You can adjust the amount of memory allocated to a VM, as well as change the characteristics of its CD-ROM and floppy drive, parallel port, serial port, sound adapter, SCSI devices, and the number of processors.

NOTE

You can adjust the number of processors from one to two in a VM only if you have at least two processors on your VM host system.

Adjusting RAM Changing the amount of RAM in a VM is so simple that it can lead to over-commitment of resources. Be cautious when adding more RAM to a VM without first considering how much physical memory is on your host system. You should need no more than 1GB of RAM allocated to the host. However, don't go below that or performance degrades, which, in turn, negatively affects your VMs.

WARNING

Do not use the VM host's virtual memory when allocating memory to VMs. Base your memory adjustments on physical RAM only.

1. To adjust the amount of RAM for a VM, navigate to the Hardware details screen shown in Figures 6-20 and 6-22.

2. Select Memory from the list and adjust the amount of RAM using the slider. Pay close attention to the minimum and maximum recommended values. See Figure 3-23.

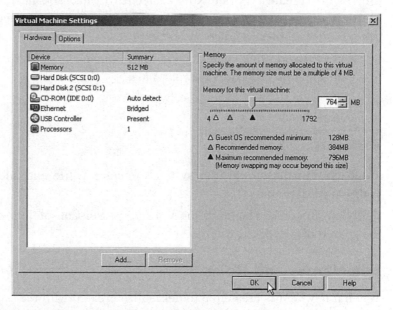

FIGURE 3-23   Adjusting memory for a VM.

You'll probably need to exceed the recommended value, but do not exceed the maximum or swapping will degrade performance for all VMs.

3. Click OK when finished.

Changing DVD/CD-ROM Characteristics   In VMware Server, you can elect to connect your virtual DVD/CD drive to a physical drive on the VM host, the client machine, or an ISO image. You can also connect the device exclusively to the current VM.

When installing a new VM, installation is quicker if you use an ISO image instead of a physical CD/DVD disk. Building an ISO repository for creating new VMs from scratch is one way to streamline this.

VIRTUAL MACHINE FILES AND FOLDERS

When you install VMware Server, a prompt asks you to name a location for your VMs. This is your VM repository. You can have more than one, but the one you name during installation is the default.

File and Folder Security

Because the installation script runs as root for VMware Server, the initial folder designated as a VM repository has *root only* privileges. If you are creating a system that other VMware Server Console users are going to use, one way to simplify the process is to create a repository for each one. If your users need a shared repository, create it as root, create a group for access to it, change group access permissions to the repository folder, and deny all other access.

Enter the following commands at the command line on the virtual host system to create a shared repository for your VMs.

```
# mkdir /VM_Shared
# groupadd vmusers
# chgrp vmusers /VM_Shared
# chmod 770 /VM_Shared
```

Then edit the virtual host system's /etc/group file and add usernames to the vmusers group entry.

Now, when users login via the VMware Server Console, they can create VMs in the shared directory (repository).

File Names and Roles

When a new VM is created, a folder is also created with the name of the VM. The folder exists under the VM repository folder. This is both an organizational and a security feature that ensures each VM has its own uniquely named folder to hold its files.

Under the VM folder, you'll have several files, depending on how large your virtual drive image is and whether the VM is powered on.

The basic files are as follows for a VM named Debian4. These files are common to all VMs:

- **Debian4.vmdk**—This is the disk definition file (Disk Descriptor File). In it are the number and filenames of the virtual disk files and the virtual drive geometry.

  For example:

  ```
  # Disk DescriptorFile
  version=1
  CID=814cf503
  parentCID=ffffffff
  createType="twoGbMaxExtentFlat"

  # Extent description
  ```

```
RW 4193792 FLAT "Debian4-f001.vmdk" 0
RW 4193792 FLAT "Debian4-f002.vmdk" 0
RW 4193792 FLAT "Debian4-f003.vmdk" 0
RW 4193792 FLAT "Debian4-f004.vmdk" 0
RW 2048 FLAT "Debian4-f005.vmdk" 0

# The Disk Data Base
#DDB

ddb.toolsVersion = "6532"
ddb.adapterType = "ide"
ddb.geometry.sectors = "63"
ddb.geometry.heads = "16"
ddb.geometry.cylinders = "16383"
ddb.virtualHWVersion = "4"
```

FLAT in the description means that the virtual drive has a static size. Each of the virtual disk files (Debian4-f00x.vmdk) listed are a maximum of 2GB in size, shown in the createType parameter as twoGbMaxExtentFlat.

- **Debian4.vmx**—The VM descriptor file. Like the .vmdk file, the .vmx file is plain text and can be edited directly. You may not edit either file when the VM is powered on.

```
#!/usr/bin/vmware
config.version = "8"
virtualHW.version = "4"
scsi0.present = "TRUE"
scsi0.virtualDev = "lsilogic"
memsize = "512"
ide0:0.present = "TRUE"
ide0:0.fileName = "Debian4-f001.vmdk"
ide1:0.present = "TRUE"
ide1:0.fileName = "/ISO/debian-40r3-amd64-kde-CD-1.iso"
ide1:0.deviceType = "cdrom-image"
floppy0.fileName = "/dev/fd0"
Ethernet0.present = "TRUE"
displayName = "Mail"
guestOS = "other26xlinux"
priority.grabbed = "normal"
priority.ungrabbed = "normal"

floppy0.present = "FALSE"

ide0:0.redo = ""
ethernet0.addressType = "generated"
uuid.location = "56 4d 93 39 d7 1e 84 95-7f 8d 0f 9a 3f 9e ae 35"
uuid.bios = "56 4d 93 39 d7 1e 84 95-7f 8d 0f 9a 3f 9e ae 35"
ethernet0.generatedAddress = "00:0c:29:9e:ae:35"
ethernet0.generatedAddressOffset = "0"
```

```
ide1:0.autodetect = "TRUE"

ide1:0.startConnected = "TRUE"
tools.syncTime = "FALSE"

uuid.action = "create"
```

- **nvram**—The VM BIOS information file. This file is binary and can't be edited directly. To change its settings, you must boot the VM and select BIOS Settings.
- **vmware.log (vmware-x.log)**—These are the log files generated when you start a VM and are generally used for troubleshooting. You may erase the log files when the VM is powered off.

Depending on your habits, needs, and VM status (Powered On or Off), you may find other files in the VM folder. The following is a list and description of those files.

- **Debian4.vmsn**—A binary snapshot state file.
- **Debian4.vmsd**—The plain-text equivalent of the .vmsn file.
- **Debian4-000002-s00x.vmdk**—A virtual disk snapshot file. The 000002 indicates this is the second snapshot. The s00x corresponds to the virtual disk part f00x.
- **Debian4.vmdk.WRITELOCK**—If this file exists, the VM is powered on.
- **.vmem**—Virtual Machine memory (RAM) file. This file is the size of the amount of RAM set in your VM.
- **.vmem-WRITELOCK**—A powered-on VM vmem file.

VMWARE SERVER IN THE REAL WORLD

It is a commonly held belief that VMware Server's sweet spot is not in production environments. That doesn't mean, however, that there isn't room for it in larger environments. The School of Electrical Engineering and Computer Science at Washington State University, for example, has found VMware Server an ideal solution for many of its users' needs.

Like many large enterprises and institutions, the school uses VMware ESX in its server room. Mail, web, authentication, and all file services for the school comes out of the server room, and it relies heavily on virtualization for these operations to be a success. It is not IT for the campus, however; and the department does not provide or oversee the network running through the building.

At one point, two admins oversaw 150 servers. At the time of this writing, 85% of all systems are virtualized. All critical services are contained within 95 VMs running on four Dell PowerEdge 2950 servers with 32GB of RAM. All four servers fit on a single 48-inch rack. Previously, four racks were needed. Not only does this save space, it also reduces power and cooling needs.

The journey has not been short. Over a ten-year period, the school has been using VMware products in some capacity. ESX has been in use for all but four of those years. When ESXi arrived on the scene, sys admins opted to stick with ESX because of its disaster recovery and high availability capabilities. A migration to vSphere is in the works, however.

This story, although interesting, is all too familiar. What is fairly unique is how the school is fitting VMware Server into its environment, demonstrating how even the largest of enterprises can benefit from this offering.

VMware Server is a free solution. But so is ESXi, and VMware Server is not anywhere near as optimized for a server environment as ESXi is. Even VMware does not position it as a solution for production environments.

In fact, the very name VMware Server is a bit of a misnomer. As noted at the beginning of this chapter, the product's roots go back to the workstation space. Later, when VMware (the product) was renamed VMware GSX, it found its way into the server realm. Although it remains adequate for a few boxes, it is not robust enough for a server environment with anything more than the most basic of needs.

For complex workstation needs, it is a different story entirely, and that is where the school has found it valuable.

The school supports the computing needs of faculty, staff, and students who are teaching or enrolled in computer science, computer engineering, and entry-level computer science required on electrical engineering. Many of these classes are UNIX based, and students are more familiar with Windows or Linux. Still, they need access to their classroom environments. Virtualization makes it much easier to access their classroom environment without having to change their operating system.

The IT department found that as tech savvy as many of these users were, they were not particularly virtualization savvy. Typically, when they were interested in trying something new, they planned to purchase new equipment.

As the economy soured and budgets took a hit, this became increasing less feasible. Some in the IT department believe end users will become more virtualization savvy when they see it will meet their goals as well as new hardware can.

The IT department has found VMware Server to be ideal for users who need to experiment with a new app or environment, or who are looking to develop a new app. So long as the scale is small, VMware Server is effective for a test environment. Thus, the systems staff began selling the solution to the faculty.

Typically, the IT staff at the school sets up the user's computer, and the user then administers it. This enables the user to accomplish whatever is needed with minimal resource consumption on the part of the IT department.

The IT staff views VMware Server as a "gateway drug," however, and it is already looking to add more computing power to its virtualization offerings. It is experimenting with a more cloud-like environment in which VMs are available to faculty via the ESX servers in the data center.

As satisfied as the school has been with VMware Server, the systems administrator responsible for it cautions about the importance of ensuring appropriate expectations. Often, users expect ESX performance and are displeased with what they get.

Assuming moderate performance is acceptable, VMware Server might even be a good candidate for an initial server virtualization foray. Despite its low price point and ease of use, it is not always ideal for small businesses with limited IT staff, which in some cases might find vSphere or vCloud better meeting its needs.

SUMMARY

This chapter introduced VMware Server and the VMware Server Console, which is the primary interface between the user and VMs. The Console is used to create, alter, remove, and edit VMs. The chapter stepped through how to create a VM from scratch, how to make changes to hardware components, and how to customize a VM for better performance. File-level composition of VMware VMs and how to secure VMs for different purposes were also covered. Finally, each VMware file type was introduced and its role in the life of a VMware VM explained.

## CHAPTER 4

VMware ESXi

VMware is the steamroller in the virtualization space, and ESX and ESXi are its flagship products, which are designed to manage huge virtual infrastructures. ESXi, the focus of this chapter, is an enterprise-level hypervisor product that VMware released as free to demonstrate the value of it products and how much real money can be saved by using them.

ESXi is a free product but is very different in scope and structure from VMware Server, which was covered in Chapter 3, "VMware Server." ESXi, as mentioned previously, is a hypervisor. It requires its very own dedicated server system capable of supporting virtual guest machines. Currently, its hardware compatibility list is somewhat limited so you'll have to install it on a system that complies with its requirements. Generally, you'll need a 64-bit CPU (with virtualization extensions); dual, quad, or more core system with 16GB RAM; and a few hundred gigabytes of disk space. ESXi supports a wide array of server-type hardware, but don't expect commodity hardware to suffice.

The difference in ESX and ESXi is that ESXi is the hypervisor only. There is no primary virtual machine (VM) or Domain0 or, in VMware terminology, the service console. You'll need to use VMware's Virtual Infrastructure Client (now known as VMware vSphere Client) to connect to and manage ESXi and your VMs. As for how ESXi works versus ESX, if you've seen ESXi through the eyes of the client software, you've seen ESX as well.

THE VIRTUAL INFRASTRUCTURE CLIENT CONSOLE

As previously mentioned, the console for ESXi is the Virtual Infrastructure Client (VIC). The VIC is a centralized management application. All interaction between you and the ESXi server takes place through this application. See Figure 4-1 for a look at the VIC.

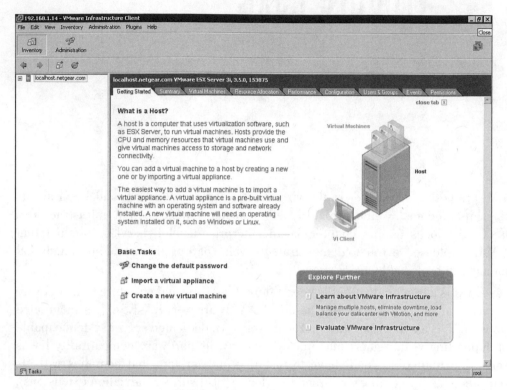

FIGURE 4-1   The VMware ESX/ESXi Virtual Infrastructure Client Console.

You'll notice that the VIC is similar to the VMware Server Console and is designed with migration from VMware Server to the enterprise products in mind.

Creating Virtual Machines

You'll spend most of your time in the VIC creating or managing VMs, so let's go through the steps required to create a new VM.

1. Begin creating a new VM by right-clicking an ESXi server listed in the left (Inventory) pane or by clicking the Create A New Virtual Machine link in the right pane on the Getting Started tab. See Figure 4-2.

    This action invokes the New Virtual Machine Wizard that steps you through the creation of your new VM.

2. You're prompted to select a Typical or Custom VM configuration for your new VM. Select Custom and click Next.

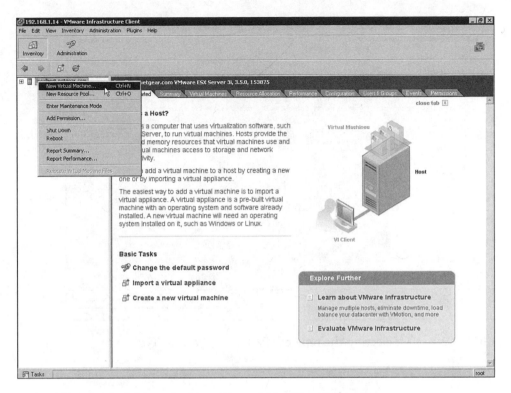

FIGURE 4-2   Invoking the New Virtual Machine Wizard.

We recommend that you always choose Custom so that you have complete control over the VM's configuration. Think of creating this VM as if you were ordering a physical system. Chances are good that you wouldn't accept a generic system, you'd ask for specific components and configurations. See Figure 4-3.

3. Name your VM (Debian 4, as seen in Figure 4-4, for example). Click Next to continue.

4. Choose a datastore (a disk volume), as shown in Figure 4-5, on which to store your new VM files. Click Next.

   If you have more than one datastore, you'll have to select one from them.

   Depending on your environment, you might have datastores designated for different purposes. One might be for web servers, whereas another might be used only for databases. If you aren't the administrator, check to find out which one is appropriate for your environment.

5. Select an operating system for your new VM. Select the specific version from the pull-down menu and click Next, as shown in Figure 4-6.

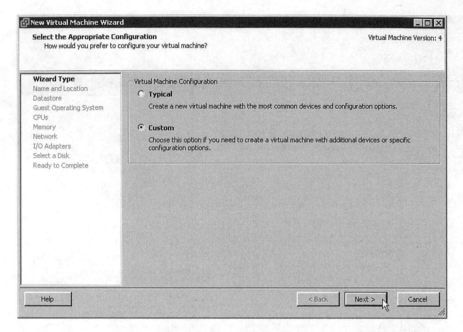

FIGURE 4-3 Selecting the type of VM configuration: Typical or Custom.

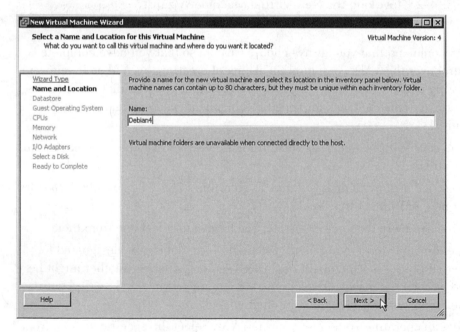

FIGURE 4-4 Naming the VM.

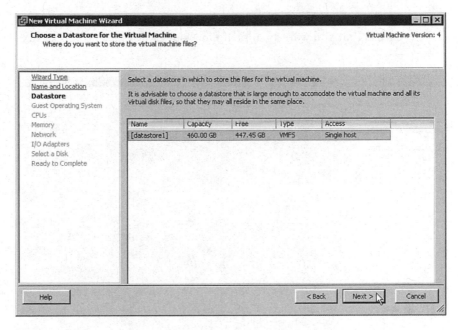

FIGURE 4-5 Selecting the datastore for the new VM.

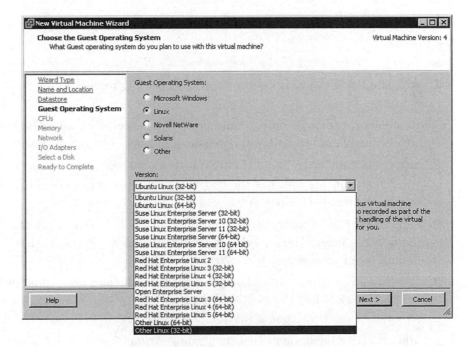

FIGURE 4-6 Selecting the operating system for the new VM.

6. In the screen shown in Figure 4-7, select the number of virtual CPUs (vCPUs) that you want to allocate for your new VM, and click Next.

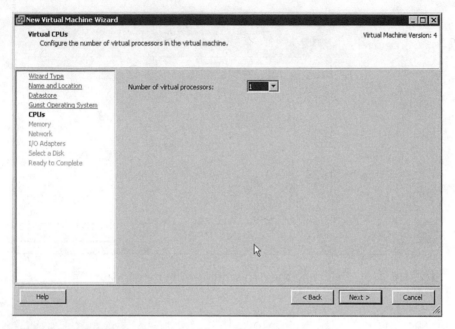

FIGURE 4-7 Selecting the number of virtual processors (vCPUs) for the new VM.

7. Allocate RAM (Memory) to your new VM. See Figure 4-8. Click Next to continue.

   Remember to allocate only the resources you'll need for your VMs. You can adjust them later (up or down) depending on usage and requirements.

8. Select the number and type of virtual network interfaces (see Figure 4-9) that you'll need for this VM. Use the check box Connect at Power On to power on the interface at boot. Click Next.

9. Select a type of I/O adapter to which your virtual disks will connect. SCSI is the default choice. The best choice for your operating system is shown as a default (see Figure 4-10). Click Next to continue.

10. This screen prompts you for how you want to set up and use virtual disks for your new VM. Select Create a New Virtual Disk and click Next to specify a size and location for your new virtual disk. See Figure 4-11.

    You also have the option to use an existing virtual disk, to use SAN (if available), or to not create a virtual disk for this VM.

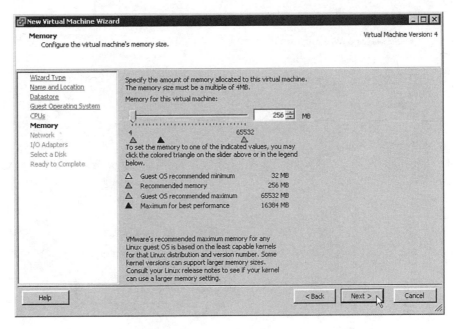

FIGURE 4-8   Allocating RAM (Memory) to the new VM.

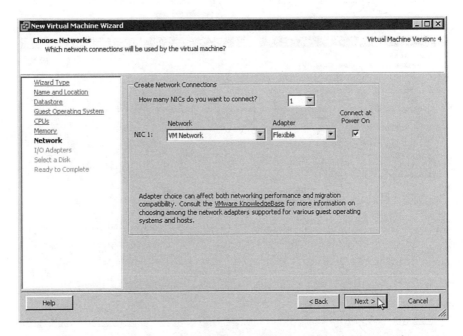

FIGURE 4-9   Selecting the number and type of virtual network interfaces.

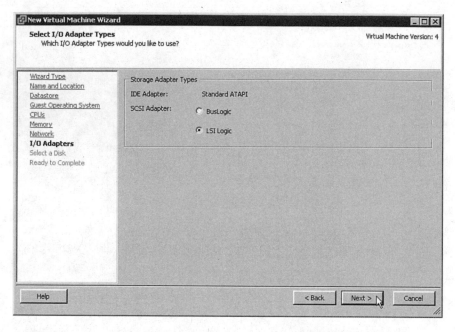

FIGURE 4-10   Selecting the I/O adapter types (default selection shown).

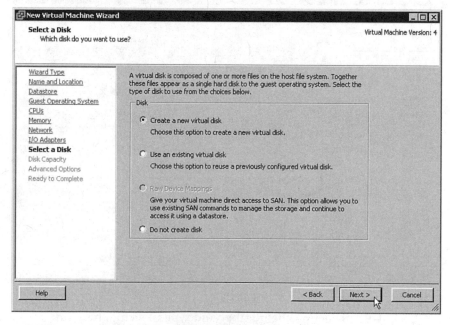

FIGURE 4-11   Creating a new virtual disk.

11. Provide a size in GB or MB and a location for your VM's virtual disk as shown in Figure 4-12. Click Next.

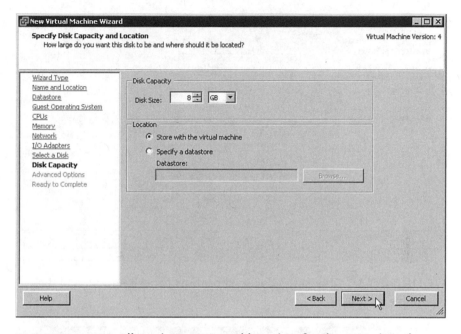

FIGURE 4-12 Allocating space and location for the new virtual disk.

12. Here you'll specify any advanced options for your virtual disk. As the information states on the screen in Figure 4-13, usually these do not need to be changed. Click Next to continue.

13. This final screen prompts you to accept your new VM settings or to edit them (see Figure 4-14). Click Finish when you're ready to create the new VM as designed.

Your VM is complete, and virtual disk space files are created. You are now ready to install the operating system to the VM. Refer to the Appendix, "Virtual Machine Installation," for those steps.

Customizing Virtual Machines

Almost no VM is perfect just the way it is from a generic wizard build, so you'll have to customize it to meet your specific needs. To edit any VM property, click Select your VM in the Inventory pane (left window) in the VI Client and click Edit the Virtual Machine Settings Before Submitting in the right window.

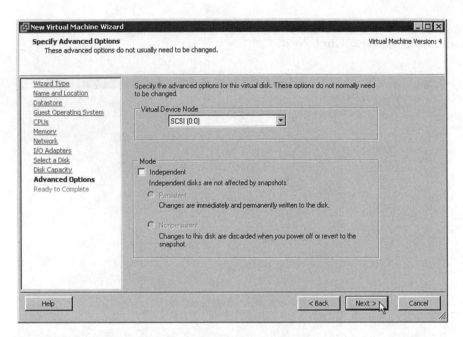

FIGURE 4-13   Choosing advanced options for the new virtual disk (defaults shown).

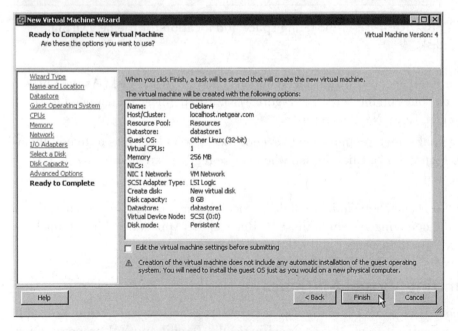

FIGURE 4-14   Examining the VM summary.

The VM's property window opens, as shown in Figure 4-15.

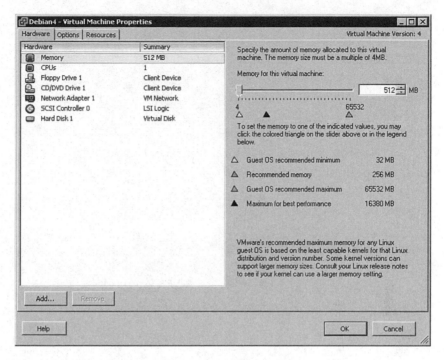

FIGURE 4-15   Editing VM properties.

On the Hardware tab, you can adjust the amount of memory, the number of CPUs, floppy disk drive support, CD/DVD drive support, network adapter properties, SCSI Controller properties, and number, size, and type of hard disks. More intriguing, though, are the advanced parameters that you can change using the Resources tab, as shown in Figure 4-16 and the next few screenshots.

By changing the number of CPU shares, you can effectively determine how much CPU processing power each VM receives so that VMs with CPU-intensive applications receive appropriate resources. A CPU share is an amount of CPU processing resources subtracted from an arbitrary total. The console operating system (the host operating system) receives 1,000 shares by default, as do all new VMs. By adjusting this number, you split the CPU's resources into a percentage of the total.

For example, if your total number of shares is 10,000, your host operating system receives 10% of the total CPU resources. You change memory shares by selecting Memory under the Resources tab, as shown in Figure 4-17.

Memory shares are assigned and calculated a bit differently. By default, memory is allocated at 10 shares per MB of VM memory. For example, if your new VM has 1GB (1024MB) of RAM, that VM receives 10×1024 = 10,240 shares of system memory.

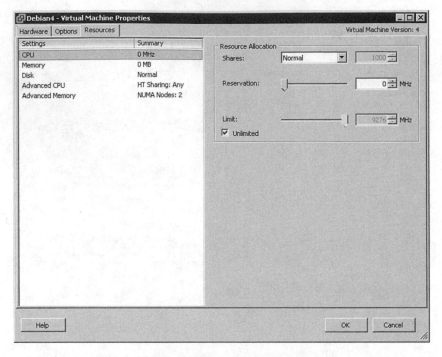

FIGURE 4-16 Changing the CPU resource allocation.

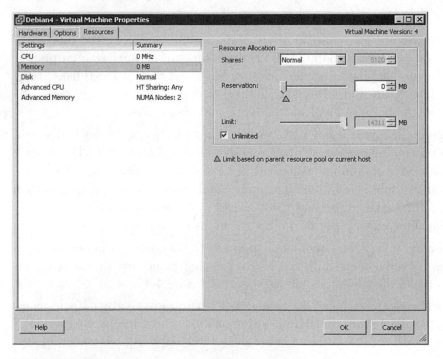

FIGURE 4-17 Changing memory resource allocation.

The use of disk shares, as shown in Figure 4-18, is used for prioritizing disk access by multiple VMs on the same datastore. To edit the settings, select Disk from the Resources menu, then double-click Shares in the right window for a drop-down menu of options (Low, Normal, High, and Custom).

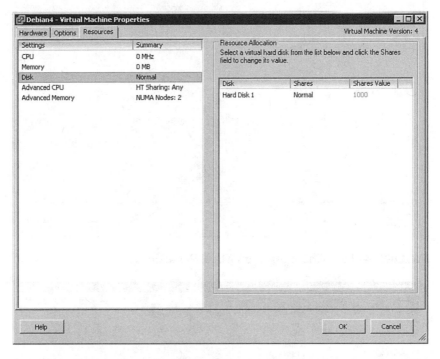

FIGURE 4-18   Changing disk resource allocation.

Disk shares are specific to each ESXi host. In other words, the disk share numbers you set on one ESXi host don't affect disk shares set on other ESXi hosts.

Figure 4-19 shows options related to changing a VM's CPU affinity, which means you can choose on which physical processor(s) your VM runs.

If you've specified CPU affinity, you might also want to associate memory allocations with a non-uniform memory access (NUMA) node. This is also known as manual memory affinity. Associating a VM with a specific NUMA node can greatly increase performance. See Figure 4-20.

To change generic VM information, select the Options tab. As shown in Figure 4-21, you can change the VM name and the Guest OS.

When you're finished editing VM settings, click OK to return to the main VI Client screen.

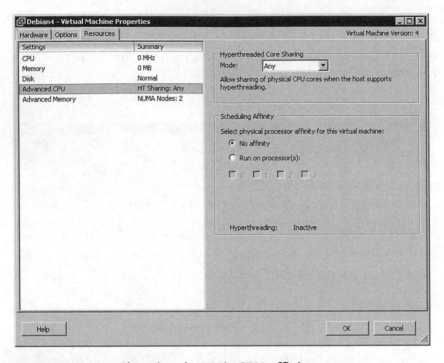

FIGURE 4-19 Changing the VM's CPU affinity.

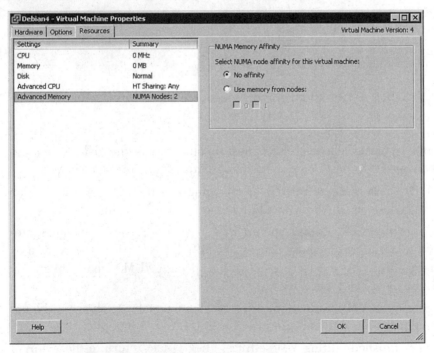

FIGURE 4-20 Changing the VM's memory affinity.

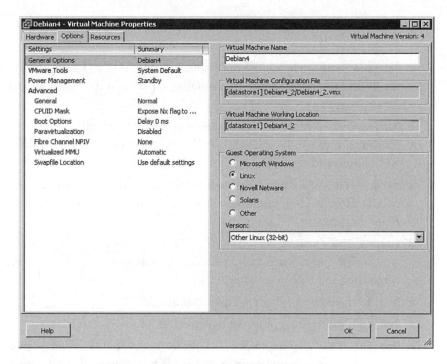

FIGURE 4-21   Changing general VM information.

VIRTUAL MACHINE FILES AND FOLDERS

After your VMs are up and running, it's time to think about file and folder security, and filenames and roles.

File and Folder Security

Because no operating system is associated with ESXi, file and folder security is handled by the VMware vStorage Virtual Machine File System (VMFS). You can't directly manipulate or look at the files, which adds the layer of security that you need for VMs and associated files.

File Names and Roles

All VMware server-level products have the same file nomenclature and format. When you create a new VM, a folder is created with the name of your VM. The folder exists under your chosen datastore or VM repository folder. This is an organizational and a security feature that ensures each VM has its own uniquely named folder to hold its own VM files.

In the datastore, you'll find several files representing your virtual drive image(s), VM description, lock files, snapshot files, a BIOS file, and a memory file.

The basic files are as follows for a VM named Debian4. These file types are common to all VMs.

- **Debian4.vmdk**—This is the disk definition file (Disk Descriptor File). In it, you'll find the number and filenames of the virtual disk files and the virtual drive geometry.

- **Debian4.vmx**—The VM descriptor file. Like the .vmdk file, the .vmx file is plain text and can be edited directly. You may not edit either file when the VM is powered on.

- **nvram**—The VM BIOS information file. This file is binary and can't be edited directly. To change its settings, you must boot the VM and select BIOS Settings.

- **vmware.log (vmware-x.log)**—These are the log files generated when you start a VM and are generally used for troubleshooting. You may erase the log files when the VM is powered off.

- **Debian4.vmsn**—A binary snapshot state file.

- **Debian4.vmsd**—The plain text equivalent of the .vmsn file.

- **Debian4-000002-s00x.vmdk**—A virtual disk snapshot file. The 000002 indicates this is the second snapshot. The s00x corresponds to the virtual disk part f00x.

- **Debian4.vmdk.WRITELOCK**—If this file exists, the VM is powered on.

- **vmem**—Virtual Machine memory (RAM) file. This file is the size of the amount of RAM set in your VM.

- **vmem-WRITELOCK**—A powered-on VM vmem file.

For a more in-depth discussion of these files and their contents, see Chapter 3.

VMWARE ESXI IN THE REAL WORLD

Based in Knoxville, TN, Jewelry Television is all about gemstones, proclaiming itself the largest retailer of loose gemstones. The company sells the jewelry through two main channels: a traditional shopping channel and its website, JTV (which also airs some of the programs shown on the TV channel); it also has a program for online affiliate sales.

Jewelry Television started out as America's Collectibles Network in the early 1990s. Back then it sold collectible items such as coins, knives, quilts, and skin care products. In 2000 it began to focus primarily on jewelry and gemstone sales, and it relaunched as Jewelry Television in the spring of 2004.

Although television remains its cornerstone (58 million U.S. households on a full-time basis), not surprisingly, a growing percentage of revenue comes from online sales. With that comes a corresponding increase in computing needs.

Three years ago, the company decided it was time to upgrade somewhere between 80 and 100 x86 machines. It opted to replace them with two new servers it describes as SAN-attached "workhorse servers" from HP running ESX.

It set out to virtualize its entire infrastructure, except where valid arguments could be made to retain a dedicated physical box. The main Oracle database, which runs on SPARC hardware, for example, remains unvirtualized. Nor is the actual storage infrastructure virtualized. Storage is impacted, however, because everything virtualized must still be stored.

The technology was an easy sell to the infrastructure group, and its members migrated easily. It took about six months to get most of the servers virtualized. The company was able to do this so quickly in part because the virtual environment mimicked physical. It was deliberately mapped out in such a way that the underlying architecture of the virtual matched that of the physical, and it was largely a matter of plugging in Ethernet links.

The bigger challenge came when it was time to migrate from ESX 2 to ESX 3. The software at the time allowed only one live migration, so it was an all-or-nothing proposition. This has since changed, and VMware has allowed live data store migration since version 3.5 using the command line (one data store to another).

The release of ESXi changed things for Jewelry Television, however.

One of the major selling points of ESX was the service console. ESXi, in contrast, runs on bare metal. Bare metal refers to a raw server system with no operating system. For administrators that rely heavily on the agents in the console (for example, for running backup), ESX is the preferred option. With the next release of ESX scheduled to be the last to have a service console, such admins are clearly in the minority.

Jewelry Television did not use any of this functionality, however. The admin, who did not take advantage of the console, viewed it as pure "bloat" and ripe for potential security vulnerabilities.

As a result, Jewelry Television decided to be ahead of the curve and go bare metal. This migration was much more straightforward than the original, because all the heavy lifting of infrastructure planning had already been done. As promised,

ESXi was up and running in less than 15 minutes. For systems on which ESXi comes preinstalled, this would be even quicker.

Software maintenance has also been simplified. With ESX, updates were constant and needed to be made to each host. ESXi, in contrast, typically has one firmware upgrade per month, which mean updates to two files and a reboot.

Although no game stoppers occurred at any point in the migration, a learning curve existed in the change between the two, because it did impact the way servers were managed. ESXi and ESX are both managed through VMware Virtual Center, and both can be managed through a remote Virtual Infrastructure Client in the same manner as environments not licensed for vCenter. However, in ESX, you can remotely connect to the service console and issue commands on the host, whereas in ESXi, a remote command line utility must be installed on the local workstation to issue remote commands against the APIs.

In addition, some of the third-party tools are not immediately compatible with ESXi. That has since changed, and all now are compatible with ESXi, including file manipulation tools. Finally, file transfer was also a somewhat kludgy process and not always as easy as it was in ESX.

The performance boost more than made up for this, however. With more computing resources available for the actual VMs, even the developers began noticing the improvements.

In and of itself, the virtualization endeavor has been successful. From an enterprise perspective, its success is even more pronounced: The company credits virtualization for enabling it to meet its goals.

IT's task was to build out an infrastructure that would support the growth of the company, and virtualizing the bulk of its infrastructure made it possible for Jewelry Television itself to grow to the size it needed to be.

Today, Jewelry Television's data center houses 70 ESXi hosts, XP desktops, close to 800 thin clients, close to 1,000 VMs—far from the two HP boxes it started out with. The bulk of its infrastructure is virtualized, including its call center, which consists of thin clients connected to a server running ESXi. The two applications that remain on dedicated servers are the customer-facing ones on its website and the main database.

In terms of hardware, with all but the most low-end servers on the market now geared toward virtualization, the choices are plentiful. Jewelry Television is by and large a Dell shop, although a few HP and Sun servers remain.

For the most part, Jewelry Television's IT infrastructure has expanded to meet its growing needs. However, with the first major build out of its network having taken place three years ago, some equipment is coming due for replacement. As hardware is cycled out, newer technology, such as Cisco's Nexxus 1000 virtual switch, will replace it. The company is also considering infrastructure changes to incorporate VMware's cloud computing infrastructure, vSphere.

Because the virtualization is so pervasive within Jewelry Television's data center, it takes great care to not differentiate between the physical and virtual, considering both to be the "data center."

It also makes patching a priority and keeps servers up to date with VMware Update Manager for updating VMware, MS WSUS for updating Windows Servers, and yum and up2date for Linux servers. Admins are careful to always maintain the same view in Virtual Center. All tools are disaster recovery services aware, with disaster recovery services and high availability used throughout.

SUMMARY

VMware's ESXi is a free enterprise-class hypervisor that has all the high-level attributes and features as VMware ESX. It lacks the console operating system (Dom0) but matches ESX in terms of performance and scalability in every other way.

In this chapter, you've learned the basics of working with ESXi and how to install and customize VMs.

CHAPTER 5

Citrix XenServer

XenServer began life as an open source project. Like so many open source projects, its roots are in research. It began life earlier this century as the XenSource project at the University of Cambridge. In 2003, it became publicly available. In the ensuing years, XenEnterprise, a commercial version of the paravirtualization-based open-source hypervisor, was born from the company that grew up closely aligned with the project. Then, in August 2007, Citrix announced plans to purchase Xen-Source. Shortly after the acquisition closed, Citrix introduced version 4 with the new branding. The open source version remains and can be found at Xen.org.

Since then, Citrix has developed an ecosystem of management tools around XenServer, keeping the same look and feel as previous versions. With the release of version 5, XenServer was made free, making it an even more desirable choice for server virtualization. XenServer, often referred to simply as Xen, is well known for its superior disk I/O, ease of use, and speed. This, perhaps, is why it is chosen in more than 95% of all clouds, including Amazon's Elastic Compute Cloud (EC2). I've personally used XenServer since version 3.x and have never been disappointed in its features, speed, or overall usability. It is a wise and frugal choice for many organizations, from those with very small server rooms to large enterprises.

XENSERVER, THE HYPERVISOR

XenServer, like ESXi, is a hypervisor, which means that the virtualization software, like ESXi, installs directly onto bare metal—a raw server system with no operating system. The operating system you interact with when you log in to the Linux-based console is itself a virtual machine (VM) installed as Domain0 (Dom0). Through this system you interact with the Hypervisor, a low-level program with which you do not interact directly.

All other VMs are user domains (DomainU or DomU) whose resources are managed by the Hypervisor. To interact fully with the XenServer, create VMs, allocate resources, add storage, monitor performance, and add various repositories you'll need to use XenCenter, which is covered in the next section.

XenCenter—The Xen Console

Xen's console is known as XenCenter. It is the graphical management interface from which you'll manage your virtual infrastructure. Figure 5-1 shows the Xen-Center console of a freshly installed XenServer with no VMs attached. The name, xenserver-kpqdpkmf, is the random name given to the XenServer upon installation. You may use this name or any other that you like—either by changing it here or during XenServer installation.

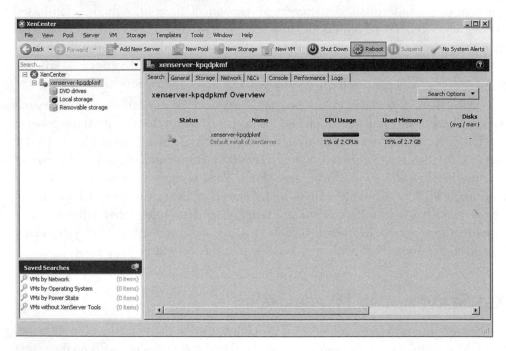

FIGURE 5-1 The XenCenter console.

To rename your XenServer in the XenCenter console, right-click the name and select Properties from the menu. The General tab opens by default. Change the name and click OK for the change to be applied. This name change has no effect on your XenServer installation or any VMs.

The XenCenter console is your main interface with XenServer. The local Xen console, shown in Figure 5-2, is limited; very few changes can be made from the local console. You'll need to use XenCenter to reap the full management capabilities.

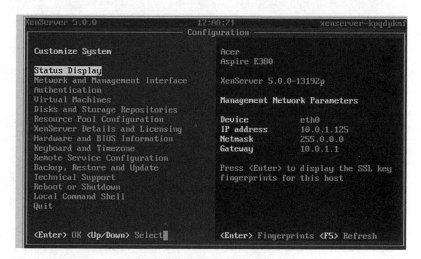

FIGURE 5-2 The local XenServer console.

Creating Virtual Machines

After XenCenter is installed and configured, getting VMs up and running is fairly straightforward. In most cases this means starting with the ISO library.

Identify an ISO Library

Unless you're installing your VMs from a local disk or CD/DVD drive, you'll need to identify an ISO Library (Repository) to XenServer. You have two possibilities for this repository: a Windows File Share via Common Internet File System (CIFS) or a UNIX-type Network File System (NFS) share. The one you select depends on where your ISO files are stored (a remote Windows system or a remote UNIX/Linux system).

To identify an ISO Library to your XenServer

1. Select the XenServer system that you want to install the new VM to by clicking it once.

2. Click the New Storage button on the XenCenter menu.

   The screen shown in Figure 5-3 appears and prompts you for the type of storage to identify to XenServer.

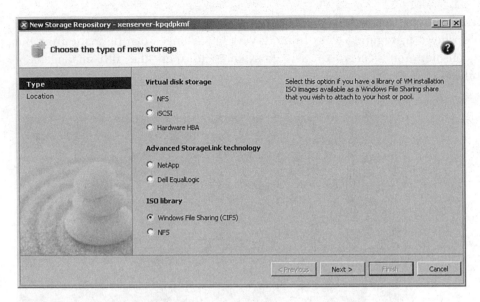

FIGURE 5-3 Select the storage type.

3. Under ISO library, select either Windows File Sharing (CIFS), as shown, or NFS, and then click Next. On the next screen, name your ISO library and supply the share name to XenServer (see Figure 5-4).

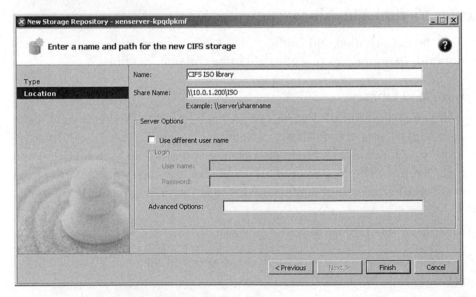

FIGURE 5-4 Name the ISO library and enter the share name.

4. Name your ISO library using any descriptive name you want.

5. Supply the share name to XenServer in the correct format for the type of share (CIFS or NFS).

   If your CIFS or NFS share require non-anonymous credentials to connect to the share that you identified, select Use Different User Name and enter the username and password in the spaces provided.

6. Click Finish.

Your ISO library will be available when you begin to install VMs, as shown in the next section. When you return to the XenCenter console, you'll see that your ISO library is now listed, as shown in Figure 5-5 (left pane).

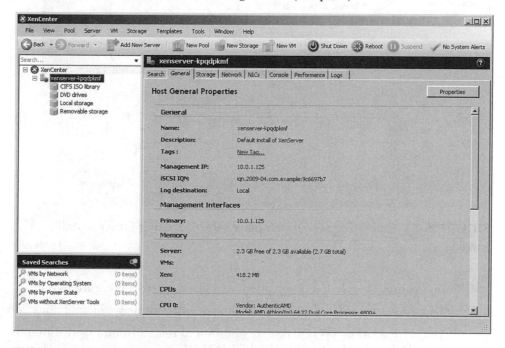

FIGURE 5-5   XenServer's asset list.

New Virtual Machine Wizard

Now you're ready to create a new VM:

1. Click New VM from the XenServer console.

   The first screen that appears in the New Virtual Machine Wizard is the one prompting you to select an Operating System Template from which to install your VM.

2. Select an operating system from the Template list. If your operating system isn't listed (ours isn't) go to step 3. If it is listed, skip step 3 and proceed to step 4.

3. Scroll all the way down to the bottom of the list, select Other Install Media, and click Next to continue, as shown in Figure 5-6.

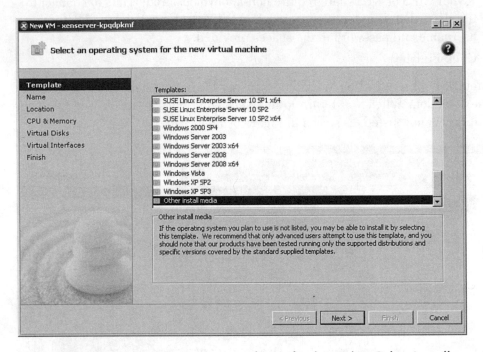

FIGURE 5-6 Operating system template selection using Other Install Media.

4. Name your VM, give it a description, and click Next. See Figure 5-7.

5. Select the source ISO image from which to install your new VM, and click Next.

   If you have a CD or DVD disk that you want to install from, insert it into the CD/DVD drive and select Physical DVD Drive. As you can see from Figure 5-8, I selected the Debian-40r3-i386-netinst.iso from the CIFS ISO library created previously.

6. As shown in Figure 5-9, select the number of virtual CPUs and initial memory allocation for your new VM. Click Next to continue.

7. Click Add to create a new Virtual Disk for your new VM.

8. Select a size for the new Virtual Disk (2.0GB, for example), select the storage location for your new VM (local storage shown), and click OK. See Figure 5-10.

   After you've selected the size and storage location of your virtual disk, you're returned to the Virtual Machine Wizard, as shown in Figure 5-11.

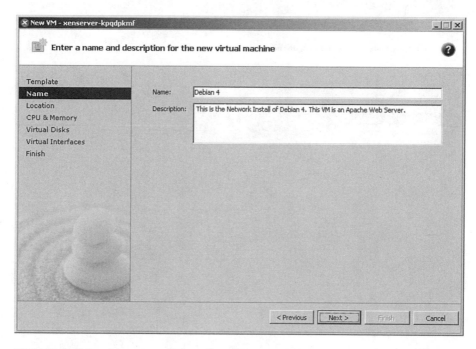

FIGURE 5-7   Name and describe the New VM.

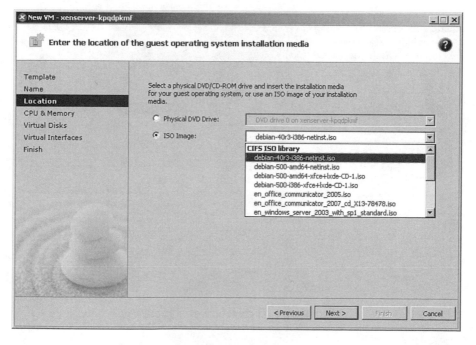

FIGURE 5-8   Select your installation media.

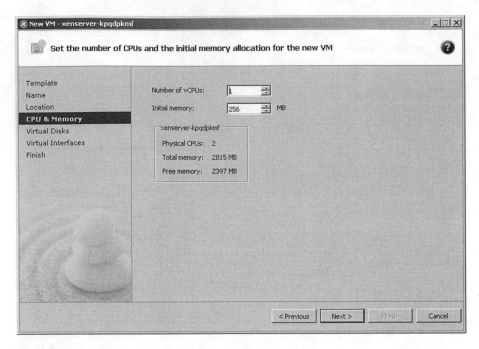

FIGURE 5-9 Select the number of virtual CPUs and memory for the new VM.

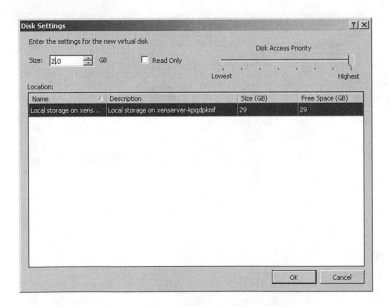

FIGURE 5-10 Select the virtual disk size and location.

9. Click Next to continue.

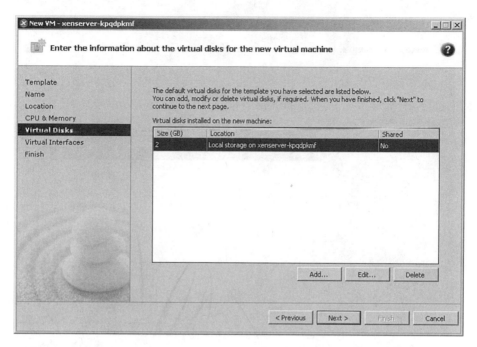

FIGURE 5-11   The Virtual Machine Wizard showing the new virtual disk.

10. Select or add a virtual network interface to your new VM, and click Next. See Figure 5-12.

    Your VM is now complete. You may, on completion of this wizard, begin installing your new VM's operating system or uncheck the Start VM Automatically box and continue.

11. Click Finish to complete the wizard.

Upon completion of the New Virtual Machine Wizard, your new VM is created with the parameters and details given while stepping through the wizard. Your new VM is listed in the XenServer asset list, as shown in Figure 5-13.

To start your new VM, select it with a single mouse click and click Start from the XenCenter menu. The VM will boot from the ISO image selected during the wizard. Refer to the Appendix, "Virtual Machine Installation," for generic VM operating system installation instructions.

Customizing Virtual Machines

VMs, like physical machines, sometimes must have their configurations changed or tweaked along the way for better performance by adding more disk space, memory, an extra CPU, or a network interface.

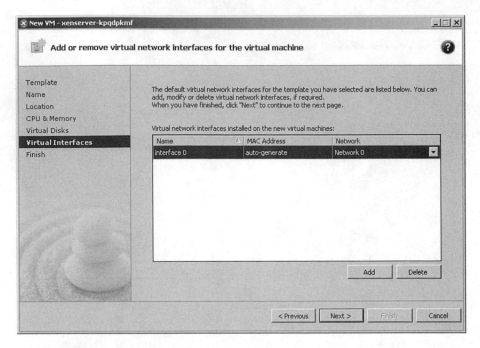

FIGURE 5-12 Select, add, or remove virtual network interfaces.

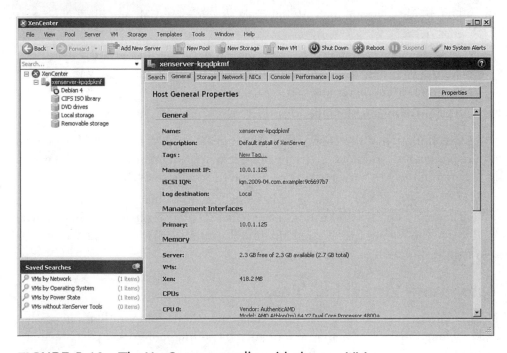

FIGURE 5-13 The XenServer asset list with the new VM.

- View your VM configuration by selecting the VM with a single mouse click. The VM may be powered on or off to view its configuration. See Figure 5-14.

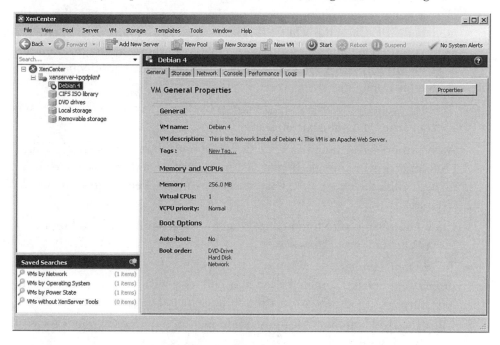

FIGURE 5-14 Virtual machine configuration.

- To rename or edit the description of your VM, click the Properties button from the VM General Properties tab. Make any changes and click OK when finished. See Figure 5-15 for your VM's properties.

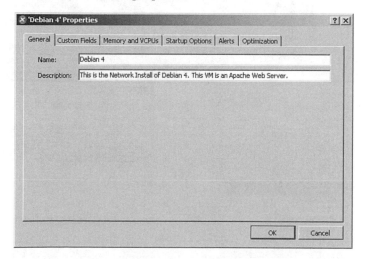

FIGURE 5-15 Virtual machine properties.

- To alter the amount of memory allocated to your VM, select the Memory and VCPUs tab.

  Here you may make changes to the memory originally allocated, the number of virtual CPUs, and the VM CPU priority. Unless you have a compelling reason to do so, don't alter the priority. An instance where you might want to alter the priority is if your VM services a CPU-intensive application (a web server, for example).

- Another property worth noting is Startup Options. On this tab, you can specify boot order and autostart on server boot.

  Autostart on server boot is a very important consideration—especially in production environments. If your VM must start when the host server is booted, click the check box. Otherwise, leave it unchecked to start your VM manually.

- Click OK when you're finished making any needed changes, and return to the VM general properties screen.

- To add more storage to a VM, click the Storage tab from the VM general properties screen. From here, you may add more virtual disks, attach available storage, or view the properties of the selected virtual disk.

- Click the Add button and fill in the information required for your new virtual disk. See Figure 5-16.

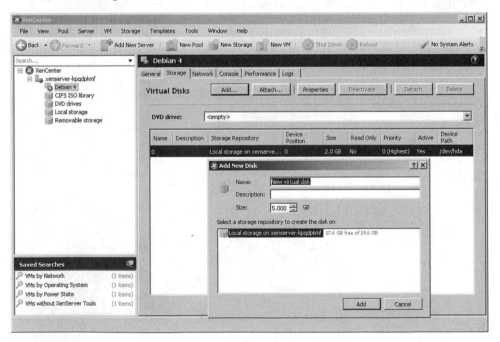

FIGURE 5-16 Adding a new virtual disk to a VM.

- When you're finished, click Add. The new virtual disk will appear in the list of virtual disks for the VM. You'll also receive a notification that the new disk will be visible to the VM upon restart of the VM. See Figure 5-17.

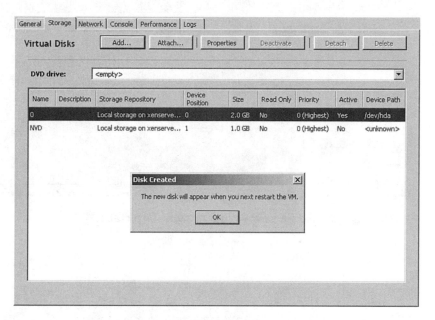

FIGURE 5-17   New virtual disk added.

- To add a new Virtual Network Interface, click the Network tab.
- Click the Add Interface button. The screen shown in Figure 5-18 allows you to add a new Virtual Network Interface.
- Select an available Network ID from the drop-down list.
- Choose an autogenerated MAC Address (recommended) or create one manually.
- Click Finish.

   You'll receive a message, shown in Figure 5-19, stating that your virtual network device changes will take effect on your next VM restart.

- Click OK to acknowledge the message.

   Note that the interface you created is not active. The message in Figure 5-19 is merely a reminder.

   Reboot your VM to see the new virtual network interface (Figure 5-20) become active and for your new virtual hard disk (Figure 5-21) to become attached to a device that your system can mount and use.

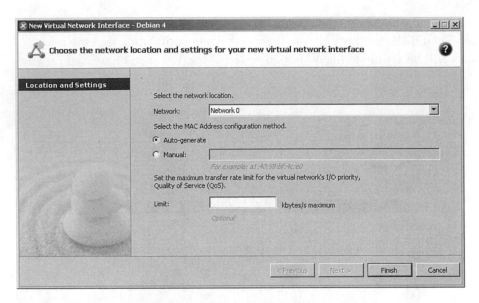

FIGURE 5-18 Add a new virtual network interface.

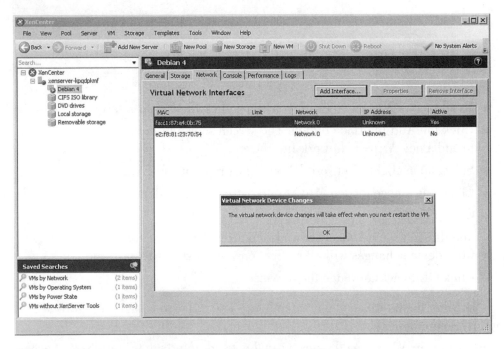

FIGURE 5-19 New virtual network interface added.

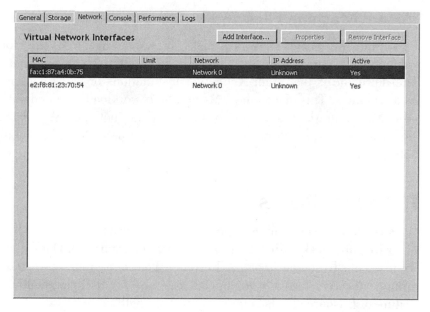

FIGURE 5-20   Virtual network interfaces (both active).

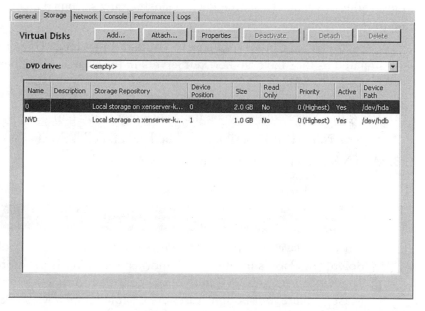

FIGURE 5-21   Virtual hard disks active and ready to use.

Virtual Machine Files and Folders

By default, XenServer uses local disks for VM storage. VMs are stored in logical volumes as separate volumes. This storage results in high-performance disk I/O. The downside is that other XenServer installations or pools cannot access these local volumes. This means the VMs and their workloads are dedicated to the specific system on which they were installed and are not agile. A VM installed onto a NFS volume, iSCSI volume, or SAN, in contrast, is agile and is capable of motion between hosts.

RESOURCE POOLS

Because XenServer is an enterprise-level hypervisor, it has more benefits than its other free and desktop-level virtualization counterparts do. One benefit is the ability to create Resource Pools. A Resource Pool is a group of virtual host systems grouped together logically to support a group of VMs dynamically. The dynamic feature of Resource Pools is their greatest strength.

It's nice that Resource Pools offer an efficient way to manage resources, but dynamic resource allocation, live migration between virtual hosts, and support for high-availability make Resource Pools a must for any serious data center virtualization project.

A Resource Pool consists of up to 16 virtual host systems. One of those systems is designated as the Master; other XenServers in the pool are Members or Slaves.

To create a new Pool

1. Click the New Pool button on the XenCenter menu bar.
2. Enter a Name and Description for the Pool and click Next.
3. Add XenServers to the new Pool and click Finish.

The first XenServer added to a Pool is designated as the Master.

NOTE

If a Pool Slave goes down, the Pool is still active. If the Pool Master goes down, the Pool is inactive until another XenServer is promoted to Master. The XenServers and VMs in the Pool continue to function in the event of a Master failure, but Pool features are disabled until a Master comes online.

VIRTUAL MACHINE TEMPLATES

Managing a large virtual infrastructure environment is, or can be, a daunting task. To simplify this task, you should implement Operating System Templates. There are several pre-built ones (remember that we bypassed them to install our VM using Other Install Media), but you can, and should, create your own.

The first step in the process is to install your VM's operating system, supporting software, updates, patches, VM tools, and applications. The second step is to convert that VM into a custom template from which you install other identical VMs. Unfortunately, it is an irreversible procedure. After your VM is converted to a template it will always be a template. If you ever need to edit your template, you'll have to delete the template, re-create the VM, convert it to a template, and create new VMs from it. Sound complicated? It isn't.

Converting a VM to a Template

If your VM is powered on, power it off. You can't convert a running VM to a template.

- When the VM is powered off, right click your VM and select Convert to Template.
- You'll receive notification that this is a one-way process. Click OK to confirm.

The VM is converted immediately to a template. Note the icon change from VM to template.

Installing a New VM from the Template

Now you're ready to install a new VM from the template.

1. Create a new VM by right-clicking the template you just created and select New VM.
2. Your new template now appears in the templates list. Select your template and click Next.
3. Name your new VM, write a description, and click Next.
4. Because you're using a template, start with an empty DVD drive. Click Next to continue.

WARNING

If you create a VM from one of the listed templates, you must provide installation media for the operating system that you select.

5. Now that you've created a Pool, you're prompted to designate a Home Server for this VM. A Home Server is the XenServer host that will originally host the VM, if possible (if adequate resources exist to host the new VM). You also have the option of selecting Automatically Select a Home Server with Available Resources. Click Next.

6. Allocate an appropriate number of CPUs and memory for the new VM. Click Next.

7. You may select, add, or remove storage (Virtual Hard Disks) and click Next.

8. You may select, add, or remove Virtual Network Interfaces and click Next.

9. Choose whether to start the VM automatically and click Finish.

Your new VM starts and is an exact clone of your Template version. When creating Templates, we suggest that you use Dynamic Host Control Protocol (DHCP) so that IP addresses are assigned to your Template VMs automatically. This prevents IP address conflicts when starting new VMs created from the Template.

XenServer in the Real World

Think ticketing sales, online or otherwise, and nine times out of ten, Ticketmaster is the first company people think of. While Ticketmaster does indeed command a whopping majority of the market, it is far from the only game in town. There are, in fact, approximately 75 ticketing system companies throughout the world, 12 of which command significant market share. None of this matters to most consumers, who never think much about who the ticket vendor is, so long as the purchasing process works as they expect it to.

One of the major players is Seatem, an international company with American owners. Some of its properties have roots that extend back to 1780 in the London theater world. The ticketing company counts itself among the top seven worldwide, and its application, the Enta Ticketing Solution, supports this. More than 50 million tickets that are sold from 250 clients in 24 countries flow through the Enta Ticketing Solution each year. Enta estimates that it services approximately 550 venues and that 65% to 70% of its purchases today are made online. This is a sharp increase from five years ago, where at most 20% of sales were made online.

Seatem's presence is strongest in the United Kingdom, where Enta UK makes use of the Enta Ticketing System to bring together the London theaters in a single pipe. Seatem is also in the process of opening an office in the Middle East, adding to its global reach, which currently extends to Australia and, of course, North America.

Enta USA is fairly new on the scene and is currently the only company in the Seatem family that is virtualized. Seatem plans to expand the model deployed in the United States in the near term. Its UK companies are using a managed system, and new clients will use a virtualized model as it is rolled out. Its Australian company is being rolled into a virtualized model now as well.

Although Enta, and Seatem, is an American company with a footprint in 540 venues in 23 countries, its actual North American presence is more recent and has quickly grown to be significant in part because it has looked beyond the typical entertainment venues and into other areas underserved by the major online ticketing outlets, such as museums. In 2007, the company began building a managed service from the ground up in Baton Rouge, Louisiana. Virtualization is a key part of it, and because ENTA was a new company, it was in the fortunate position of being able to build its data center from scratch.

Early on, the company opted to build its software infrastructure around Citrix. "Citrix gurus" on staff were already familiar with the software. Because Enta functions much like an MSP (its actual customers are venues, not end users) and it intended to build a cloud-like infrastructure, Xen seemed a natural fit.

Indeed, when Enta launched its virtualization efforts in the third quarter of 2008, few technical hitches occurred. There were, however, some hiccups on the human element side. The company that built it was the only Citrix shop in the area. Because of its staff members' claimed qualifications, Enta hired the company to do the Xen install.

The consultants muddled through, taking three times as long as estimated. Eventually, Enta was up and running. Since then, their technical team has worked with Citrix support to get XenServer running even more efficiently.

Unlike most companies that get started with virtualization by dabbling, Enta went in whole hog, virtualizing 80% of customer-facing apps. All the web servers and sites are virtualized, and credit cards are processed on virtual servers.

Because of the nature of what it was virtualizing, it was even more important that it work. Customers don't care about the back end, so long as their transaction is accomplished smoothly and securely.

To accomplish this, Enta has six HP quad-core boxes running enterprise editions of the full suite of Xen software. Three have 96GB of RAM and are running between 14 and 18 VMs. The other three have 64GB of RAM and are running between 10 and 14 VMs. The number of virtual servers fluctuates because of constant dynamic provisioning. Enta makes full use of the provisioning tools found in the management console to reallocate resources on-the-fly.

The servers connect to a SAN, which is backed up to another SAN every 15 seconds, and then to tape each night. Two database servers are hooked into the SAN and backed up to the second SAN as well. The database servers are not virtualized at this time and most likely will not be for security reasons.

Should a VM crash, the software has been configured to automatically create another image and take that image to the second server, theoretically not impacting the end user experience. Following this model, the tech team found it easier to protect one box housing 12 VMs compared to 12 physical servers.

Since the initial rollout, Enta has made a number of changes. First, it began cultivating its Xen talent in-house, hiring an admin self-taught in Xen. Next, it began documenting the what and how of everything that was virtualized. Enta plans to continue to grow its virtual infrastructure, particularly in the area of web ticketing.

The other big change on the horizon involves moving away from a Citrix architecture to .NET architecture. This will not impact its virtualization choices directly, because it involves the databases, but it will change the way data is delivered to clients.

Enta USA is already moving away from Citrix as a way to save money. Servicing its customers through Citrix's access portal costs Enta approximately $130 per user for them to connect to application. .NET costs considerably less. Enta has already begun the transition to .NET, with an even split between web-based and Citrix management.

Even if cost-savings was not the primary driver in why Enta virtualized, it has not gone unnoticed. Virtualization has, in fact, saved Enta a great deal of money. Not only has the company been able to get by with less hardware, but it has also been able to pay less in licensing fees for its software, because fewer OS instances have been required. This cost savings is passed along to end users; Enta's clients' handling fees are typically in the $2.50 to $3 range. That's something that customers certainly do notice.

SUMMARY

XenServer is an extremely powerful and versatile hypervisor and now that it's free, it's the perfect choice for almost any data center application, particularly those running in a cloud-based environment. For high-availability, notifications, and certain storage options, you'll need to upgrade to Citrix Essentials, which is a commercial product enhancement to XenServer. This chapter is by no means an exhaustive treatment of XenServer and its many spectacular features, but it does step you through how to get up, running, and productive in a short amount of time.

This chapter provided an introduction to Citrix XenServer and its method of handling VMs. It examined the basics of the XenCenter console, as well as how to create VMs and how to create a Template from a VM.

## CHAPTER 6

Microsoft Virtual PC

Virtual PC (VPC) was Microsoft's original entry into the virtualization market. Never an innovator, Microsoft was fairly late to the virtualization party. In 2003 it acquired Connectix, a company that developed virtualization software for Windows and Macintosh environments. Three years later, Microsoft released Virtual PC 2004 as an emulation suite for Mac OS X on PowerPC and a virtualization suite for Windows. The Windows version was free; the Mac version was not. A month later it announced the Macintosh version would not be ported to Intel-based Macs, which were replacing PowerPC-based Macs, thus cutting out the non-Windows market.

In early 2007, Microsoft released VPC 2007, the current version in production. As expected, Virtual PC 2007 is available only for the Windows platform. Microsoft bills it as "Windows only"; however, most x86 operating systems, including Linux, can run inside VPC, although Microsoft does not officially support them. Key functionality new in this release includes support for Windows Vista as both a host operating system and guest, support for 64-bit host operating systems, support for hardware-assisted virtualization, network-based installation of a guest operating system, and the capability to run virtual machines (VM) on multiple monitors. At this time, support for linked disks in a VM was eliminated.

In mid-May 2008, Microsoft released Virtual PC 2007 Service Pack 1, which basically added support for service packs of already supported operating systems.

Originally viewed as a desktop product, VPC has also been getting some play as a server virtualization platform. It was never intended to be used as a server product, however. That was Virtual Server and, later, Hyper-V's domain. Hyper-V will be examined in Chapter 7, "Microsoft Hyper-V."

In its original release VPC was essentially a standalone product. This will change with the release of Windows 7, where VPC gets a slight name change

(Windows Virtual PC) and fills a vital role: It facilitates the much publicized Windows XP mode and integrates it into the new operating system to enable virtualization. Other key capabilities include USB and multithread support, as well as folder integration between a host and its guests.

At the time of this writing, a beta version has recently become available for download on Microsoft's website, www.microsoft.com/windows/virtual-pc/download. aspx. Because this is a beta and subject to change, this chapter will focus on Microsoft Virtual PC 2007, not Windows Virtual PC.

THE VPC CONSOLE

The VPC Console is almost minimalist in size but not in function. The console, like most hosted virtualization software applications, keeps a list of all VMs, running or not, in its main window. This console is the primary interface for VM management, but VPC VMs can be managed at the command line as well.

Figure 6-1 is a snapshot of our VPC Console. You can see that several VMs are listed, and only one is currently running.

FIGURE 6-1   The Microsoft VPC Console.

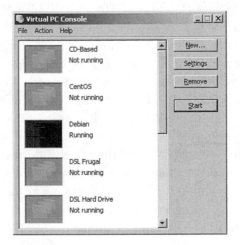

Unlike other virtualization software consoles, Microsoft VPC launches each VM in its own window. Individual VM windows present advantages and disadvantages for users. Some think that it makes their workspace too cluttered, whereas others think that individual windows give each VM its own identity, defining it more as a whole machine unto itself. Hyper-V, in contrast, has a console similar to other vendors' virtualization software, where all VMs are centrally managed and run from the console interface application.

Creating Virtual Machines

VPC offers three options when creating a new VM. All use the New Virtual Machine Wizard.

- Create a VM with custom settings.
- Create a VM using the default settings
- Import an existing VM.

New Virtual Machine Wizard

To create a new VM, follow these steps:

1. Launch the VPC application and click Next on the Welcome screen.
2. Click New to start the New Virtual Machine Wizard.
3. Select one of the three options for creating a new VM and click Next.

   For this first example, we are going to create a custom VM (Option 1: Create a Virtual Machine). See Figure 6-2.

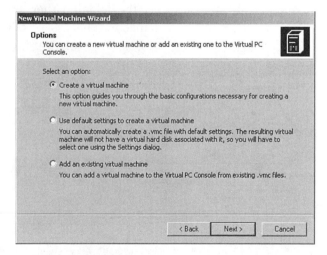

FIGURE 6-2   The Microsoft VPC New Virtual Machine Wizard.

   As shown in Figure 6-3, enter the name of your new VM. We are installing Fedora XFCE (a version of Fedora Linux with the XFCE window manager).

4. Name the VM (for example Fedora_XFCE) and click Next.

   The default location for all VPC VM .vmc files is C:\My Documents\My Virtual Machines. Browse to and select a new location if you prefer. If you accept this location, it doesn't mean your virtual disk(s) can't reside in another location.

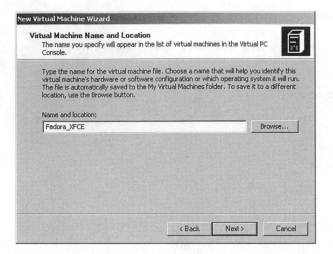

FIGURE 6-3 Naming the VM.

The wizard attempts to identify your operating system by the name you supply. If it can't, you'll see the default, Other, as the identified system. Use the drop-down menu to change it, if necessary. See Figure 6-4.

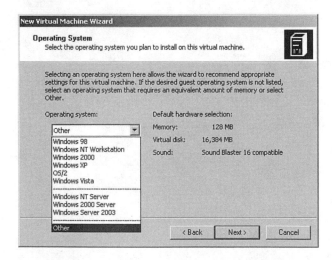

FIGURE 6-4 Select the operating system for the new VM.

5. Select the correct operating system for your new VM and click Next.

Notice that the default memory (RAM) is set to 128MB and the virtual disk is 16GB. We will adjust those values in subsequent screens.

As Figure 6-5 illustrates, you can either accept the recommended RAM or adjust it by selecting Adjusting the RAM and using the slider bar to increase or decrease the allotted RAM for the VM.

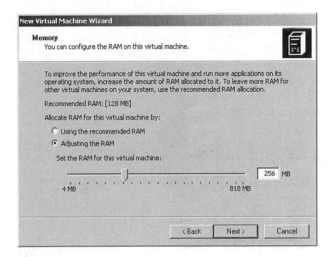

FIGURE 6-5   Adjusting the Amount of RAM for the VM.

6. Select Adjusting the RAM.

7. Use the slider bar to increase the amount of RAM to 256MB and click Next.

   The next screen, Figure 6-6, is the Virtual Hard Disk Options screen, where you can choose an existing virtual hard disk or create a new one. If you create several of the same size of virtual disks for your VMs, you should have a "golden" virtual disk that you copy into your destination folder for use with all VMs. Doing this also speeds the process of creating VMs.

8. Select A New Virtual Hard Disk and click Next.

   Select a location for your virtual hard disk. This disk can be located on any drive that has sufficient space and where you have write permission. As shown in Figure 6-7, I am using Drive G:, a local drive, to store my new VM.

9. Enter, or browse to, the location for your new virtual disk.

10. Enter a size in MB (Megabytes) for the new virtual disk and click Next.

    The wizard completes, and your VM is created. See Figure 6-8.

    Your new VM is ready to start and install or customize. Consult the Appendix, "Virtual Machine Installation," for step-by-step guidance in how to do that.

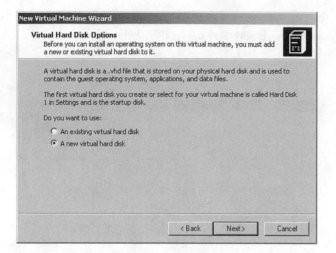

FIGURE 6-6   The Virtual Hard Disk Options screen.

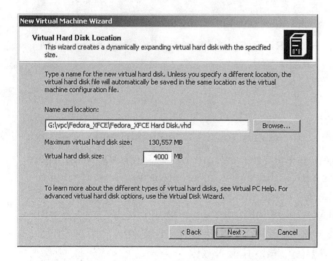

FIGURE 6-7   Select the location and size for the virtual disk.

Installing the Virtual Machine's Operating System

Installing a new VM is a little different in VPC in that you can't directly alter the behavior of the CD/DVD drive using the Settings button on the console. Because you need some sort of installation media from which to install the VM, this is an important step. You can't preselect an ISO or alternative drive to boot from until you start the VM.

FIGURE 6-8 New VM in inventory.

To see how this works, consider the following example:

1. Select the VM you want to install an operating system into and click the Start button.

   The VM launches, as shown in Figure 6-9.

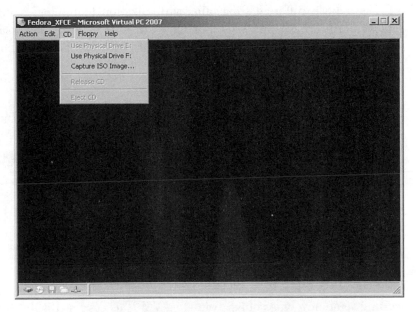

FIGURE 6-9 Altering the boot options for a running VM.

2. Click CD from the powered-on VM menu, and select the physical drive or ISO image from which to boot.

If you select Capture ISO Image, you are given a browse window from which to navigate and select your ISO image.

Should you miss your opportunity to select a drive or ISO image before the VM boots, it will attempt a network boot (PXE—Preboot Execution Environment). Click Action, Pause to pause the boot process. Locate your ISO or select the physical CD drive. Click Action, Reset to restart the boot process.

The VM will boot from your media and installation can begin.

Importing a Virtual Machine

There is no *native* way to import another vendor's VM into VPC. A few third-party applications exist that can make the transition by copying VM disks and converting them to the new format.

Customizing Virtual Machines

After your VM is established, it is far from permanent. The beauty of virtualization is that hardware can be easily added and removed or reconfigured.

Removing Hardware from a Virtual Machine

VPC is a little different from other virtualization technologies in that you don't remove hardware from its VMs, but simply disable it. When it's disabled, the hardware doesn't show up in the VM's list of hardware and isn't detected by hardware detection scans in any operating system.

To disable hardware components in a VM:

1. Open the VPC Console, select a VM, and click the Settings button.

   The Setting for Your Virtual Machine opens and presents you with a centralized applet for customizing your VM's hardware settings. See Figure 6-10.

2. Select Sound from the list, and deselect Enable Sound Card in the right pane.

You'll notice that the Current Value for Sound changes from Enabled to Disabled. See Figure 6-11.

When the VM is booted, sound will not be available.

Adding Hardware to a Virtual Machine

Adding some new types of hardware to a VM is as easy as disabling them; you simply select the component you want to add.

To add a parallel port to your VM:

1. Select LPT1 from the list. The current value is None.

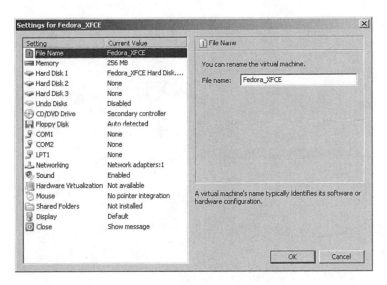

FIGURE 6-10   VM hardware settings screen.

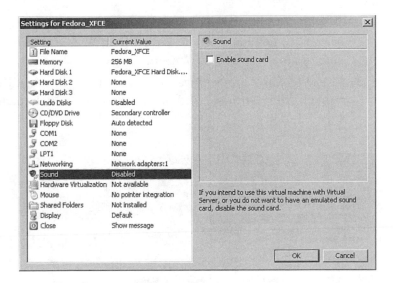

FIGURE 6-11   Disabling sound in a VM.

2. Select Physical Parallel Port in the right pane, as shown in Figure 6-12.

   The LPT1 port is now enabled and will be detected on the next boot of the VM.

   Probably the most popular additional hardware item added to a VM is a hard disk. VPC allows three hard disks (drives). They are all IDE-type drives and will translate as such if you migrate a VPC VM to a different vendor's virtualization software.

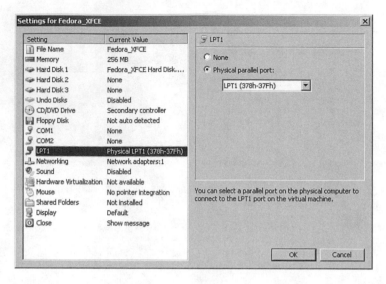

FIGURE 6-12 Adding an LPT port to the VM.

To add an additional hard disk, you can either select one created previously or create a new one with the Virtual Disk Wizard. The following example employs the Virtual Disk Wizard.

3. From the Hardware Settings window from step 2, select Hard Disk 2, and then click the Virtual Disk Wizard button in the right pane, as shown in Figure 6-13.

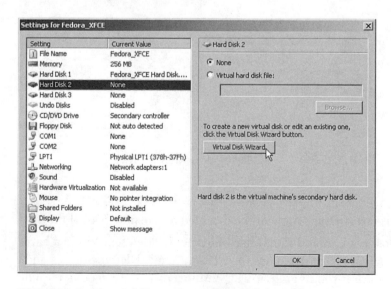

FIGURE 6-13 Adding a new virtual disk to the VM.

The Virtual Disk Wizard launches and displays the Virtual Disk Wizard Welcome screen (not shown).

4. Click Next on the Virtual Disk Welcome screen.

On the next screen, Disk Options, you have the option of creating a new virtual disk or editing an existing virtual disk.

5. Select Create a New Virtual Disk and click Next.

6. Select the Virtual Disk Type to create (virtual hard disk or virtual floppy disk) and click Next.

7. Browse to or enter a location for your virtual hard disk, name the new virtual hard disk with the .vhd extension (for example, G:\vpc\Fedora_XFCE\ Disk2.vhd) as shown in Figure 6-14, and click Next.

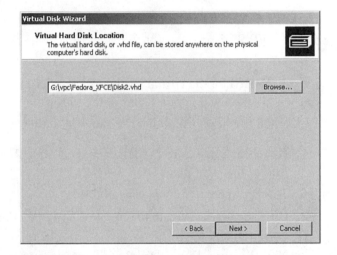

FIGURE 6-14 Selecting the location and name for the new virtual hard disk.

8. Select Fixed Size and click Next.

9. Enter a size for the new virtual hard disk in megabytes, as shown in Figure 6-15, and click Next.

After you've clicked Next, you're presented with a summary screen showing the details of your new virtual hard disk (not shown). If you need to make any changes to the disk, click Back; otherwise, click Finish on the Summary screen to create the new disk.

10. Click Finish to complete the Virtual Disk Wizard (Summary screen not shown).

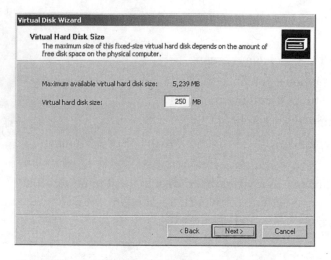

FIGURE 6-15 Choosing the size of the new virtual hard disk.

All 250MB for the virtual hard disk (Disk2.vhd) is now allocated. The hard disk you just created will not be listed in the hardware inventory.

To add the new virtual disk to your VM, follow these steps:

1. Refer back to Figure 6-13, select Hard Disk 2, and select Virtual Hard Disk File in the right pane.

   The Browse button is now available.

2. Click Browse, navigate to (or enter) G:\vpc\Fedora_XFCE\Disk2.vhd, for example, and click Open.

   Now the virtual disk, Disk2.vhd, appears in the hardware inventory list.

3. Click OK to confirm your selection and make the change permanent.

Reconfiguring Virtual Machine Hardware

VPC has an array of parameters that can be changed or reconfigured. You can adjust RAM, change the name of your VM, change a dynamic hard disk to a fixed-sized one, change the number and type of network adapters, enable pointer integration, alter characteristics of COM ports, and more. We will highlight two popular changes: adjusting the amount of RAM allocated to a VM and changing a dynamic virtual hard disk to a fixed-sized one.

Adjusting RAM   Adjusting RAM is a straightforward process in VPC.

1. Select Memory from the hardware inventory list.

2. Increase the amount of RAM to 384MB by entering 384 into the RAM field. See Figure 6-16.

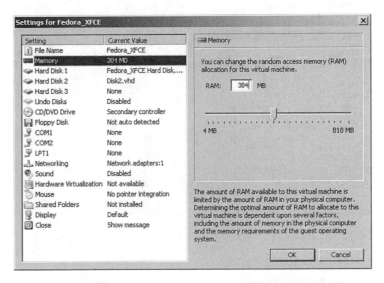

FIGURE 6-16 Adjusting the amount of RAM for a VM.

You can also use the slider bar to perform this function.

On the next boot, the VM will automatically recognize and use the new RAM.

Changing a Dynamically Expanding Virtual Hard Disk to a Fixed Size For this example, assume a new 100MB dynamically expanding virtual hard disk (Disk3.vhd) has been created based on the instructions in the section "Adding Hardware to a Virtual Machine."

To convert the disk from dynamically expanding to fixed size, follow these steps:

1. Select the disk in the VM's hardware inventory list. See Figure 6-17.

2. Click the Virtual Disk Wizard button in the right pane.

3. Click Next on the Welcome screen.

4. Select Edit an Existing Virtual Disk and click Next.

5. Browse to or enter the full path to the selected virtual disk and click Next.

6. On the Virtual Disk Information and Options screen, shown in Figure 6-18, select Convert It to a Fixed-Size Virtual Hard Disk and click Next.

7. Accept the default Replacing the Current File and click Next.

8. Click Finish to start the conversion process.

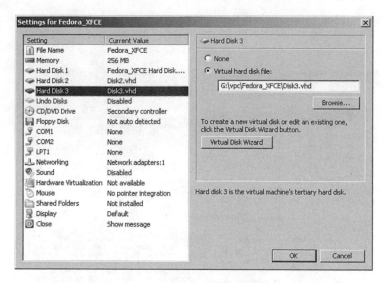

FIGURE 6-17 Select the dynamic disk for conversion.

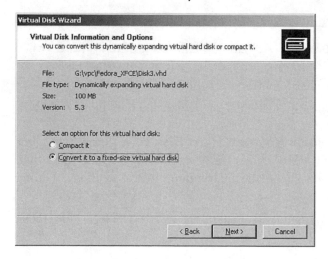

FIGURE 6-18 Preparing to convert a dynamically expanding disk to fixed size.

If everything goes well, you'll receive the message The Virtual Hard Disk Was Converted Successfully.

9. Click Close to acknowledge the message.

VIRTUAL MACHINE FILES AND FOLDERS

The default location for Microsoft VPC files is C:\My Documents\My Virtual Machines. This location is where the definition files are stored. Hard disk files may be (and should be) stored elsewhere for performance enhancement.

File and Folder Security

Any serious virtualization solution will be installed on a server, and an administrator will most likely install software such as VPC. An Administrator's My Documents files aren't accessible to other system users; therefore, the definition files are protected by design.

All VM virtual disk files should be placed in a parent folder that only the Administrator can access. All folders under the parent inherit permissions accordingly.

File Names and Roles

The VM definition file that resides in the My Virtual Machines folder is an XML file that describes all the attributes for a VM. The file is plain text and is editable with any text editor. The entire contents of the file are too long to list here, but Listing 6-1 offers a glimpse with an excerpt from our sample VM.

Generally, only two types of files are associated with any VM: the VMC and the VHD files.

- <VirtualMachineName>.vmc—The VM configuration (vmc) or definition file
- <VirtualMachineName>.vhd—A virtual disk file associated with a specific VM

LISTING 6-1   Excerpt from Virtual Machine Definition File: Fedora_XFCE.vmc

```xml
<?xml version="1.0" encoding="UTF-16"?>
<!- Microsoft Virtual Machine Options and Settings ->
<preferences>
    <version type="string">2.0</version>
    <alerts>
        <notifications>
            <no_boot_disk type="boolean">true</no_boot_disk>
        </notifications>
    </alerts>
    <hardware>
        <memory>
            <ram_size type="integer">256</ram_size>
        </memory>
        <pci_bus>
            <ethernet_adapter>
                <controller_count type="integer">1</controller_count>
                <ethernet_controller id="0">
                    <virtual_network>
                        <id
type="bytes">A39EDD46A0C811DB825EAB789EA38CC0</id>
                        <name type="string">SiS 900-Based PCI Fast
Ethernet Adapter</name>
                    </virtual_network>
```

```
                        <ethernet_card_address
type="bytes">0003FF126268</ethernet_card_address>
                </ethernet_controller>
        </ethernet_adapter>
        <video_adapter>
                <vram_size type="integer">8</vram_size>
        </video_adapter>
```

SUMMARY

This chapter introduces Microsoft's VPC—Microsoft's original virtualization solution product. The VPC Console is the centralized interface to all your VMs.

You stepped through how to create a VM from scratch, how to make changes to hardware components, and how to customize a VM.

The chapter concludes with a look at VPC's files and security information.

## CHAPTER 7

Microsoft Hyper-V

Hyper-V is Microsoft's entry into the server virtualization space. Its desktop virtualization product, Virtual PC (covered in Chapter 6, "Microsoft Virtual PC"), has enjoyed widespread success but can't compare to a server-based hypervisor product. Hyper-V is, as the name implies, a true Windows-based hypervisor. You'll need a dedicated, 64-bit, multicore processor, high-capacity server system on which to install it. Windows 2008 ships Hyper-V ready.

Hyper-V should prove to be a formidable player in the server virtualization market because it includes native support for Windows virtualization. It is a typical Microsoft application in that it is easy to use, intuitive, and has native hooks into the Windows operating system.

THE CONSOLE

The Hyper-V console (shown in Figure 7-1) is your single interface for creating and managing virtual machines (VM). To open the Hyper-V Manager, Click Start, Programs, Administrative Tools, Hyper-V Manager.

The console (Hyper-V Manager) is where you manage (create, edit, delete) your VMs and is your interface to the consoles of your VMs. VMs, correctly configured, can be accessed via network protocols (SSH, Terminal Services, HTTP). In the next section, you'll learn how to create a VM.

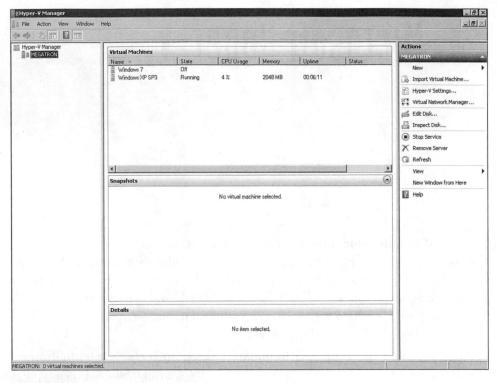

FIGURE 7-1   The Hyper-V Manager console.

Creating Virtual Machines

After you've logged in to your Windows 2008 Server and opened the Hyper-V console application, you're ready to begin creating and working with VMs.

1. To create a new VM, select your Windows 2008 server from the inventory in the left window, as shown in Figure 7-2, right-click it, and select New, Virtual Machine.

2. The New Virtual Machine Wizard launches and you're presented with the Before You Begin screen, as shown in Figure 7-3. Click Next to continue.

3. The next step is to name your VM and to select where to store it. See Figure 7-4 for an example.

4. If you aren't sure where to store your new VM, click the Browse button and select a location. Click Next to continue.

5. Allocate RAM to your new VM by entering the amount of RAM in megabytes (MB). See Figure 7-5.

6. Click Next to continue.

FIGURE 7-2 Creating a new VM.

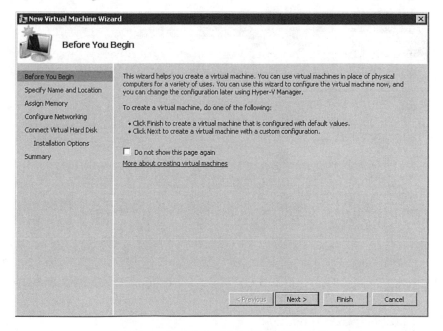

FIGURE 7-3 Starting the Virtual Machine Wizard.

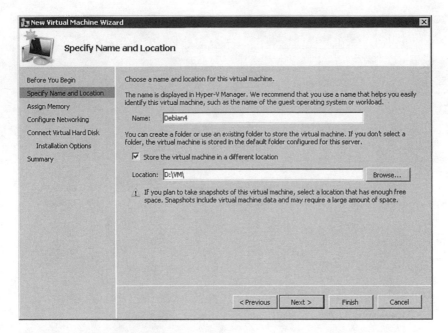

FIGURE 7-4 Specifying the VM name and location.

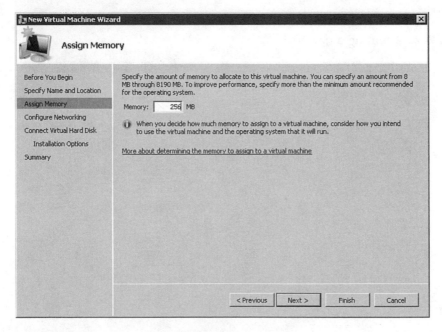

FIGURE 7-5 Allocating RAM to the new VM.

7. On the next screen, Configure Networking, as shown in Figure 7-6, select a network connection from the drop-down list. All possible host network connections will be shown in your list.

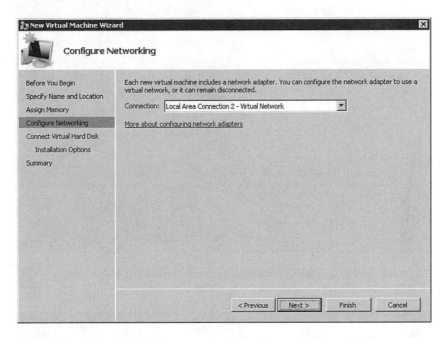

FIGURE 7-6   Selecting a network connection for the VM.

8. After you've selected a network connection, click Next to go to the next screen.

9. Your next task is to create a virtual hard disk for your new VM. To do this, name the virtual hard disk, select a location for the new disk, and enter a size in gigabytes (GB) for the disk. See Figure 7-7.

10. If you want to select and use an existing virtual hard disk, select that option, browse to the disk you want to use, and select it. You also have the option of not creating a virtual hard disk at this time.

11. Click Next when you're finished. As shown in Figure 7-8, the next screen allows you to choose installation media from which to install your VM's operating system.

12. Select from a physical CD/DVD drive, an ISO file, a floppy disk, or from a network-based installation server. You also have the option of creating the VM without specifying any installation media.

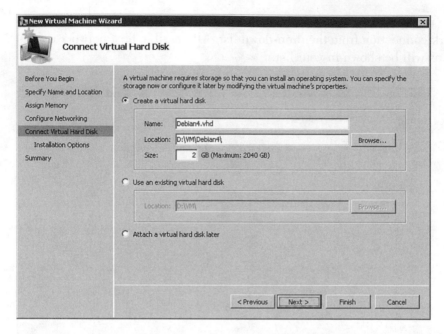

FIGURE 7-7   Creating a new virtual hard disk for the VM.

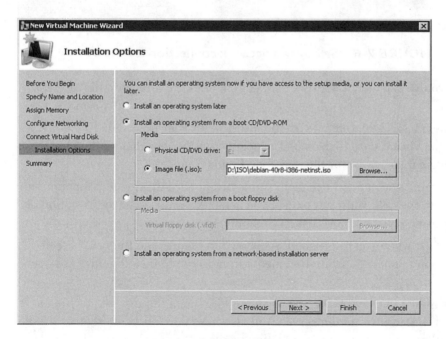

FIGURE 7-8   Selecting installation media.

13. Click Next to continue. Your new VM is ready for creation. The summary page for your new VM is shown in Figure 7-9.

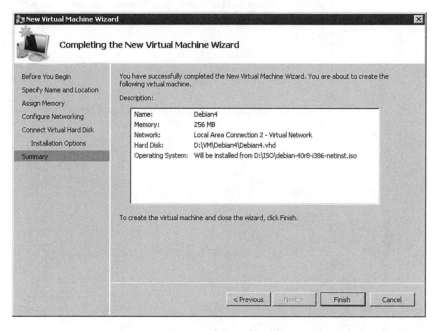

FIGURE 7-9   Completing the New Virtual Machine Wizard.

14. If you're satisfied with your new VM's configuration, click Finish. You can also click Previous to go back and correct or edit any of the settings for this VM prior to its creation.

15. Click Finish to create the new VM. Figure 7-10 shows your new VM in the inventory. Notice that its state is Off.

16. To connect to your new VM's console, select your new VM from the inventory and click the Connect option in the right (Actions) window.

17. As shown in Figure 7-11, select Start from the Actions menu to start the VM.

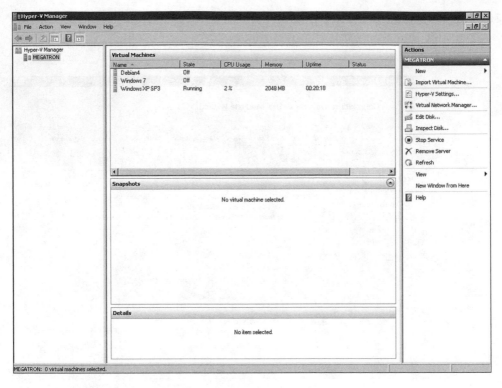

FIGURE 7-10   Inspecting the VM inventory.

Customizing Virtual Machines

With the VM still powered off, you can edit the VM settings or properties by selecting Settings in the Actions menu. All editable settings for the VM are displayed in a new window, as shown in Figure 7-12.

Fortunately, the Settings screen is self-explanatory. For each hardware type, there is a full explanation of your options for adding or changing a setting for the VM. One of the best features of Hyper-V is the capability to change the BIOS attribute of boot order from this screen. As you can see from Figure 7-12, the current setting is to Boot from CD, which is handy for the first boot to installation media.

In contrast, in other virtualization software applications, you have to power on the VM and act quickly to enter the BIOS to make this same change. For more detailed instructions in how to proceed through the installation, consult the Appendix, "Virtual Machine Installation."

FIGURE 7-11   Connecting to the VM's console.

VIRTUAL MACHINE FILES AND FOLDERS

The default location for VM virtual hard disk files is your chosen location for your VMs. For example, D:\VM, as shown in the previous section, is the repository we selected when building the VM.

File and Folder Security

Security on files and folders in Hyper-V is standard Windows security. The VM files are owned by Administrator or by the user that creates the VM.

File Names and Roles

Hyper-V virtual hard disk files are named with the same convention as Virtual PC virtual hard disk (.vhd) files. Unlike Virtual PC (covered in Chapter 6), Hyper-V doesn't make use of the VM configuration (.vmc) files. Instead, it uses cryptically named XML files to hold the VM configuration information.

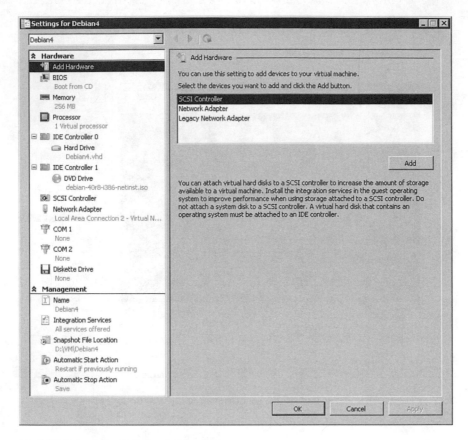

FIGURE 7-12 Editing VM settings.

SUMMARY

Hyper-V ushers in a new era of Windows virtualization a la Microsoft. For Windows virtualization, there might be nothing better, but recently Microsoft has made agreements with Red Hat and Citrix to ensure cross-compatibility that many enterprise users demand from such a product. This new era of forced compatibility with non-Microsoft operating systems might be exactly what systems integrators and resellers historically have wished for.

Only maturity and third-party management applications will make Hyper-V the enterprise tool that developers and marketers foresee it becoming. Hyper-V is easy to install and use, but only time will tell if it is capable of usurping market share from its competitors.

## CHAPTER 8

VirtualBox

Sun Microsystems is no stranger to virtualization. First came operating-system-level virtualization in the form of Solaris Containers, and Zones, in Solaris 10 in 2005. In February 2008, Sun acquired Innotek, a German software developer, and with that its x86 virtualization software package, VirtualBox. Sun rolled VirtualBox into its xVM group, which consists of four x86 virtualization technologies: xVM Server (a bare-metal hypervisor), xVM Ops Center (a data center automation tool), Sun VDI software (a desktop virtualization offering), and xVM VirtualBox.

VirtualBox can be configured for server, desktop, and embedded environments. It is available in an open source version (in both executable and source code) and a commercial version (via RDP Server, USB support, USB over RDP, and Serial ATA controller).

VirtualBox at the time of this writing is in version 2.2. It is available for Windows, Linux, Macintosh, and OpenSolaris hosts and supports myriad guest operating systems, including Windows (NT 4.0, 2000, XP, Server 2003, Vista, and Windows 7), DOS/Windows 3.x, Linux (2.4 and 2.6), Solaris and OpenSolaris, and OpenBSD.

THE VIRTUALBOX SERVER CONSOLE

The VirtualBox Server Console, also known as the VirtualBox graphical user interface, is a very attractive console—possibly one of the most attractive and intuitive out there. Although this isn't a review, per se, it bears mentioning that VirtualBox is visually pleasing and easy to use. The designers of VirtualBox thought out the detail, color, and layout of the product from top to bottom, as Figure 8-1 demonstrates.

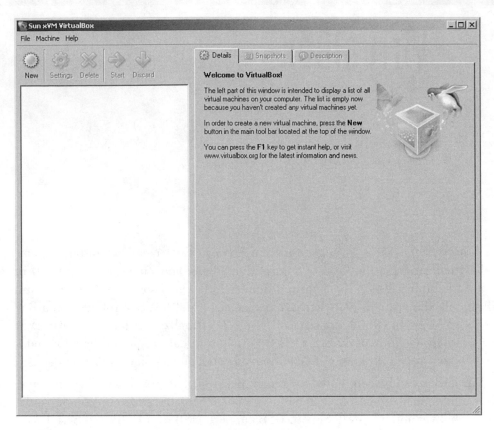

FIGURE 8-1 The Sun xVM VirtualBox console.

Admittedly, the console looks more impressive when populated with virtual machines (VM). About all you can do at this point is set file location preferences or create a new VM.

To set file location preferences, follow these steps:

1. From the Console menu, select File, Preferences to launch the VirtualBox Preferences applet shown in Figure 8-2.

2. Accept or change the locations of your virtual disk image (VDI) and your virtual machine definition files.

NOTE

VRDPAuth is the location of the remote display protocol (RDP) authentication library. The default setting is acceptable for most installations.

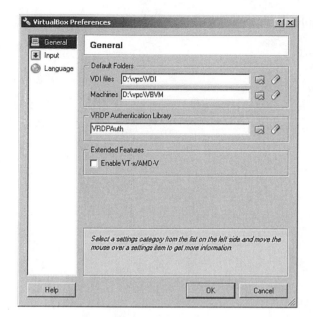

FIGURE 8-2 The VirtualBox Preferences screen.

If you're running VirtualBox on a new system with an Intel or AMD CPU with VM extensions (check your CPU model's documentation to be sure), enabling the extended features offers better VM performance.

The Input menu selection allows you to choose a hot key to define keyboard capture for VMs. The default is the right Ctrl key.

3. Click OK to accept your changes.

Creating Virtual Machines

VirtualBox is similar to other virtualization software applications in that it provides a centralized management console, a Virtual Machine Creation Wizard, and the capability to import other types of VMs. After a VM is created, the interface provides a single page management tool you can work with.

Virtual Machine Wizard

To create a new VM, follow these steps:

1. Click the New button on the VirtualBox console to launch the New Virtual Machine Wizard.

2. Click Next on the New Virtual Machine Welcome screen.

3. Name your new VM (for example, Fedora_XFCE).

4. Select an OS Type (for example, Fedora) from the drop-down options as listed here, and click Next.

Other/Unknown
DOS
Windows 3.1
Windows 95
Windows 98
Windows Me
Windows NT 4
Windows XP
Windows Server 2003
Windows Vista
Windows Server 2008
OS/2 Warp 3
OS/2 Warp 4
OS/2 Warp 4.5
eComStation
Linux 2.2
Linux 2.4
Linux 2.6
Arch Linux
Debian
openSUSE
Fedora
Gentoo Linux
Mandriva
Red Hat
Ubuntu
Xandros
FreeBSD
OpenBSD
NetBSD
Netware
Solaris
L4

5. Allocate RAM to your VM by entering the amount into the field or using the slider bar, and click Next to continue.

The recommended RAM is already set up for you by the wizard, as shown in Figure 8-3.

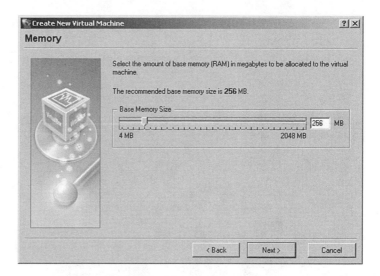

FIGURE 8-3 Allocating memory (RAM) to a VM.

The next step is to create or select a virtual disk for the new VM. As Figure 8-4 shows, no virtual disk exists yet; you must create one. When one does exist, you can select it from the drop-down list or by browsing to one and selecting it for use.

FIGURE 8-4 Virtual Hard Disk decision screen.

6. Click the New button on the Virtual Hard Disk screen as shown in Figure 8-4.

7. Click Next on the Welcome to the Create New Virtual Disk Wizard screen.

8. On the Virtual Disk Image Type screen, select Fixed-Size Image, and click Next.

9. On the screen shown in Figure 8-5, name your VDIfile.

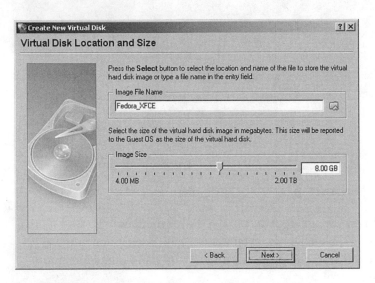

FIGURE 8-5 Supplying a name, location, and size for a virtual disk.

A default name is supplied for you (Fedora_XFCE).

10. Also on this screen, adjust the size of the virtual disk to fit your needs.

   The recommended size is supplied for you. Use the slider bar or enter the exact size in MB, GB, or TB.

11. Click Next to continue.

12. Click Finish to create the virtual disk.

   You are now returned to the New Virtual Machine Wizard at the point where you left. Your new virtual disk is selected for you.

13. Click Next to continue.

14. Take a final look and double-check your VM parameter. Click Finish on the Summary screen to complete the wizard.

You are then returned to the main VirtualBox console screen. The new VM will be listed as inventory in the left pane, and its associated hardware will be in the right pane. See Figure 8-6.

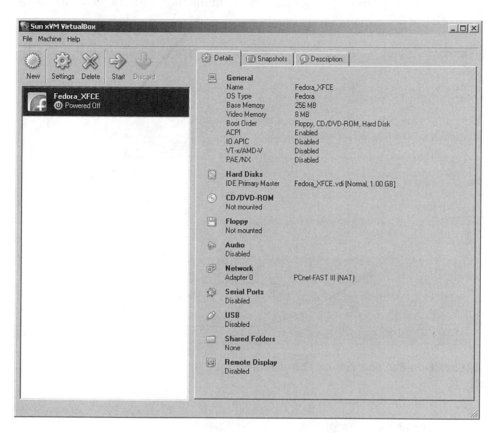

FIGURE 8-6   VirtualBox console with VM and hardware list.

Importing a Virtual Machine

You can import VMware VM disk images (VMDK) files into VirtualBox via the Virtual Disk Manager (VDM). VDM is an applet that allows you to manage VDIs separately from individual VMs. The VDM keeps its own inventory of your VDIs, including virtual hard disks, CD/DVD images (ISO files), and floppy disk images.

The following example makes use of an existing VMware VM running Damn Small Linux (DSL) version 3.3 with a 2.4 kernel.

To import a VMware virtual disk, follow these steps:

1. Click File, Virtual Disk Manager from the VirtualBox menu.

   The Virtual Disk Manager launches and displays current VDIs, as shown in Figure 8-7.

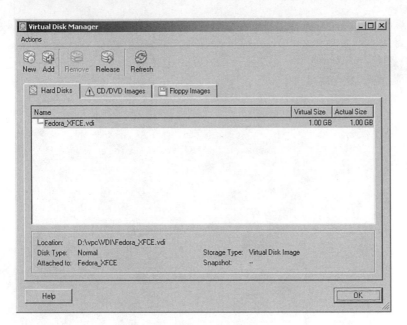

FIGURE 8-7   The Virtual Disk Manager.

2. Click the Add icon or select Actions, Add from the menu.

   A Browse window opens.

3. Navigate to, select, and open a VMware VDI (.vmdk file).

   The disk image immediately appears in the Virtual Disk Manager, as shown in Figure 8-8.

4. Click OK on the Virtual Disk Manager to return to the VM inventory page.

   You'll notice your inventory page hasn't changed. You still have only one VM in the list. The Virtual Disk Manager imported the disk image but not the definition file. You have to create a new definition file by invoking the New Virtual Machine Wizard.

   By importing a virtual disk, or selecting an existing disk during VM creation, the wizard is significantly abbreviated.

5. Start the Virtual Machine Wizard by selecting File, New from the Virtual-Box menu.

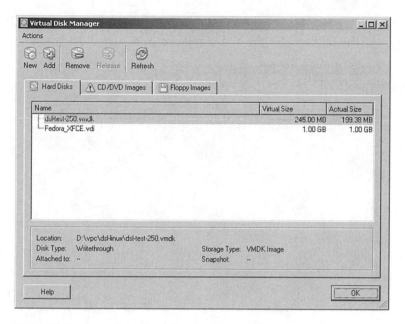

FIGURE 8-8 Virtual Disk Manager with VDIs.

6. Click Next on the Virtual Machine Wizard Welcome screen.

7. Enter a name for the new VM into the Name field (for example, DSL 3.3).

8. Select an operating system from the drop-down menu (for example, Linux 2.4) and click Next. See Figure 8-9.

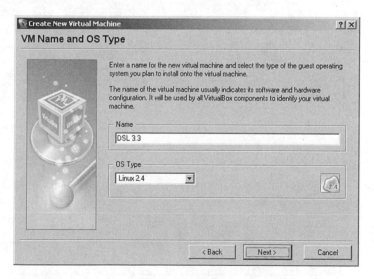

FIGURE 8-9 Choosing the Virtual Machine Name and OS Type.

9. Use the slider bar (or enter the amount directly into the MB field) to adjust the memory for the VM, as shown in Figure 8-10, and click Next.

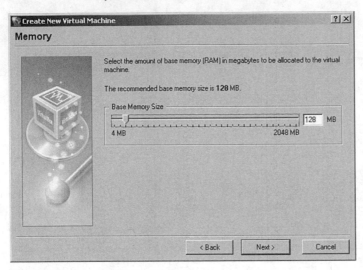

FIGURE 8-10 Adjusting the memory for the new VM.

10. Choose an existing virtual hard disk from the Virtual Disk Manager inventory and click Select, as shown in Figure 8-11.

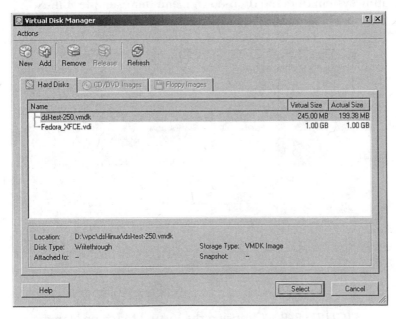

FIGURE 8-11 Selecting the virtual disk for the imported VM.

11. Click Next on the Virtual Hard Disk screen.

12. Click Finish to complete the wizard and add the new VM to inventory.

13. Start or customize the VM.

Customizing Virtual Machines

All customization of VMs is done via the VirtualBox console. The right pane of the VirtualBox console lists all of a VM's hardware and the status of each item. Each hardware item listed is a clickable link that opens a settings page from which you can edit all hardware settings. The particular item you click has focus when the Settings screen is opened, but you can select any item from the list for editing. Figure 8-12 shows CD/DVD-ROM selected from the list.

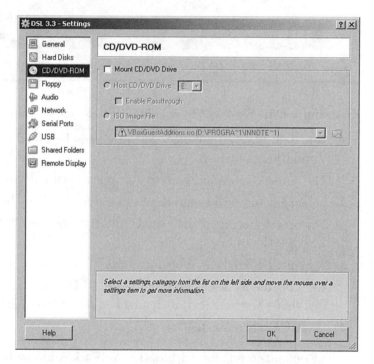

FIGURE 8-12 Virtual machine Settings page with CD/DVD-ROM focus.

Removing Hardware from a Virtual Machine

VirtualBox, by default, starts out a newly created VM with most of its available hardware either disabled or not mounted. This is often the most stable and highest performing configuration for a VM. Each VM is equipped with RAM, video memory, a hard disk, and a network adapter.

In this example, you'll remove the network adapter for a VM.

1. Select a VM from your inventory and click Network in the right pane to open the Settings screen.
2. Deselect the Enable Network Adapter check box on the Adapter0 tab.

   All options are immediately grayed out.
3. Click OK to accept the change.

The network adapter is now disabled and will not function when the VM boots.

Adding Hardware to a Virtual Machine

Enabling or mounting hardware effectively *adds* the hardware to your VM. This section steps through how to enable a USB device and connect to your VM using various network protocols.

NOTE

Your VM must be powered off to make any changes to the hardware.

Enabling a USB Device To enable a USB device on your VM, follow these steps:

1. Select the VM you want to work with, and click USB in the right pane of the VirtualBox console.

   The screen shown in Figure 8-13 appears with all options disabled.
2. Select Enable USB Controller by clicking the check box.

   You may optionally enable any USB 2.0 controller by also selecting Enable USB 2.0 Controller.
3. Add any USB device filters for your USB devices.

   Clicking the icon, as shown in Figure 8-14, results in a list of USB devices that this VM can detect when attached to the host machine.
4. Click OK when finished.

The default setting for Adapter 0 is Network Address Translation (NAT), which is adequate in most cases. With NAT, you can browse the Internet, connect to external resources, receive software updates, and more. What you cannot do is connect directly to the VM without some NAT port-forwarding magic to make it happen.

Establishing NAT Port Forwarding The following example demonstrates how to implement NAT port forwarding for a VM so that connectivity to the VM's network services is possible. NAT port-forwarding setup must be performed with the VM powered off.

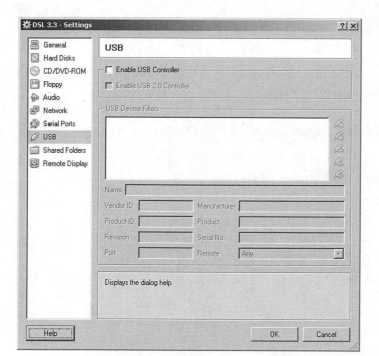

FIGURE 8-13
USB device enable-
ment options.

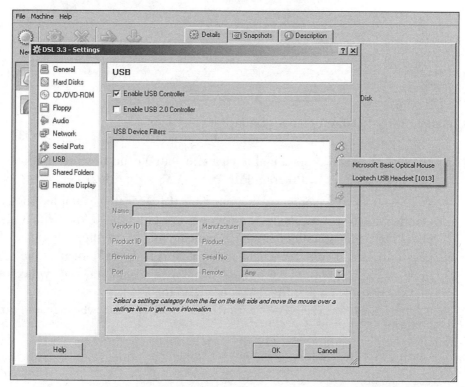

FIGURE 8-14 Detectable USB devices.

To set up NAT port forwarding for SSH (Secure Shell) and RDP (Remote Desktop Protocol):

1. Click the Network link in the right pane of your VM, as shown in Figure 8-15, to check the default adapter settings.

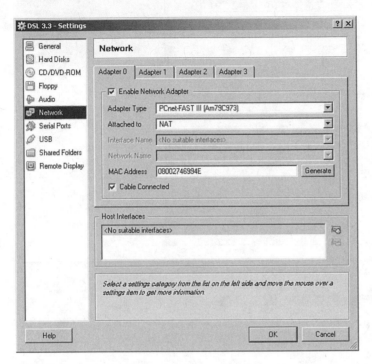

FIGURE 8-15   Default Network Adapter 0 settings.

2. Open a command prompt and navigate to your VirtualBox installation directory (for example, C:\Program Files\Sun\xVM VirtualBox).

We'll be using the command-line interface (CLI) for this example. The command-line tool VBoxManage is a very powerful ally in working with VMs. It offers more functionality than the graphical tool. To see the wide range of possibilities and complete command syntax, type VBoxManage at the prompt. To get a better view of the VBoxManage command and syntax, redirect the output to a text file that is easier to read.

```
C:\Program Files\Sun\xVM VirtualBox> VBoxManage > vboxmanage.txt
<ENTER>
```

3. Enter the following three commands exactly as shown:

```
VBoxManage setextradata "DSL 3.3"
"VBoxInternal/Devices/pcnet/0/LUN#0/Config/dslssh/Protocol" TCP
```

```
VBoxManage setextradata "DSL 3.3"
"VBoxInternal/Devices/pcnet/0/LUN#0/Config/dslssh/GuestPort" 22
VBoxManage setextradata "DSL 3.3"
"VBoxInternal/Devices/pcnet/0/LUN#0/Config/dslssh/HostPort" 2222
```

Now you can ssh to your VM via the forwarded ports you have created.

4. Connect to the VM using the following syntax:

```
ssh <VM Host IP Address> -p 2222 -l <VM Username>
```

This is the way it looks on our computer:

```
ssh 10.0.1.200 -p 2222 -l khess
```

5. Log in to the remote host with your password.

The preceding instructions deserve some clarification because they are somewhat cryptic in nature. The VBoxManage command sets up a protocol, a listening port to forward to your VM (Guest), and a listening port on your VM Host. To set up any network service for a VM, you must change the following:

The VM Name ("DSL 3.3")—It is the VM Name.

The VM Number—Start at 0 for the first one.

The LUN (Logical Unit Number)—Each service needs its own unique number.

The Service Name—A unique name to identify the service (dslssh).

Protocol—Can be TCP or UDP.

GuestPort—The Standard TCP/UDP Listening Port on the VM.

HostPort—The Listening TCP/UDP Port on the Host Computer (Must be > 1024).

Setting Up RDP You may configure more than one network service for a VM. The following example illustrates how to set up a second network service using RDP, which allows a console view of your VM. Windows computers have the RDP service that is sometimes referred to as Terminal Services. On Windows workstations and UNIX/Linux VMs, RDP is remote control, but on Windows Servers, it is a remote desktop terminal.

To set up RDP to your VM, follow these steps:

1. Click Remote Display in the right pane of the console.

2. Select Enable VRDP Server by clicking the check box.

3. Change Null to External in the Authentication Method drop-down.

Null means that no authentication is necessary to connect to the service. Always change this to External. By changing this setting to External, you'll need a valid user account on the VM that uses a password.

4. Click OK to accept the changes and return to the console.

5. Open a command prompt and navigate to your VirtualBox installation directory (For example, C:\Program Files\Sun\xVM VirtualBox).

6. Enter the following three commands exactly as shown:

```
VBoxManage setextradata "DSL 3.3"
"VBoxInternal/Devices/pcnet/0/LUN#1/Config/dslrdp/Protocol" TCP
VBoxManage setextradata "DSL 3.3"
"VBoxInternal/Devices/pcnet/0/LUN#1/Config/dslrdp/GuestPort" 3389
VBoxManage setextradata "DSL 3.3"
"VBoxInternal/Devices/pcnet/0/LUN#1/Config/dslrdp/HostPort" 4389
```

Notice the changes needed to create the new service. The LUN changes from 0 to 1 and dslssh to dslrdp, GuestPort, and HostPort. The GuestPort is 3389 because that is the standard TCP port for RDP; 4389 was chosen because it is not currently in use by the host computer and it is similar to the RDP port.

7. Power on your VM.

When the VM is completely up and running, you may connect via RDP. On Windows, don't use the graphical version of the Remote Desktop Connection tool. The command-line version is in your path. The proper way to invoke it for our setup is

```
mstsc /v:Host Computer IP Address:4389
mstsc /v:10.0.1.200:4389
```

For a UNIX/Linux computer, the simplest form of a connection string is

```
rdesktop Host Computer IP Address:4389
rdesktop 10.0.1.200:4389
```

After it is invoked, you'll be prompted for a username and password, and then your VM appears just as it does in the console. When you're finished with a Windows workstation or UNIX/Linux RDP session, just close the window—there is no need to logout or shutdown. Remember, you are on the actual machine as if you were operating the VM from the console. An RDP server session is a terminal (not a remote control) session, so in that instance, you would logoff.

Reconfiguring Virtual Machine Hardware

VMs are usually built for specific tasks; therefore, their resource requirements are often far less than those of their physical counterparts. After an assessment is made, RAM, disk space, and peripheral adjustments can be made with minimal effort. Reconfiguring VM hardware is a necessary part of managing VMs.

In this section, we address how to adjust VM RAM and how to alter CD/DVD-ROM characteristics.

Adjusting RAM   Follow these steps to adjust the RAM of a VM:

1. Click the General link on the right pane of the console.

2. Figure 8-16 shows the Basic RAM adjustments you can make using the familiar slider bar or entry field. An added bonus here is that you can adjust the amount of video RAM for your VM using the same simple methods.

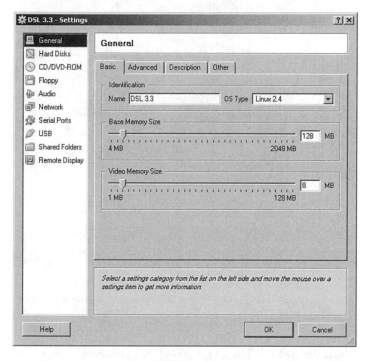

FIGURE 8-16   Virtual machine RAM settings.

3. Adjust the VM RAM and video RAM and click OK to accept the changes.

Changing DVD/CD-ROM Characteristics   CD/DVD-ROM drives are not mounted by default in VirtualBox VMs. This is a feature that has performance implications because every time a CD or DVD is inserted into the host drive, it seeks and mounts it automatically. If you have several VMs, this can result in a per-formance hit for all VMs. The way to mitigate this behavior is to disable Autoplay on the host machine for all CD/DVD drives and other media.

You have a few options for working with CD/DVD drives:

■ Mount and select the Host CD/DVD Drive.

■ Enable Passthrough.

- Select an ISO image from which to boot or install an operating system.
- Select an ISO image from which to install software.
- Select VBoxGuestAdditions ISO from which you install VirtualBox Tools.

See Figure 8-17 for the CD/DVD-ROM Settings screen.

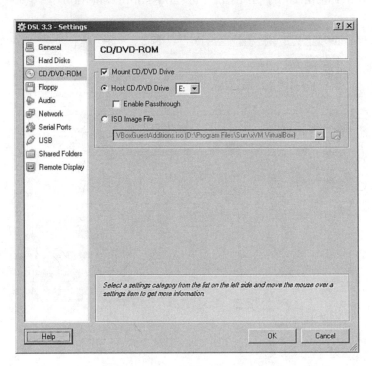

FIGURE 8-17 The CD/DVD-ROM Settings screen.

You may mount the Host CD/DVD drive and select, if more than one, the drive letter of the drive you want to use for the VM. Note that you're choosing the host's drive letter, not the VM's drive letter. UNIX and Linux machines, for example, don't use drive letters.

If you want the VM to be able to burn data CDs or DVDs, check the Enable Passthrough check box.

Selecting ISO Image File allows you to browse to an ISO image from which to boot your VM. You can also select an ISO image for an installed VM to allow access to a CD/DVD from which you can install software.

The default setting for ISO Image File is VBoxGuestAdditions.iso. This ISO image is available for installing VirtualBox software. The Guest Additions are add-on programs and drivers that enhance the VM's performance and usability.

VIRTUAL MACHINE FILES AND FOLDERS

After you've established and configured your VMs (see the Appendix, "Virtual Machine Installation," for step-by-step guidance in how to get the VM's operating system up and running), you must decide how you're going to handle the files and folders on which the VDIs reside.

File and Folder Security

On a Windows system, you'll have to alter the permissions for the folders containing the VDIs and the VM definition files. My suggestion is to restrict those directories to administrators only. All other users should utilize the VMs via remote network connectivity protocols, such as RDP and SSH.

On a UNIX or Linux system, your home folder is protected by the default operating system permissions, but the folder containing the VDI files must be protected. Again, my suggestion is to make the VDI files accessible only to the administrator (root user).

File Names and Roles

At the beginning of this chapter, in the section "The VirtualBox Server Console," we selected the locations for our virtual disks (D:\vpc\VDI) and our VMs (D:\vpc\VBVM). Under the VDI folder are your VM disk images. For our example, DSL 3.3.vdi is the VDI file. All VDI files are located here, although you may specify alternative locations for them. Your VM definition files are under the VBVM folder, with each VM having its own directory (VBMV\DSL 3.3) and XML files. In addition, a Logs folder contains the current and previous three log files for your VM.

NOTE

The XML file is a plain-text file that defines your VM. If you ever have a problem starting a VM, this is the place to start troubleshooting. Remove any offending entries and restart the VM.

On UNIX and Linux, all VirtualBox definition files are under a folder named .VirtualBox. It is a hidden folder located in your home directory. The VDI files are under the folder specified during installation.

VIRTUALBOX IN THE REAL WORLD

Musicmetric is all about data. The London-based startup provides analytics for the music industry. It collects large volumes of trending data and parses it for artists, agencies, labels, and pretty much anyone interested in the music industry. Its algorithms, which it guards closely, can measure everything from an artist's popularity to the effectiveness of a marketing campaign. It also makes some of its data available via MuZoid, a Twitter app where users put in an artist and it spits out other similar music the user might enjoy.

Despite musicmetric's data-centric business model, like most startups, it did not have a lot of cash to burn on hardware or software. When it launched in February 2009, the bulk of its server room came from the Sun Startup Essentials program, which gets companies up and running on Sun Microsystems' hardware at a greatly reduced cost. The program provides greatly discounted servers and storage, open source software, discounted partner hosting, and free technical advice and training.

Currently, musicmetric is running nine servers at a collocation facility with more on order, as well as another four at it offices. The servers bring enough raw iron for day-to-day use of data collection and analytics. But compute power is the key asset of musicmetric's business, whether for development efforts or number crunching. This meant the company needed to find a way to access increased compute power as needed.

At first, using a cloud model was considered and used, but the company quickly determined that having cloud available on a 24/7 basis wasn't financially feasible. It does, however, intend to use cloud in short periods on large projects. The needs of a given task will determine whether cloud is to be used. It will likely come into play with disaster recovery, for example, but not for autofailover. In addition, down the road, any old equipment lying about may be added to the mix as a resource.

The other option was to buy additional servers, but that, too, represented significant expense for something that was not 100% needed all the time.

One other issue for musicmetric was finding a way to meet the computing needs of its developers. Development is an operational expense for the company, and server capabilities are needed for almost half of its nine employees. Because today's desktop machines have capabilities that surpass the servers of only a few years ago, musicmetric found it was able to use desktop PCs running Windows, Solaris, and Linux on the back end to accomplish its needs.

But although the desktop machines are adequate for development, they are not up to snuff for data crunching. As developer boxes, they also aren't all being used at full capacity all the time. Rather than invest in additional hardware, musicmetric looked for a way to harness their compute cycles to accomplish the necessary tasks.

Sun's VirtualBox was believed to be well suited for the task. Two other checks in VirtualBox's favor were that musicmetric was already dealing with Sun through the hardware program, and VirtualBox is free.

Ironically, most of the systems running VirtualBox are Dell PCs, not Sun products. Nor are they running Solaris, although musicmetric does have several Sun workstations.

Originally, the desktops were running Windows, but later most were reinstalled with Linux, with Windows running inside Linux using VirtualBox. This resulted in the "more technical" users running Linux desktops powered by Ubuntu and Fedora Core 11. This will also enable the much sought-after cycle stealing that helped tip the ball into VirtualBox's court in the first place.

There was another reason VirtualBox was chosen: musicmetric wanted to be able to test its apps in as close to a live environment as possible. Its T1-architecture-based Sun servers cannot be directly replicated using the x86-based VirtualBox. VirtualBox does, however, allow Open Solaris to be replicated locally, making it an ideal tool for testing and development purposes, thus accomplishing two goals at once.

Investing in powerful desktops proved to be a frugal move from this angle as well. It meant that a massive capital outlay was unnecessary, because virtualization did not need to take place on the actual server. It also meant musicmetric had more choices open to it.

For example, vSphere, the latest offering from VMware (which also represents the vendor's strategy shift from the server to the cloud), was found to be cost prohibitive for musicmetric's budget. Moreover, musicmetric saw vSphere's emphasis was failover, which musicmetric is not handling within the cloud—not flexibility, which was its key goal for its virtual environment.

VirtualBox, in contrast, not only offered flexibility but was also found to be straightforward and easy to use. And it didn't hurt in the selection process that the software is free.

Perhaps the final straw in VirtualBox's favor was CTO's preferred computing environment. Mac users are a loyal bunch, and the CTO of musicmetric is a Mac user. The dearth of Mac offerings, and their price tag when they are present, is often a barrier. This, too, was in VirtualBox's favor because unlike comparable virtualization environments such as VMware Fusion and Parallels, it is free.

Today, nearly half of musicmetric's employees are using VirtualBox for a variety of tasks. VirtualBox environments are used for development, but they are also used for system administration. It is used for Java development as well as Open Solaris work. In addition to moving to Linux on the desktop, musicmetric is in the early stages of implementing Apache Hadoop, a distributed computation platform.

The goal for flexibility has been met, and the company is indeed getting the most bang for its buck (or in this case, pound) out of its hardware. All hardware is fully specked, and each computer has two monitors, enabling the user to see both a given VM and the whole box.

But all x86 hardware has access to VirtualBox. For most Windows apps, this means not having to dedicate an entire box to running a Windows server. An admin can put the desired bits in a VM, effectively doubling up on the number of servers.

Although musicmetric is using VirtualBox in the least expensive way possible, even with the most minimal setup, it found it a snap to use. The VirtualBox installer is included. The simplest way to use it is with predefined images (which musicmetric has used often): Install it, point it at the image, and be up and running.

VirtualBox is not without its limitations. In the current environment, only a single core is supported. Sun's release notes, however, reveal plans to change it in future versions.

Summary

This chapter's focus was Sun's xVM VirtualBox software. The chapter introduced the console, its design, and its features. It stepped through creating, importing, and customizing a VM with the software.

The chapter also discussed how to use NAT port forwarding to gain LAN access to a VM's services. VBoxManage, the command-line utility, was used to create the forwarded ports. If you choose VirtualBox as your virtualization solution, it is important to be very familiar with this utility.

Finally, the chapter provided an overview of the files involved, the roles they play, the security information associated with VirtualBox's VDI and XML definition files, and concluded with a look at how one company is using VirtualBox.

Part II

Applying Virtualization

## CHAPTER 9

Server Virtualization in Action

This chapter enters the mix of solving problems with virtual machines (VM) and services. We've chosen solutions that are somewhat generic in nature and thus applicable to the widest range of situations. The software we will use to demonstrate those solutions are VMware Server and Microsoft Virtual PC. In this and the two subsequent chapters, the software is ancillary to the solution and should not be viewed as an endorsement of a particular solution or company. In this case, VMware Server and Virtual PC were chosen because they are free and work well with a variety of guest operating systems. There is also a huge repository of VM templates, server appliances, and images available for both platforms.

This chapter illustrates how to create and configure dedicated virtualized servers; then it covers migrating physical machines to virtual ones. It also provides an overview of backup and recovery, server appliances, VM migration, tuning, and concludes with a look at VM security.

CONFIGURING DEDICATED SERVERS WITH VIRTUALIZATION

This section is probably going to take the most time to absorb because it is such a shift from tradition. The next server you create and use will not be a physical one with a system board, drives that you plug in, or memory boards that snap into place. You won't need to worry about downloading drivers for that video card, network card, or controllers of any kind. In fact, there might not be any hardware compatibility troubleshooting whatsoever.

These days we hardly even bother with CD/DVD drives to install an OS. ISO images are much easier to deal with, and there is hardly a point in searching for a disk that might be scratched in some vital area, making installation frustrating, if not impossible.

A dedicated virtual server (system) is one that, like a physical server, is dedicated to a job or jobs for which it is designed. Configuring a virtual dedicated server is much the same as configuring a physical dedicated server. After installation, the server needs security patches, software updates, and service pruning. *Service pruning* is halting or removing unneeded services from your system.

Service pruning is necessary to reduce the number of potential vulnerabilities that exist with some network services. You should install and run only the services you need for your dedicated server to perform its designated function.

In this first dedicated server example, a Debian system is installed to function as a mail server. Debian was chosen because it installs quickly without a lot of superfluous services and software. We used an ISO image to install from and boot the VM.

Preparing the Virtual Machine

To do this in VMware Server, create a new VM and, when it is complete, browse to your ISO image under Edit Virtual Machine Settings from the main VMware Server screen, and change as shown in Figure 9-1.

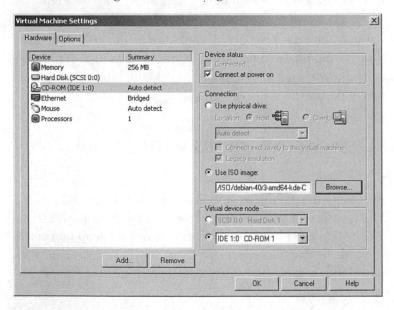

FIGURE 9-1 Selecting the ISO image from which to boot in VMware.

Or, if you're using Virtual PC, you need to start the new VM, then choose CD, Capture ISO Image before the VM boots. See Figure 9-2.

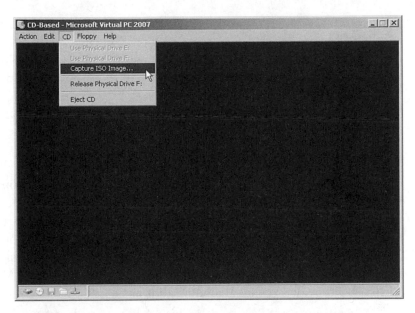

FIGURE 9-2   Capturing the ISO image in Virtual PC.

If your VM doesn't boot to the ISO image in VMware, you will need to set the VM to boot to the CD/DVD drive using VMware's Boot Menu. To get to the Boot Menu, press ESC when the VM begins to boot, as shown in Figure 9-3, and then select CD-ROM Drive.

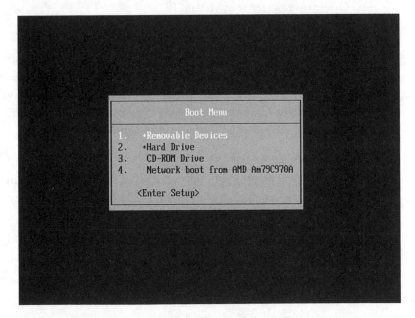

FIGURE 9-3   Press ESC for Boot Menu.

NOTE

The booting VM must have focus before you're able to press ESC and select from the Boot Menu. You give the VM focus by clicking the VM with your mouse.

The VM will now boot from the ISO image. Follow this same procedure to boot from the CD/DVD drive if you have a physical CD or DVD disk from which to boot.

After the new VM boots to the CD image, install the operating system as you would for a physical system. In the case of a Linux installation, you may find that on first boot the X Window system (graphical interface) starts incorrectly or fails to start altogether. This is because the video setup is incorrect or not supported. VMware and Virtual PC have additional software available to assist you in setting up your system for unsupported hardware. VMware includes VMware Tools and Virtual PC provides Virtual Machine Additions.

To install Virtual PC's Virtual Machine Additions, select Action, Install or Update Virtual Machine Additions, Continue. The installation should start automatically.

NOTE

Virtual Machine Additions are available only for DOS, OS2, and Windows Operating Systems in Virtual PC.

Installing VMware's Tools for Windows computers is a simple task—click VM, Install VMware Tools. You may be prompted to reboot when the installation completes. The installation begins and proceeds automatically with only a few interactions from you. Linux, however, is more complex, depending on the distribution. Here's how to install VMware Tools for any Linux distribution:

1. Click VM, Install VMware Tools, Install.

   The dialog box disappears and it looks as if VMware Tools are installing for you in the background, but they aren't. The Tools are now available to you in a virtual CD format.

2. Mount your CD/DVD drive (if it doesn't automatically mount and open for you). Enter the following code:

   ```
   # mount cdrom or mount /dev/cdrom.
   ```

   Two files on the virtual CD contain the VMware Tools: VMwareTools-(version).rpm and VMwareTools-(version).tar.gz. You can install the rpm directly, if your distribution supports it. The tar.gz file is the source code for the VMware Tools and the only way we have ever been successful at installing them. Your experience may vary.

The prerequisites for a successful installation include, but may not be limited to, the following:

- A C compiler (gcc).
- Kernel sources.
- Kernel header sources.
- Others—Check your error messages.

3. Copy the tar.gz file to a directory on your hard drive, unzip, and untar it.

4. CD into the vmware-tools-distrib directory and execute the install script using the following code:

```
# ./vmware-install.pl
```

The script will guide you through a series of installation questions. Use the default answer unless you know how to answer the prompts for your system. If all goes well, your installation should proceed without issue. If you get errors, you will have to download and install any missing pieces.

5. Check for the vmware-guestd after installation by entering the following:

```
# ps -ef |grep vmware
```

You should see a response similar to the following:

```
/usr/sbin/vmware-guestd -background /var/run/vmware-guestd.pid
```

Now that you have successfully installed VMware Tools, you can install the video support drivers so your X Window interface will work properly. To get to that, enter

```
# apt-get install xserver-xorg-video-vmware
```

Reboot your VM or restart your X server to initialize the new video support. Your graphical interface should fire up and prompt you for a username and password. A graphical interface isn't necessary to any functions of a dedicated server, but it's nice to have for performing some administrative tasks (creating new users, sharing folders, printer setup) in a busy environment.

Whether you use Windows, Linux, or some other operating system, your virtual server is now ready for dedicated service.

Dedicating the Server

Depending on your operating system and choices during installation, it takes only 15 to 45 minutes to completely install and prepare a VM for this next critical step in the process of creating a dedicated system.

For our Debian-based mail server, we must prune out all unnecessary daemons (services) and check for open ports that may offer an attacker opportunity to hack our system. We downloaded and installed the NMap network security auditing tool from www.nmap.org. This tool is available as source code, Linux/UNIX packages, and as a Windows installer.

The NMap tool assists you in checking your new system for open TCP and UDP network ports so that you can make informed decisions about which ones to turn off. When we performed an intense scan of my new Debian system, we found that we had three open ports. Table 9-1 shows the output from NMap for that system.

TABLE 9-1   NMap Results for Debian Mail Server Scan

Port	Protocol	State	Service	Version
22	tcp	Open	Ssh	OpenSSH
25	tcp	Open	Smtp	Postfix smtpd
111	tcp	Open	rpcbind	

Although we have three open ports, only two are essential: SMTP and SSH. You could argue that SSH is not absolutely necessary, but we prefer to keep it. rpcbind (rpc.statd) is a good candidate for removal because the mail server does not require Network File System (NFS) or any other Remote Procedure Call (RPC) program to operate normally.

The same service pruning can be done for Windows systems, although more caution should be taken when doing so. Disabling required services can be devastating to a Windows system. We scanned a virtual Windows 2003 server that acts as an Active Directory server with NMap. Table 9-2 shows the results. The server is a default installation to which Active Directory was added upon initial configuration. No other services were configured for it.

TABLE 9-2   NMap Results for Windows 2003 Active Directory Server Scan

Port	Protocol	State	Service	Version
53	tcp	Open	Domain	Microsoft DNS
88	tcp	Open	kerberos-sec	Kerberos-sec
135	tcp	Open	Msrpc	RPC

TABLE 9-2   Continued

PORT	PROTOCOL	STATE	SERVICE	VERSION
139	tcp	Open	netbios-ssn	
389	tcp	Open	Ldap	LDAP
445	tcp	Open	microsoft-ds	Directory Services
464	tcp	Open	kpasswd5	
593	tcp	Open	ncacn_http	RPC over HTTP
636	tcp	Open	Tcpwrapped	
1025	tcp	Open	Msrpc	RPC
1027	tcp	Open	ncacn_http	RPC over HTTP
3268	tcp	Open	Ldap	LDAP
3269	tcp	Open	Rpcbind	

Table 9-3 is an NMap scan of a Windows 2003 system default installation.

TABLE 9-3   NMap Results for Windows 2003 Server Scan

PORT	PROTOCOL	STATE	SERVICE	VERSION
135	tcp	Open	Msrpc	RPC
139	tcp	Open	netbios-ssn	
445	tcp	Open	microsoft-ds	Directory Services
1025	tcp	Open	Msrpc	RPC
1026	tcp	Open	ncacn_http	RPC

Although this is not a book on security, it bears mentioning that ports 135 and 445 should be blocked from the Internet. Port 445 is deeply embedded in Windows and is almost impossible to turn off without negative consequences, so your best option is to block it via firewall. Port 135, on the other hand, may be turned off without ill effects. At a minimum, it should be blocked via firewall from the Internet. When it comes to Internet security, you should expose only those ports that need exposure.

After you have removed any offending services from your system, it's ready for business as a dedicated virtual server.

DEPLOYING SERVER APPLIANCES

Related to dedicated virtual servers are server appliances. Server appliances are open source (usually) VMs created for a specific function. They are downloadable VM images that serve as web database servers, blog servers, content management system application servers, and even file and print servers, to name a few. They are designed to be smaller and to perform a singular function, which makes them perfect candidates for projects that would otherwise require a physical system that would likely be underutilized.

Server Appliances are ready to use as soon as they're downloaded, unzipped, and opened in your virtualization software console.

Table 9-4 lists some sites from where you can download server appliances:

TABLE 9-4 Websites Offering Downloadable Server Appliances

Site Name	URL	Description
Jumpbox	www.jumpbox.net	Open source server appliances
ThoughtPolice	www.thoughtpolice.co.uk	VMware images of popular open source systems
VirtualAppliances	www.virtualappliances.net	Offering specialized open source server solutions
VMware	www.vmware.com/appliances	VMware and community server appliances

SERVER APPLIANCES: A WORD OF CAUTION

Server Appliances must be subjected to the same rigorous security sweeps and pruning as other servers. Don't trust them just because they are prepackaged.

ADJUSTING AND TUNING VIRTUAL SERVERS

The next item of business you'll need to tackle for your dedicated VMs is adjusting and tuning. You'll need to do this after the system has been up and running for a few weeks so that you'll have a feel for baseline performance. You need to monitor performance with a performance-monitoring tool such as Orca (www.orcaware.com/orca).

Tools like Orca give you a continuous (hourly, daily, monthly, quarterly, and yearly) view into system performance. Not only can you keep an eye on performance peaks and valleys, you can also determine the best times for backups and maintenance. You'll also know when to add more RAM, more disk, more CPU, or even another VM to share the load.

So how do you tune a VM? The answer is, "almost the same as a physical machine."

RAM

Adding RAM can be the easiest way to boost performance in physical and virtual systems. Your host system must have sufficient RAM for itself plus enough to run each guest efficiently and have room for growth. Often, but not always, adding more RAM can refresh sluggish systems. RAM is a cheap commodity and it has the highest performance boost per dollar of any performance enhancing adjustment. However, RAM is not always the culprit, as Chapter 12, "Form-Factor Choices and Their Implications," will discuss, and adding RAM without knowing the root cause could have little impact.

Virtual Machine Add-ons or Tools

Adding your chosen platform's VM tools is often ignored as a performance-increasing tweak. After installation, even before patching or updating, you should install the VM tools. Your overall experience with the VM's performance will increase.

Drivers in these tools and add-ons boost and optimize video performance, as well as enhance mouse performance and transitions between host and guest, and deliver time synchronization improvements between host and guest.

Virtual Disks

Virtual drive configuration is also important. Stick with fixed-size virtual disks. Dynamic disks are nice to have, but you take a performance hit when using them. You can always add more disk space by creating another virtual drive for your VM.

Virtual Machine Pagefiles and Swap Space

Pagefiles and swap space should be configured as separate drives. This is a bit trickier on Windows systems because you'll get drive full errors, although they can be turned off. A separate drive for swap space and pagefiles makes your system run more efficiently because it has a separate drive to use for paging. Using a separate partition won't help performance like it does with physical machines. Using more than one drive for swap space also increases performance. Keep separate swap space drives to 2GB.

Host Machine Performance Tuning

Some system administrators are disappointed with virtualization performance because they assume that purchasing a physical system for their VM host with lots of RAM and disk space is the key to happy VMs. You must build your VM host with virtualization in mind.

CPU

These days most CPUs are designed with virtualization in mind—64-bit multi-processor host machines should always be used. A two-processor system is good for testing and initial deployment, but for production, you need to use (at a minimum) quad-processor systems. The host machine's performance should also be monitored closely for those same peaks and valleys. An overloaded host system will result in poorly performing guest systems. Chapter 12 discusses this in greater detail.

RAM

With RAM consumption on the rise for applications and operating systems, there is generally no such thing as too much RAM. Purchase and install the maximum amount of RAM for your host system.

Disks

Drives and drive configuration are often overlooked as a potential performance bottleneck. Drives and configurations should be chosen with care. SCSI drives still outperform even the highest-end IDE drives. Purchase the fastest, widest data transfer rate, highest cache drives you can afford for your host system. One of the biggest complaints against virtualization is sluggish disk I/O. VM disks will never perform like physical disks, but you can ensure that you have the optimum speed available by choosing high-performance drive technology.

Disk Configuration and Controllers

Drive configuration is also very important to performance. The host operating system should be physically separate from any guest machines. Partitions are not good enough. You need to separate them physically on different drives and even different controllers.

Defragmentation and Optimization

On Windows platforms, you should keep your drives defragmented. Fragmentation of a drive, virtual or physical, kills performance. The built-in Windows defragmentation program is good for a start, but if you experience disk lag after defragmenting, get a third-party disk defragmentation and optimization utility. Use it for both phys-ical and virtual systems.

Virus Scanning

Disable virus scanning of your VM environment. You do not need to scan your vir-tual disk files for viruses. Virus scanning produces a performance hit for virtual disks. If you feel compelled to scan the partition or disk where your VMs live, do a daily sweep of them just before you perform backups.

Server Dedication

Your VM host system should be dedicated to the task of being a VM host with no other jobs. It should not be a mail server, a proxy server, and a file server all in one. Network traffic from your LAN—such as file copying, mail, and disk I/O—has a negative effect on the host's performance, which is reflected in each running VM.

Network Optimization

Sharing NICs with the host or other VMs has a negative impact on network through-put. Dedicate a physical NIC to each VM where possible, especially where the VM is highly network traffic dependent (such as a web server, application server, or ter-minal server).

SECURING VIRTUAL SERVERS

A common myth among those new to virtualization is that VMs are somehow more secure than a physical system. You may have noticed that security was not listed as one of my reasons for using virtualization software in Chapter 1, "To Virtualize or Not to Virtualize?" Security was intentionally left out of that list because security isn't a good reason to consider virtualization.

If someone has physical access to a system, its security is compromised. Drives can be removed, systems can be rebooted, power can be switched off, network cables unplugged, and so on. However, the same is true for your VM host system. It is vulnerable to all those issues as a single point of failure for all VMs residing on it. Because physical security is roughly equivalent on physical and VMs, it is ruled out as an issue.

Network security is a major vulnerability for physical systems. It is no less so on virtual ones. Why, you ask? It's because each VM has at least one virtual NIC that connects to a physical counterpart on the host machine. Some malware writers are clever enough to find out if a system is virtual and, in turn, use that system to attack its own host and other VMs.

Block or Remove Services

The removal and blocking of services and ports was discussed in the "Configuring Dedicated Servers with Virtualization" section. Following are some basic principles for blocking or removing services. To get started:

- Remove services that are unnecessary to the system's function.
- Use a firewall to block all incoming traffic to your LAN.
- Open firewall exceptions (holes) to provide incoming access to a service.
- Regularly use a port scanner (security auditing tool) to monitor exposed ports.

Use Antivirus Software

Use antivirus software on VMs just as you would on physical ones. This statement isn't in conflict with one made earlier about turning off virus scanning for VMs. That referred to turning off scanning VM disk images with the *host* system's antivirus software. It may sound like a case of splitting hairs, but there is a distinct difference.

VMs must have their own antivirus service running to prevent infections from outside sources. With antivirus software installed on each VM, there is no need to have the host server scan the VM files.

Perform Regular System Security Audits

A system audit is not the same as a network sweep to find open ports, renegade services, or NICs in promiscuous mode. System audits involve checking the system for spyware, viruses, and malware of all kinds. It also includes checking user accounts for violations of security policy.

Any account with Administrator or root equivalent should be disabled. Unused accounts should be deactivated or removed completely. VM user accounts get overlooked by administrators who assume for whatever reason VMs are inherently more secure.

VM Backup

Backup and recovery strategies are as varied as political opinions and just as debatable. Ultimately, the process you use depends largely on what you already have in place and the virtualization technology you've selected.

Following are three basic backup strategies for VMs:

- Backup of virtual disk files via file copy
- Backup software running in the VM
- Backup solution from virtualization vendor

File Copy

Simple file copy is perhaps the easiest and most straightforward method of VM backup. You can copy live images on a UNIX/Linux host environment but not on a Windows one. On Windows, the VM must be powered off to make a copy, so if you use Windows as your VM host, you'll have to find some other method of performing backups.

With VMware, you can create a Snapshot of a live VM and do a file copy backup of the Snapshot files. A Snapshot is an exact copy of the running VM at a particular point in time. It is a live backup. Usually Snapshots are taken before some significant event for the VM, such as applying a service pack or patch, installing new software, or removing software. Should something go wrong in the process, you can revert to the Snapshot. Reverting to the Snapshot restores the VM to the point at which the Snapshot was taken.

Chapter 3, "VMware Server," explained the following file types in detail.

Filename

.vmsn – VM state file.

<VM Name>-00000X-s00x.vmdk

Where X is the Snapshot number and x is the disk image number. The disk image number corresponds to the regular disk image number.

VM Backup Software

This method treats the VM like a physical system with its own installed backup software. The software copies selected files and folders to tape, network attached storage, or other media just as it would in a physical machine. This is the least efficient method of backing up VM data. Normally, you make a backup of an entire VM so it can be restored quickly to its productive state.

Vendor Backup Solution

Most likely, your virtualization vendor can recommend a viable backup solution or has already provided one bundled with the virtualization software. Backup and restore modules may be included with the virtualization software or as an add-on for an additional cost.

Check with your vendor for its VM backup solution. That solution is generally the safest and most reliable for its software. Mixing virtualization software and other virtualization vendor backup solutions piecemeal adds another level of complexity and multiple points of failure. You should consider it only when the vendor certifies your VMs can be backed up and restored in a reliable manner.

MIGRATING VMS TO NEW SERVERS

What happens when your VM host system needs to be replaced? What do you do if you decide to change host platforms from Windows to Linux? What do you do if one VM host gets overloaded?

The answer to these questions is in the topic—you migrate the VMs to new servers. Depending on your virtualization solution, this can be painful or of no consequence at all. Some virtualization vendors support only Windows or UNIX. Some virtualization solutions aren't much more than placeholders for VMs with little or no extra support for migration or pooling.

File Copy Migration

The most direct method of migration to a new VM host server (system) is to copy the VM to the new server. This is the same method used for direct backups. Copy the VM to the new server, open the virtualization software console, and import or open the copied VM. Your VM is now migrated to a new host system.

Virtualization Software Migration

If your virtualization software supports moving VMs to a new host server, then employ it. Permissions, paths, identities, and the like will be migrated to the new system without the need for an import or manual intervention. The VM migrates to the new server without issue.

Clearly, this is the best method, if available to you as a part of your virtualization software solution, as an add-on, a third-party module, or as an external program. Using your virtualization software, you can move VMs that are powered off; in some cases, you can move a live VM to a new server.

In the next section, you'll discover ways to migrate physical machines to virtual ones.

MIGRATING PHYSICAL TO VIRTUAL (P2V)

Physical systems that are about to be replaced are perfect candidates for virtualization. You can migrate the entire system to a VM, test it with the physical system still intact, and then allow the workload to move to the VM when you're satisfied with the results.

CD-Based P2V Migration (Cold Cloning)

Traditionally, to migrate a physical machine to a virtual one, the physical system boots from a live CD and migrates to the virtual server host machine over the network via a conversion wizard. This is called cold cloning. The physical machine's operating system must be offline so an image copy can be made of its disks and their contents. This is still a current method for converting physical machines to VMs.

Although it's not possible to demo a CD-based migration in a book, it is possible to offer an example of such a CD and explain the steps, as Figure 9-4 does.

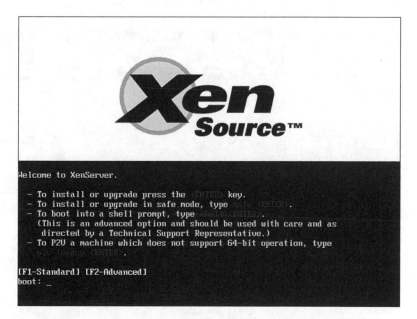

FIGURE 9-4 The Xen bootable CD P2V initial conversion screen.

The CD boots into a minimal operating system and prompts for source machine (physical machine), new VM, and target machine (VM host) information. Follow the onscreen prompts to begin the migration.

Live P2V Migration (Hot Cloning)

Recent advances enable live P2V conversions, also called hot cloning. VMware has a product called VMware Converter that allows you to grab a Windows system image and convert it to a VM while it is live and operating. The real beauty of VMware Converter is that it can run on a remote system that is neither the physical system being converted nor the VM host server accepting the new VM. VMware Converter is a free download from the VMware website, but if you purchase the Enterprise version, you also get a bootable CD image for creating cold clones.

This section explains how to hot clone a Microsoft Windows 2003 Server using the VMware Converter application. The server is cloned from a workstation and then sent to the VM host server.

The VMware Converter converts live physical machines (P2V), live VMs (V2V), and powered off VMs. It also migrates powered-off third-party VMs and images.

Figure 9-5 shows the VMware Converter main screen where you click Import Machine to begin creating a new migration task.

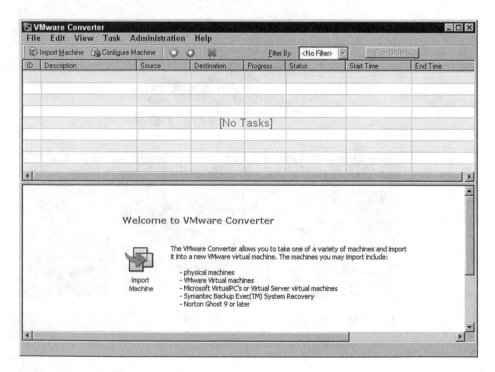

FIGURE 9-5 The Main VMware Converter main screen.

The first step in the Import Machine Wizard is to select your source machine (the system you want to clone). If you are cloning a powered-on third-party VM

(Virtual PC, VirtualBox, or the like), select Physical Machine for the source (see Figure 9-6).

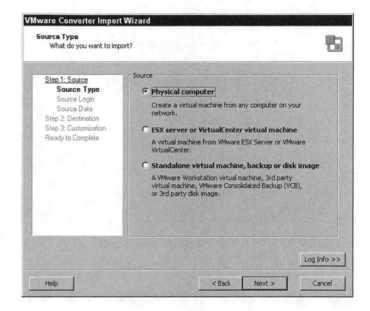

FIGURE 9-6   Select the type of source machine to clone.

You will then be prompted for specific system information for the source machine, as Figure 9-7 illustrates. Enter the Name or IP Address and the login information. You must have administrative access to the source machine.

Next, as the prompt in Figure 9-8 shows, you must grant permission to install the VMware Conversion agent on the source machine and indicate whether you want the agent automatically installed or if you'll do it manually.

Next, you'll be prompted to select the volumes (drives) from your source machine to convert, as Figure 9-9 shows. You may choose any or all volumes and resize them.

The source server's C: drive is low on disk space, but it is possible to expand that drive when it is migrated. Figure 9-10 shows where the volume is expanded from 5.84GB to 8GB.

Next you will be prompted for a destination system type, as shown in Figure 9-11. In this example, VMware Server 1.x is in use.

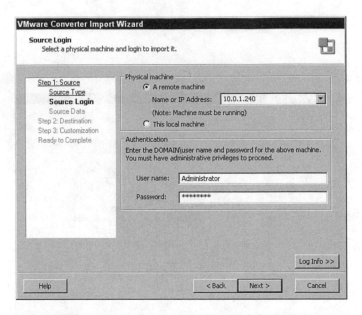

FIGURE 9-7 Source machine name and login information.

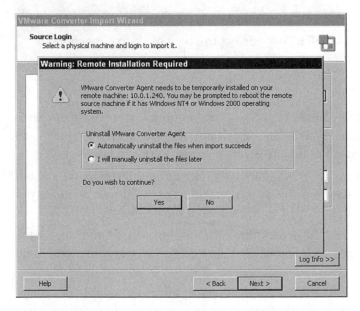

FIGURE 9-8 Agent installation and removal screen.

Then, as shown in Figure 9-12, you will be prompted for the location and name of the new VM. The location is a share on the virtual host machine.

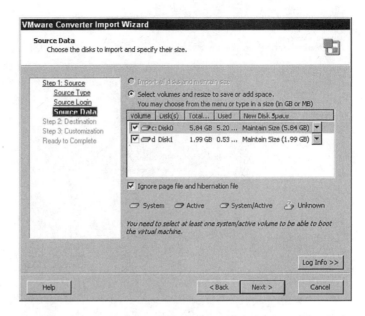

FIGURE 9-9   Volume migration selection and resize screen.

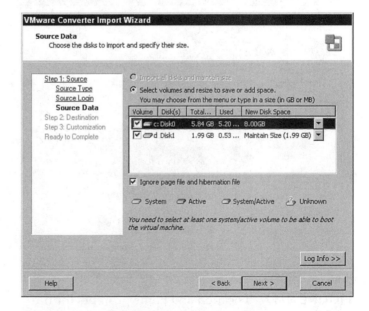

FIGURE 9-10   Expanding the source's volume for migration.

Next up, as shown in Figure 9-13, comes a decision discussed previously: static versus dynamically expanding drives. Static drives yield better disk I/O performance, and for that they are generally recommended.

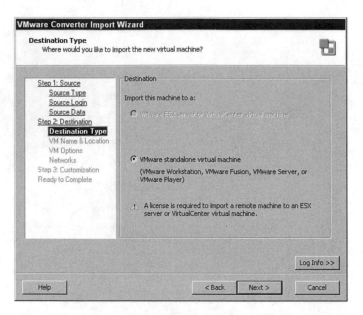

FIGURE 9-11 Select the VM host server type.

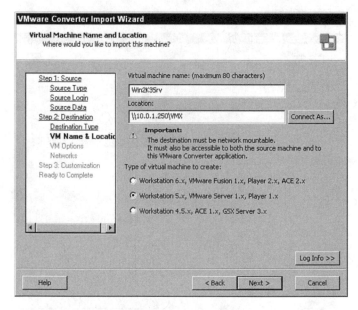

FIGURE 9-12 Location and name prompts for the
new virtual machine.

Now it's time to make your network connectivity choices. Figure 9-14 presents the options available to the new VM. You are asked for the number of NICs, the type of addressing (Bridged, NAT, or Host-Only), and if the NIC is to be powered on at boot.

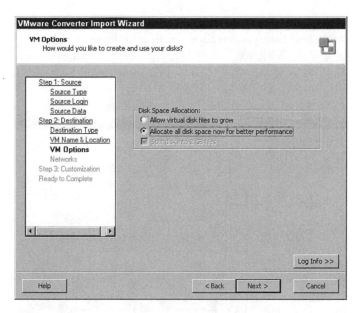

FIGURE 9-13   Select the type of disk space allocation for the new VM.

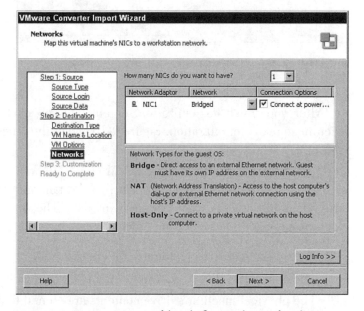

FIGURE 9-14   Networking information selection screen.

Click Next to continue, and the next screen, as shown in Figure 9-15, prompts you for information concerning specific settings for the new VM. You can change the machine's identity, IP address, create a new SID, and so on. To do this, you must download the sysprep files specific to the operating system you are migrating to the new VM. Without those files, you can't continue those steps in the wizard. If you don't have those files, deselect Generate New Security ID (SID) and continue.

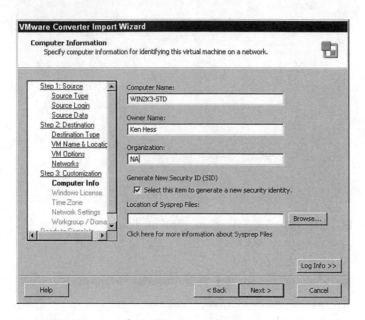

FIGURE 9-15 The VM customization screen.

After you finish customization, or elect for no customization, your physical machine is ready for migration. Figure 9-16 shows the migration progress screen for your new VM.

If you follow the progress of your VM migration on the VM host machine, you'll notice the virtual drives seem to appear in a short amount of time. Those are just the base image files and they don't contain any data. The wizard migrates your physical machine's image in the following order.

1. Empty virtual drives (volumes) are created.
2. The converter takes a snapshot of the physical machine.
3. The physical machine's drive contents are cloned to the new virtual volumes.

VMware doesn't have a monopoly on Live P2V migration. Third-party vendors such as PlateSpin (now owned by Novell) at www.novell.com and Vizioncore's vConverter can be found at (www.vizioncore.com); they also perform live P2V, V2P, and, in the case of PlateSpin, V2P migrations.

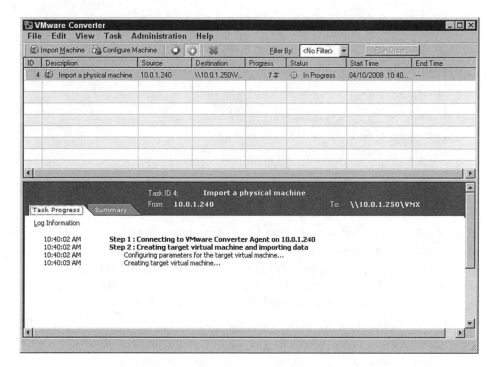

FIGURE 9-16   VMware Converter VM creation progress.

Live migration software prompts you for source, VM, and target system information much the same as the cold clone CD prompts do. The major advantages of live P2V conversions are that you can clone a system while it is up and running—although performance will suffer somewhat while the image is being copied to the VM host—and you can clone a remote system to the VM host. You must have administrative access to the source system for hot cloning.

Manual Cloning

A third method exists for migrating a physical machine to a virtual one. Sometimes it's impossible to reboot a system and keep it in a nonproductive state for a long period (hours). And live P2V conversion software isn't available for all operating systems. This method requires manual creation of the VM (manual cloning) and manual workload migration from physical to virtual.

This is the most primitive and time-consuming method. It is also prone to errors and omissions. Often, key components are left out of a manual migration so, if possible, use one of the automated methods.

If you must perform a manual clone, here is a checklist for you to use for that process. This checklist will help you remember to gather the required information to successfully complete a manual cloning.

- Operating system, version, and patch level
- Required services, shares, servers, or daemons
- User and group accounts
- Machine, workgroup, and domain names
- IP addresses, default gateway, and DNS info
- Drive sizes, partitions, file system type
- Number of CPUs and amount of memory (RAM)

SUMMARY

This chapter examined server virtualization from dedicated virtual server systems to migration of physical to VMs. It also introduced the concept of ready-made VM images known as virtual appliances. From there, we covered tuning your VMs, VM security—with discussion that VMs are no more or less secure than physical systems and backup. The chapter concluded with a look at system migration.

The next chapter covers the concept and practice of desktop virtualization. We'll discuss techniques and strategies on how to virtualize your corporate desktop environment. Cost savings and user training are also discussed.

## CHAPTER 10

Desktop Virtualization in Action

Server virtualization is not the only virtualization option. Virtualizing the desktop is another popular endeavor in the world of virtualization. Desktop virtualization has been around for decades. Previously, it was referred to as terminal services computing or thin-client computing. It is also where VMware and Microsoft cut their virtual teeth.

Desktop virtualization, briefly, is moving a traditional desktop operating system from local hardware to a remote server system. The remote desktop is accessed by utilizing some lightweight client in the form of a small or minimal operating system (smart terminal) or a dumb terminal that has only enough programming to inform it of the whereabouts of the desktop.

Desktop virtualization is attractive to enterprises because it promises to minimize costs associated with managing hundreds or thousands of desktop computers, operating systems, patches, software, and user support issues. The unfortunate truth is that, depending on the way desktop virtualization is implemented, the cost savings may disappoint all but the most pessimistic onlooker.

This chapter examines several methods of desktop virtualization and describes how each is implemented. The pros and cons of each solution are discussed so that when the time comes to put a project plan together, you can make an informed decision and have a smoother transition to virtualized desktops.

TERMINAL SERVICES

Terminal services, the oldest type of desktop virtualization, still may be the best all-around solution available for most applications. The speed, centralized management, lack of specialized or extensive user training, and overall user satisfaction may be hard to beat by other forms of desktop virtualization.

You may recognize the term *terminal services* from Windows Terminal Server or Windows Terminal Services, but the concept and the practice predates Windows by a decade or more. Terminal servers are server systems with terminal services enabled. The terminal server may be UNIX, Linux, or Windows. The desktop experience you receive depends on the terminal server's operating system. You can't get a Linux desktop from a Windows Terminal Server, nor can you get a Windows desktop from a UNIX or Linux Terminal Server.

After you connect to a terminal server, your user experience depends largely on the administrator who set it up and any corporate standards that may be enforced. For a Windows Terminal Server, you'll see a standard Windows desktop with the familiar look and feel of a standard Windows desktop operating system. The behavior of the desktop, applications, and printing are the same as if you were using a local computer. More often than not, users report that the terminal server is far faster than their old desktop computer, and they are quite pleased with the perceived upgrade.

Smart Terminal

A smart terminal is a minimal computer equipped with a minimal operating system—perhaps even an embedded one. A smart terminal has limited processing power because its entire job is to connect you to a remote server system. The operating system is graphical and has a small number of icons or hyperlinks that you can use to connect to different resources.

Smart terminals connect to Terminal Servers by some protocol—Citrix ICA, RDP, VNC, XDMCP, and the like. Users, after authentication, are presented with a desktop and all the applications they would see if they had logged on locally to the remote system. Remote terminal services are very fast and efficient for the end user. Modern Terminal Servers can even redirect sound to the user's terminal for an almost local desktop experience. Video quality is also very high—24-bit color is standard.

Prices for such hardware are falling while functionality is ever increasing. You can purchase smart terminals for about the same price as a low-end desktop computer. The terminal has fewer moving parts and has a longer life expectancy than a standard desktop computer.

Dumb Terminal

Classic dumb terminals are almost nonexistent these days. Thin clients have taken their place as the next-generation dumb terminals. These devices have a small set of utilities embedded in them so that they can be configured locally, remotely, via a web browser, or some other proprietary provisioning software.

After the terminal is provisioned or configured, the user is automatically directed to the appropriate server when the unit is powered on. These devices are generally single-homed (configured for a single Terminal Server), unlike the smart terminals that can connect to a user-selectable array of available resources.

Dumb terminals are very cost effective, typically priced in the $200 USD neighborhood. Minimal cost, minimal configuration, and practically no maintenance make this an excellent choice for a desktop virtualization solution. The major drawback to a dumb terminal is that it is single-homed.

Terminal services receive high praise for speed, productivity, and ease of administration. Consider this desktop virtualization solution near perfect for all bandwidth situations from dial-up to Gigabit Ethernet LANs.

HOSTED DESKTOP

The hosted desktop is the current VMware and Xen method of desktop virtualization. On the virtual machine (VM) host server system, you have several—possibly dozens—of desktop VMs. Users connect via thin clients (smart terminal, dumb terminal, or client software) to their specific VM and run their desktop as if it were local to them, with a few exceptions. The most notable exception is that thin clients have no local CD/DVD or floppy drives. This aspect of virtualized desktops is confusing and frustrating for some users who are used to having local drives from which they can copy files to their desktop computers or to the server system. Most hardware thin clients are equipped with USB ports, so the capability to copy files to and from the virtual desktop or server system still exists.

Second, but less devastating than the lack of a CD or floppy drive, is that many of the new-generation hardware thin client devices also lack an operating system. The devices are remotely programmed to connect to a VM server system, connect to the appropriate VM, and present the user with the desktop system.

Hosted desktop operating systems offer little in the way of saving administrative time and effort, because each individual VM still has its own set of applications, including the operating system itself, antivirus software, an Internet browser, and other programs specific to an individual desktop computer. The VM still needs periodic maintenance, patches, defragmentation, and so on. So where's the savings? It's in hardware maintenance for those individual desktop computers.

Thin client hardware offers ease of administration, no moving parts, and most, if not all, are optimized for a Virtual Desktop Infrastructure (VDI) and are priced at or below the price of a standard desktop computer. A thin client device lasts two to three times longer than a standard desktop.

Desktop computer components typically carry a one-year warranty and therefore begin to fail when the hardware is one year and one day old. Most thin-client devices carry a three-year warranty and have an expected life of five to six years. Laptop computers have a very short life expectancy (about 18 months) because of breakage, loss, failure, and obsolescence, but there are some thin-client laptop computers available for users that require mobility.

Hosted desktop solutions are popular, but they are the least efficient in terms of resource usage, flexibility, and overall cost savings. You should explore all the other desktop virtualization possibilities before plunging headlong into this solution.

WEB-BASED SOLUTIONS

Web-based solutions are relatively new players in the virtualization arena, but they are gaining ground at a rapid pace. Online service companies are gaining trust, and the quality of online applications has increased to the point where many rival their locally installed counterparts. This section looks at hosted web applications and hosted web pseudo-desktop systems.

Hosted Web Applications

Hosted web applications are applications installed and used on remote server systems. Word processing, databases, spreadsheets, customer relationship management (CRM) presentations, and calendars are some of the applications currently being hosted by online providers. Although hosted web applications are not explicitly considered desktop virtualization per se, they are an extension of desktop virtualization. Hosted applications take much of the responsibility away from local staff and users and place it directly on the hosted service company.

Type "hosted applications" into any search engine, and you'll see hundreds of links to such services. Have an idea or list of applications and services you need before beginning your online search. When you've narrowed your search down to a few candidates for your hosted service, remember to ask about your Service Level Agreement (SLA) terms.

Your SLA describes the service you're paying for when you enter into the hosting contract. The SLA should describe uptime or availability (should be very close to 100%), backup and restore procedures, help desk and customer service availability, and security information. Pay extra attention to indemnification and hold harmless clauses that may state that the hosting company isn't responsible for any losses or damage to files.

Hosted applications are another way to enhance your virtualization strategy and lower maintenance costs associated with application support.

Hosted Web-Based Pseudo-Desktop Systems

Web-based pseudo-desktops are the newest entry into the desktop virtualization world. You can access your desktop from anywhere with a web browser. These web-based desktops are best described as pseudo-desktop systems because they aren't operating systems at all—they are Web 2.0 applications that mimic the look and feel of a desktop operating system. Being purely web-based, they are very fast and quite enjoyable to use.

Unless you've seen one of these, the concept may seem a little odd at first, but most work quite well and offer an impressive collection of applications. The following three figures are the best examples we've seen of this technology. Figure 10-1 is a screenshot of the icloud CloudOS from Xcerion. The service is still in beta and you have to sign up as a developer if you want to use it. The website is at www.icloud.com.

The icloud Cloud OS Desktop includes, as you can see, a live calendar, clock, international time information, and several applications, including an application builder. Windows and Linux users alike will enjoy using this web-based system.

The next system we have used is StartForce.com's Online Desktop. This offering is interesting because of the level of detail in mimicking a standard Windows or Linux (KDE) desktop experience. Figure 10-2 shows you the standard StartForce Online Desktop.

StartForce Online Desktop feels comfortable at any resolution and has several familiar applications, such as a web browser, an audio player, and an instant messenger. It has the familiar naming and behavior expected from a regular desktop computer. Handy icons on the desktop enable users to provide feedback, to request a new feature in StartForce, or to participate in one of the many forums that have sprouted up in response to this service.

The final online desktop system reviewed here is AjaxWindows. AjaxWindows has more in the way of useful applications than any of the other systems we have seen, but it seems less stable to me. We are hopeful that the maintainers will continue to upgrade this service and make it as stable and fast as StartForce. Figure 10-3 shows you my AjaxWindows Desktop.

FIGURE 10-1 My Cloud OS Desktop.

Check out AjaxWindows Desktop at www.ajaxwindows.com.

Two other web-based desktop systems we have looked at briefly deserve some mention here: Ghost (Global Hosted Operating System) at http://g.ho.st and the Ulteo Online Desktop at www.ulteo.com. Both of these services receive good reviews and awards, and they are definitely worth a look.

Web-based desktop systems are a viable option for those of you looking to totally virtualize your desktop environment and user experience. These services offer a generous amount of storage space and unlimited access at no charge. In the future, the services will most likely offer a premium support option, more storage space, and more options for those willing to pay a small fee.

FIGURE 10-2   The StartForce Online Desktop.

LOCALIZED VIRTUAL DESKTOPS

A localized virtual desktop is a virtual desktop operating system that is run locally on a system with or without any underlying operating system to support it. There are several methods of creating and running a localized virtual desktop. The three methods we'll explore in this section are Live CD, live operating system distribution on a USB drive, and desktop virtualization software running a VM.

Live CD

Live CDs have been around for a while and some are quite cleverly conceived and constructed, but none (that we're aware of) run as a live VM. You have to reboot your host computer with the Live CD in the CD/DVD drive and allow the operating system on the Live CD to become your new desktop OS.

A Live CD is a virtual desktop in that you can't save info generated from it because it is a read-only system. It's useful in situations where you need a desktop OS for remote connectivity to other systems such as websites, network drives, or other systems via VNC, RDP, SSH, or other remote protocols.

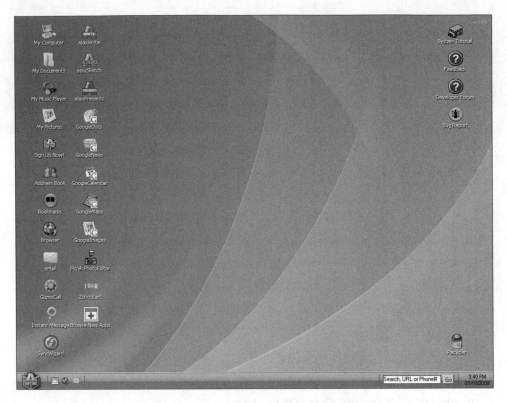

FIGURE 10-3 The AjaxWindows Desktop with standard icons and applications.

To use a Live CD as your desktop OS, select and download a Live CD distribution, burn it to a CD, and boot your computer from the Live CD. Alternatively, you can use virtualization software to boot from the ISO image or from the CD itself.

The best Live CD we've seen is Damn Small Linux (DSL) (www.damnsmalllinux. org). You can operate the very small (~50MB) system from a small format CD, install it to a hard drive, or install it on a pen drive (USB drive—see the next section "Live USB"). Figure 10-4 shows the basic DSL desktop apps and the right-click menu for accessing various programs and utilities.

DSL is perfect for desktop virtualization because it is loaded with remote connectivity applications such as VNC, Rdesktop, FTP, Telnet, SMBclient, Instant Messaging, and Internet browsers. DSL can be used as a desktop system itself or used as a client system to connect to remote UNIX, Linux, or Windows server systems.

Based on the Debian Linux (www.debian.org) distribution, DSL has excellent hardware detection and supports a wide range of devices and peripherals.

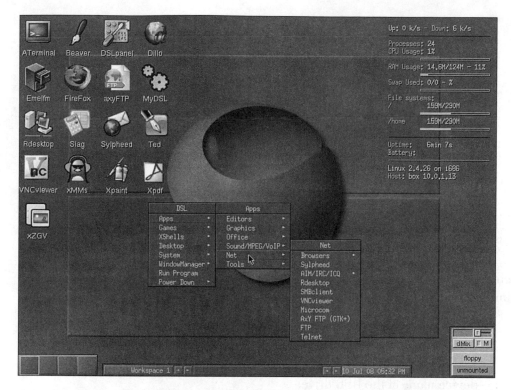

FIGURE 10-4 The Damn Small Linux Desktop and right-click menu.

If you need or want something more complete, nothing beats Knoppix for a loaded system. Knoppix can be downloaded from www.knoppix.net. The Knoppix Live CD contains hundreds of software programs and utilities to deliver a full desktop experience. It also has all the remote connectivity applications to get you connected to any remote system.

Live USB

USB drives are used in much the same way as Live CDs, except that you may use the operating system on the USB drive simultaneously with your existing desktop OS. As stated in the previous section, DSL offers a USB drive installation option.

To install DSL to a USB drive, follow these steps:

1. Download the Live DSL CD, burn it to media, and boot it on your system.
2. Insert the USB drive into a USB slot on your computer.
3. Right-click your mouse to launch the menus.
4. Select Apps, Tools, Install to USB Pendrive, Install to USB-Zip Pendrive, or Install to USB-HDD Pendrive.

NOTE

This procedure won't work in a VM unless your virtualization software has the capability to use USB devices.

Some computers allow you to boot from a USB drive, in which case you would have access only to the USB-hosted OS. In either case, the following instructions will transfer the Linux image to a USB drive for you. (If you use DSL, you don't have to do this.)

The process is straightforward for Windows or Linux as a host. First, select a Linux distribution that provides support for Live USB drives, download it, and install it to the USB drives using the UNIX *dd* program to convert and copy the file.

For Windows hosts, install CygWin or dd.exe for Windows from www.chrysocome.net/download. After you have a working copy of dd.exe and the usb image file, follow these steps:

On Linux hosts:

1. Insert the USB drive into a USB port on the computer.

2. Open a Terminal window and issue the dmesg command to discover the device name of the USB drive.

   It is usually /dev/sdx where *x* is the device letter starting with *a*. For this example, we are assuming it is /dev/sda.

3. Issue the following command to transfer the image to the USB drive:

   ```
   dd if=image_name.img of=/dev/sda
   ```

   You'll have to mount the drive to use it, if it is a live guest distribution.
   ```
   mount /dev/sda /mnt/usb
   ```

Depending on the Linux distribution you're using for the USB live system, you may be able to start the new operating system now. If it is a boot-only distribution, you'll have to reboot your computer and configure your BIOS to boot from the USB device.

The preferable way to use the USB drive is to boot a live operating system while still using your host OS normally. Whether your USB drive system is dedicated or guest depends on your application for the USB system—full desktop or VM.

Virtualization Software

Running virtualization software on a desktop operating system to run another OS in a VM is similar to running server-based virtualization software on a server system.

NOTE

Enter the full path to dd.exe or make sure that the Cygwin\bin or dd.exe is in your path. You will also need to enter the full path to your downloaded image file if it isn't in your current directory.

1. Click Start, Run, type cmd in the Open field, and click OK.

This launches your Command window.

2. Insert the USB drive into a USB port on your computer.

The computer automatically assigns a drive letter to the USB drive when inserted.

```
dd if=image_name.img od=x:
```

Image.img is the name of the USB Linux distribution image you downloaded, and x: is the drive letter assigned to your USB drive.

For Windows desktop operating systems, you'll need to use a package like Microsoft's Virtual PC, VMware Server, Sun's VirtualBox, or VMware Player. VMware Player allows you to use a premade VM and run it without installing any other virtualization software. It doesn't allow you to create VMs, but you can run almost any VMware-created or compatible VM. For Linux desktops, you can use Sun's VirtualBox, VMware Server, or VMware Player.

Using virtualization software to use another desktop operating system while maintaining your current one is highly liberating. It allows you to enjoy the flexibility and freedom of using both operating systems simultaneously. Using VMs in this manner will also allow you to connect to different remote networks with your VMs.

For example, you have a Windows desktop that you use for normal productive work, but you also need to connect to another network via VPN to perform other tasks. If you have two computers, your problem is solved; use the other computer. A single computer running a VM can do the same job without the extra hardware clutter or additional energy costs. The VM in this example can be any operating system that fills your needs.

Using VMware Player, you can download and use prebuilt VMs from VMware's website. Most of the pre-built VMs available are Linux-based because no licensing requirements are associated with its use for any purpose. You can run only prebuilt VMs with VMware Player. You can't use ISO images, import VMs, or create new VMs with VMware Player. Figure 10-5 shows your available options: Open a VM, download a virtual appliance from VMware, open a recently used VM, or download and use the featured virtual appliance.

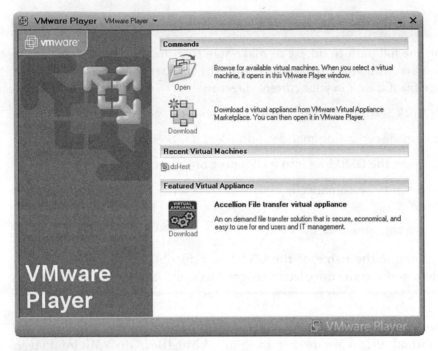

FIGURE 10-5   VMware Player Virtual Machine options.

Figure 10-6 is a screenshot of VMware Player using a DSL virtual machine named dsl-test.

VMware Player allows you to use your CD drive, floppy drive, network interface, and Bluetooth Adapter in an on-demand fashion by using the toolbar located along the top frame of the Player.

Localized virtual desktops offer an inexpensive, portable, and easy-to-use virtual desktop alternative. You are limited to Linux-related distributions for Live CDs and USB-oriented systems, but they provide a very low-cost way to connect to remote systems of any type.

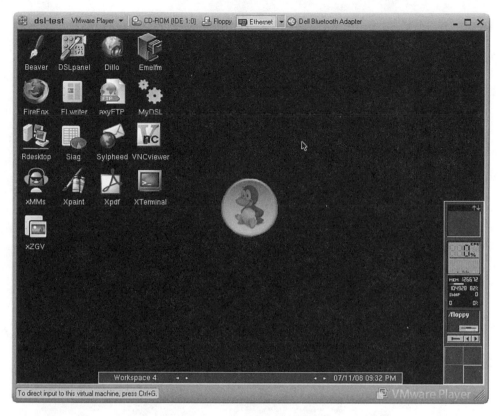

FIGURE 10-6 VMware Player running a DSL Virtual Machine.

SUMMARY

This chapter offered an overview of the different types and applications available in the desktop virtualization realm. This space, like any of virtualization, has its positive and negative sides.

Converting from traditional to virtual desktops and applications takes a change of mind for you, your management, and your users—especially your users. A gentle introduction, training, and a virtual sandbox for users to test and become comfortable with the idea has great value and will likely save you a lot of grief later. Gain user buy-in, and your most difficult problems are solved—implementation is easy by comparison.

## CHAPTER 11

Network and Storage Virtualization in Action

This chapter covers network and storage virtualization from a 10,000-foot view, as far as the details and definitions are concerned. From a virtualization strategy point of view, however, we're going in for a fly-by. Not every network needs a VPN, VLAN, leveraged storage device, or some of the other components discussed here. For those that do, this information will help you implement them successfully.

Other concepts presented in this chapter don't lend themselves well to physical demonstrations, or sufficient information can be found elsewhere to illustrate certain points. Those concepts we will observe and navigate past.

VIRTUAL PRIVATE NETWORK (VPN)

VPNs have been around for some time now and are still the accepted method to connect remote users and remote offices to a central office network. VPNs are secure and efficient by nature and require minimal setup for server and client systems alike. Setting up a VPN server as a VM is desirable from a financial, administrative, and security standpoint.

Because a VPN server incurs almost no overhead, you can use a virtual appliance that is dedicated to the job of authenticating users and granting access to specific resources. Some VPN virtual appliances use as little as 100MB of disk space and 40MB of RAM. There are several ways to implement a VPN service for your network, involving either hardware or software.

Hardware VPN

A hardware VPN solution involves the purchase and setup of hardware devices to create your VPN solution. VPN routers available through several vendors allow you to plug in the device on your network, configure it via a web browser or utility, and grant access to network resources.

On the low end of the VPN device spectrum, you may spend about $175 USD for a 30-user VPN router. Higher-end devices will cost several thousand dollars (USD) but the features, support, warranties, number of users, and product life are greater.

A hardware VPN solution can be a good solution for remote users and remote office connectivity to a central office. The disadvantages of hardware VPN are costs and administrative overhead—including training for administrators and time for configuration and maintenance. Each branch office will need its own VPN device for remote connectivity; single roaming remote users will not. This section's discussion will focus on software VPN services.

Software VPN

Software VPN solutions are less expensive using VPN server systems but are no less cumbersome to set up than their hardware counterparts. The greater advantage of software VPNs is recovery time. Restoring a VPN virtual machine (VM) requires only a few minutes of time, whereas getting a hardware VPN solution repaired and back online may take days or weeks unless you purchase a service contract through the vendor, which adds considerably to the cost of the device.

Setting up a VPN server VM with Windows 2003 Server is a simple process. The following steps guide you through creating a VPN service and then connecting a Windows XP client to the server via VPN.

 NOTE

Before you begin this setup, you'll need two Ethernet connections configured for the VM. One must be connected out to the Internet or to a firewall that is Internet connected. The second Ethernet connection must be configured to access the internal network of interest for the VPN. The wizard sets up routing services and configuration as you go through it.

VPN Server Setup

To set up your VPN software, follow these steps:

1. In your Windows 2003 Server VM, click Start, Settings, Control Panel, Network Connections.

2. Double-click the New Connection Wizard icon.

3. Click Next on the Welcome screen.

   Figure 11-1 is the Network Connection Type selection screen.

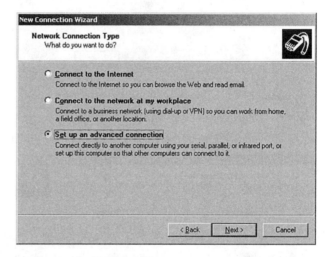

FIGURE 11-1   Setting up the Network Connection Type (Advanced).

4. Select Set Up an Advanced Connection and click Next to accept and continue.

   The next screen, shown in Figure 11-2, allows you to select your connection option for the VPN server.

5. Select Accept Incoming Connections and click Next to continue.

   Figure 11-3 is a remnant from the old days when serial and parallel ports were used for connectivity.

6. Do not select Direct Parallel. Click Next to continue.

   You will then see the screen depicted in Figure 11-4, which tells the firewall to allow or deny VPN ports for connectivity to this server.

7. Select Allow Virtual Private Connections and click Next.

   You may see the pop-up informational message shown in Figure 11-5. It is notification that you'll need to manage future incoming VPN connections via the Local User Manager or via Remote Access Policies.

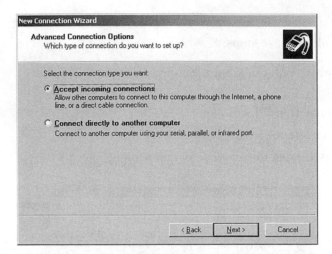

FIGURE 11-2 The Advanced Connection Options screen.

FIGURE 11-3 The Devices for Incoming Connections screen.

8. Click OK on this information screen to continue with the New Connection Wizard.

   The next screen, shown in Figure 11-6, allows you to select VPN users while still in the New Connection Wizard. As the informational pop-up (Figure 11-5) stated, you'll need to configure future VPN users through the Local User Console or Remote Access Policies.

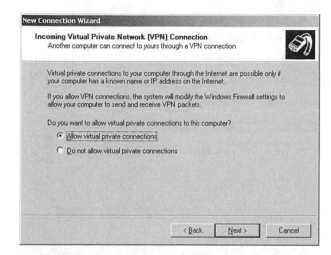

FIGURE 11-4   The Incoming Virtual Private
Network (VPN) Connections screen.

FIGURE 11-5   Incoming Connections informational notification.

FIGURE 11-6   The VPN User Permissions
screen.

9. Select all current users who'll use VPN connectivity to this VPN server system. Click Next when finished.

   Figure 11-7 is the wizard screen where you select all protocols that users are allowed to use when connected to this VPN server system.

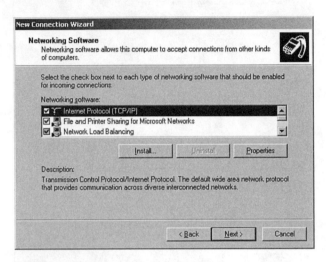

FIGURE 11-7 The Networking Software for incoming connections screen.

10. Install or remove any protocols or software on this screen. When finished, click Next to continue.

11. Click Finish on the next screen to complete the New Connection Wizard.

NOTE

Unless your VPN server is directly connected to the Internet, you'll have to configure your external firewall to forward all PPTP (TCP/IP Port: 1723) traffic to your VPN server's Internet-facing IP address.

L2TP uses TCP/IP Port 1701.

VPN Windows Client Setup

Now that you've completed the server side of the VPN setup, let's move on to the client portion.

1. On your Windows XP computer click Start, Settings, Control Panel, Network Connections, Create a New Connection.

   The New Connection Wizard launches and presents you with the Welcome Screen.

2. Click Next on the Welcome Screen.

   The Network Connection Type screen presents you with several options for remote connectivity, as shown in Figure 11-8.

FIGURE 11-8 Selecting the Network Connection Type for a VPN connection.

3. Select Connect to the Network at My Workplace and click Next.

   The screen shown in Figure 11-9 prompts for the method you'll use to connect to your workplace network.

4. Select Virtual Private Network Connection and click Next. You will be prompted for a connection name, as shown in Figure 11-10.

5. Enter a descriptive name for your new VPN connection and click Next to continue.

6. The next screen, shown in Figure 11-11, prompts for a Fully Qualified Domain Name (FQDN) or IP address that will allow you to connect to your VPN server. Enter the information and click Next.

7. Select Add a Shortcut to This Connection to My Desktop, and click Finish to complete the wizard.

8. Open the VPN to Main Office icon on your desktop.

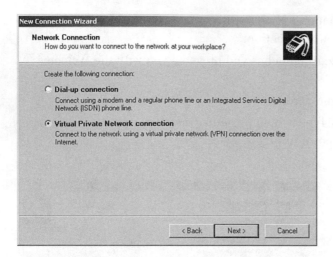

FIGURE 11-9   Select your connection method.

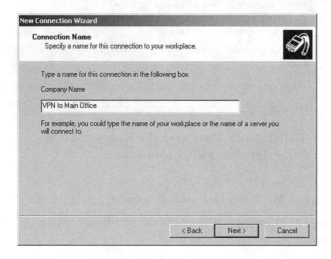

FIGURE 11-10   Name the VPN connection.

9. Enter your username and password for your local user account on the VPN server system.

10. Click Connect.

You'll see the connection taking place, and in a few seconds, if all went well, your connection will be complete.

You can now use all the services that you selected in Figure 11-7 when you configured the VPN server.

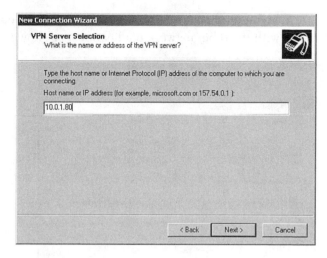

FIGURE 11-11   The VPN Server Selection screen.

On the Windows 2003 Server, you can see who is connected into the server by opening Network Connections in Control Panel. See Figure 11-12 to see a server with no connections.

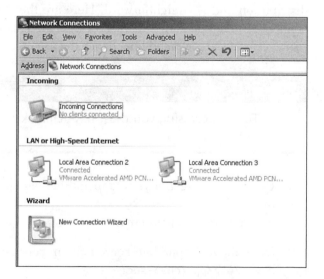

FIGURE 11-12   Windows 2003 VPN Server Network Connections.

When a user connects to the VPN server, the connection and protocol will be listed with the other network connections, as shown in Figure 11-13.

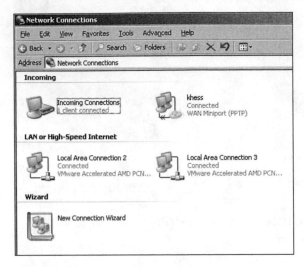

FIGURE 11-13 Network Connections with connected user.

VPN Linux Client Setup

Yes, it's true—you *can* connect to a Windows VPN via PPTP in much the same way you connect from a Windows XP computer. This method works on every major Linux distribution and is straightforward. Here are the steps to get your Linux computer connected to a Windows VPN server system. This entire process requires sudo or root access at the command line, hence the use of the # sign when issuing commands.

NOTE

To be successful, you must have Linux kernel 2.16.15 or later and ppp version 2.4.2 or later.

1. Use either apt-get or yum to install the necessary packages (using sudo or root access).
   ```
   # yum install pptp-linux
   ```

2. Open the /etc/ppp/chap-secrets file in your favorite editor.
   ```
   # vi /etc/ppp/chap-secrets
   ```

3. Enter your authentication information into the /etc/ppp/chap-secrets file with the following:

Use the format: username VPN Server Name password *

khess WIN2K3-VPN connectme *

The username and password are your login credentials on the Windows VPN server system.

If you use Windows Domain Authentication, enter the information into the chap-secrets file as shown next.

```
CORP\\khess WIN2K3-VPN connectme *
```

CORP is the domain name.

4. Save and exit the chap-secrets file.

5. Open a new file for your new connection under /etc/ppp/peers.

```
vi /etc/ppp/peers/win-vpn
```

You can use any name you want. We used win-vpn because it's short and descriptive.

6. Enter your connection information into the /etc/ppp/peers/win-vpn file.

```
pty "pptp win2k3-vpn –nolaunchpppd"
name khess
remotename WIN2K3-VPN
require-mppe-128
file /etc/ppp/options.pptp
ipparam win-vpn
```

7. Save and exit the win-vpn file.

8. Check the /etc/ppp/options.pptp file to be sure it has the following entries and that they are uncommented:

```
lock
noauth
refuse-eap
refuse-chap
refuse-mschap
nobsdcomp
nodeflate
require-mppe-128
```

Using these settings require the use of MSCHAP-V2, a more secure authentication protocol.

9. Try out your new VPN connection with the following command:

```
# pppd call win-vpn
```

10. To see your connection status, use

```
# tail -f /var/log/messages
```

This command allows you to watch system messages as they are sent to the system log.

You should see messages similar to the following confirming a successful connection to your VPN server.

```
Jul 24 16:49:25 debian4 pppd[3790]: pppd 2.4.4 started by root, uid 0
Jul 24 16:49:25 debian4 pppd[3790]: Using interface ppp0
Jul 24 16:49:25 debian4 pppd[3790]: Connect: ppp0 <-> /dev/pts/1
Jul 24 16:49:41 debian4 pppd[3790]: CHAP authentication succeeded
Jul 24 16:49:41 debian4 pppd[3790]: MPPE 128-bit stateless compression
enabled
Jul 24 16:49:43 debian4 pppd[3790]: found interface eth0 for proxy arp
Jul 24 16:49:43 debian4 pppd[3790]: local  IP address 10.0.1.52
Jul 24 16:49:43 debian4 pppd[3790]: remote IP address 10.0.1.101
```

It may take a few seconds for the CHAP authentication succeeded to appear, but once it does, you have successfully authenticated to the Windows VPN server (or domain).

VIRTUAL LOCAL AREA NETWORK (VLAN)

VLANs are used on larger networks to segment, or isolate, traffic into separate broadcast domains. VLANs are usually created using intelligent switches, but you can also create them with physical or VMs. VLAN trunking is included in Linux kernel versions 2.4.14 and later, and in all 2.6 versions. You can also create VLANs using Windows servers, but you must have NICs that support VLAN creation (for example, the Intel Pro Series).

In VMware Server, you can create VLANs within the VMware environment, allow VMs to participate in standard VLANs, or create a combination of the two. VMs may participate in VLANs like any physical system by virtue of its IP address.

Standard VLAN

For example, if you create VLAN 10 in your switch and assign the IP address range of 192.168.1.0/24, any host that you place into that network range will be a member of VLAN 10. There is nothing else special needed to place a device into a VLAN. The switch handles the traffic to the VLAN.

VMware VLAN

An extremely interesting aspect of VMware products is that you can create VLANs within the software itself for very efficient VM to VM communications. You do this by creating a virtual switch through which all inter-VM communications will take place. The VMware VLAN is not accessible outside the VLAN.

The following steps describe how to set up a VLAN between VMs in VMware Server.

1. Choose two or more VMs from your VMware Inventory that will participate in the VLAN.

2. Add a new Ethernet Adapter to each VM.

3. When prompted for the new Ethernet Adapter properties, select Custom: Specific Virtual Network under Network Connection, and choose a device from the list as shown in Figure 11-14. Here, /dev/vmnet2 was selected as the virtual switch identity.

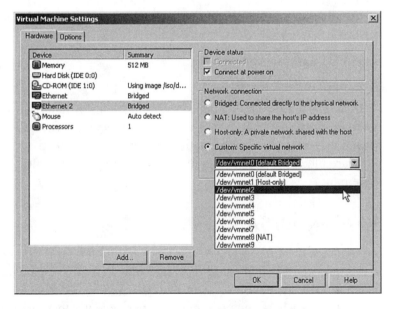

FIGURE 11-14   Select a virtual switch device from the drop-down list.

4. Start up the VMs.

5. Change the IP addresses for the Ethernet Adapters connected to the VLAN (/dev/vmnet2).

You don't need a default gateway for the new adapter's settings, but if your operating system gives you an error, use the IP address of the adapter as your gateway address.

6. Apply the changes.

7. Test connectivity by pinging the VLAN interface of another VM.

Your VMware-only VLAN is complete.

Combination VLAN

A combination VLAN can be a valuable asset in creating a more secure environment for certain services. To see how this works, remove or disable the primary Ethernet Adapter on one of your VMs from the previous example.

You still have VMware VLAN connectivity between the VMs using /dev/vmnet2. You now have one VM with dual connectivity and one with VLAN-only connectivity. The only system that may contact the VLAN-only is the VM connected to it via the /dev/vmnet2 VLAN.

To illustrate the level of security for the isolated system, consider the following scenario:

- VM1 has dual connectivity.
- VM2 is VLAN only.

VM1 is a web application server that calls a database on VM2. VM2 is a database-only server system. On VM2, implement a firewall that allows only the incoming port for web application to database connectivity. All other incoming ports are blocked. This results in a very secure environment for the database server system.

SAN AND VSAN

Storage area networking (SAN) has been around for a few years now. It has matured and grown more popular in larger networks as a way of moving away from server-based storage to network-based storage. Server-based storage is traditional file server storage where you are connected permanently to a server that shares its local disks to users for file storage. Network-based storage is storage that is not local to any one server but spread throughout a network in the form of disk arrays, tape libraries, optical disk arrays, and various types of network attached storage devices.

Smaller networks rarely use SANs because of the sheer cost and complexity of the equipment involved in the process. Typically, as networks grow and evolve, the following progressive steps are taken toward SAN architecture:

- Server-based storage
- Network attached storage (NAS)
- Storage area networks
- Virtual storage area networks (VSANs)

Generally, there must be some significant advantage to virtualized storage for large, complex networks. The major payoffs are in storage management and in the segregation of network traffic within a SAN. When you split up a large SAN into segments or VSANs, you not only have a more manageable SAN infrastructure, you also improve the performance and scalability of your SAN.

Devices that are used in SANs use special communications protocols to transfer data via the network. Fibre Channel and iSCSI are the two major protocols used in SANs.

VLANs and VSANs are very similar in that they are logical separations of devices and traffic into a network compartment. VLAN and VSAN creation occurs at the switch level. Individual storage devices are grouped into a logical unit (VSAN) with a unique ID number. The switch is then responsible for forwarding the data to the correct VSAN by ID.

The VSAN enables SAN managers to administer SANs with greater efficiency because the VSAN removes the location issue from the SAN. It also allows maintenance to occur without interruption—for example, by replacing, adding, or removing storage devices without bringing an entire SAN down to do so.

Data Transportation

Data transport speeds are very high using FCP (Gbps), but Fibre Channel Host Bus Adapters and switches are expensive. The additional architecture is also very complicated compared to other technologies. Although prices are coming down and speeds are going up, it may be wiser to leverage existing architecture using iSCSI. iSCSI is implemented with existing switches, NICs, and the speeds can approach Fibre Channel if you use Gigabit components.

To gain greater throughput, you can bind two or more NICs together to create a larger data pipe to the iSCSI device.

Fibre Channel and iSCSI devices are suitable for storing and running live VMs. Disk I/O is sufficient to sustain an acceptable read and write throughput. Many companies store disk I/O intensive databases and applications on such devices with great success.

NAS

Network attached storage (NAS) devices usually don't participate in SANs because of the protocols they use to transfer data. NAS devices use Network File System (NFS), Common Internet File System (CIFS), or HTTP. NAS server systems transfer data via these protocols over standard TCP/IP at Ethernet speeds.

This transfer rate makes NAS suitable for use as a file server and storage for nightly backups, but it is not suitable as a storage device for live applications or as a storage medium for live VMs. The exception to the previous statement is for VMs that rely on network connectivity more than they do on disk I/O. Network speeds to and from a NAS are insufficient to allow for anything but a small amount of disk I/O—especially for disk writes. A moderate amount of disk reads may be performed without significant latency if the amount of data is relatively small.

SUMMARY

Network and storage virtualization are now common terms within larger networks. Perhaps the most familiar term in network virtualization is the virtual private network, the VPN. Today, with the ubiquitous nature of broadband Internet connectivity from home and office, VPN is generally the accepted method for remote access to a central location.

Growing networks create the need for segmentation and isolation for security and network traffic management. VLANs have come to our rescue in this area. VLANs are relatively inexpensive and easy to set up and maintain—even for nonenterprise networks.

Virtual storage networks grow out of standard storage networks when administrative needs dictate such action. Virtualizing the SAN streamlines administrative tasks related to the SAN and creates storage stealth so that the actual location of storage devices is no longer relevant.

Part III

Building the Virtual Infrastructure: Hardware's Role in Virtualization

## CHAPTER 12

Form-Factor Choices and Their Implications

If you've recently bought new x86 hardware you can probably skip this chapter; chances are it's well suited for virtualization, and it's also highly unlikely you'll receive additional money for new equipment.

If the servers you're planning to virtualize have been hanging around since they were last used for Y2K, or if they were purchased in the dot-com boom, don't even consider using them except maybe for test and dev for inconsequential applications. For all practical purposes, if you're going to effectively implement a virtualization strategy (and by strategy, we mean anything more than ten boxes), hardware that came out in the past three years is in order.

The adage stating that there's no such thing as a free lunch applies quite strongly here. If your organization opts to move forward with insufficient investment in hardware, whether it be using what's on hand or buying the least-expensive hardware possible, bear in mind that you will likely pay down the road, and in areas beyond hardware. Don't underestimate the potential cost of man hours necessary to troubleshoot, or personnel issues and lost sales due to potential downtime.

This chapter looks in general at x86 form-factor choices, from towers and racks versus blades, to sockets and cores and why they matter when it comes to virtualization. You'll learn how to best determine your needs and how to ensure that you are setting up a scalable infrastructure. The subsequent chapter will take a general look at what each of the major server vendors has to offer and where virtualization fits with their strategy. We also discuss cloud computing, which is a way to outsource the heavy lifting inherent in virtualization and one that is emerging as an option for cash strapped enterprises.

This is a fast-moving marketplace, so we have tried to be both general and current. Before making any purchases, be sure to consult with the vendors to ensure that their offerings still comply with your needs.

TOWERS, RACKS, AND BLADES

Three major footprint options exist for today's servers: towers, racks, and blades. Some OEMs have comparable offerings across all three platforms, and some release to the various form-factor based on anticipated need. Numerous hybrid options also exist, such as Dell's PowerEdge 2900 III, which Dell describes as a Rack Mountable Tower, and some options don't fall neatly into any other category. However, if you're looking to virtualize within an x86 environment, chances are you're looking at one of these form factors.

All things being equal, blades are often touted as the most ideal hardware for virtualization, although the particulars of a given situation might dictate otherwise.

Tower servers are generally the most low end of servers, and in most cases are the least likely candidates for virtualization. A tower server occupies the same footprint as a desktop CPU. In some cases, especially for SMBs, it may even be a repurposed desktop CPU, but more likely it was built specifically as a server. A tower server is well suited for test and dev or any other standalone virtualization endeavor because it's both easily moved and self-contained. On a virtualized network its advantages are few: It takes up more real estate than a server sitting in a rack or a blade chassis, and it adds an additional layer of complexity to the cabling and peripheral management.

Thus, if your data center is typical, chances are that most of your servers sit in racks. A rack server takes up far less space than a tower server; it generally runs quieter and is easier to manage from a physical infrastructure perspective. The majority of servers in use in data centers are rack servers, and not surprisingly, or perhaps as a result, the majority of newer servers with a respectable amount of processing power are designed that way.

A server rack can be as small as four units (or 4U) high, but in a large data center, it is more typical for racks to go from floor to ceiling and be only partially filled because of power and cooling constraints or for scalability reasons. Within the rack, server size can vary, and servers can occupy as little as one slot or as many slots as there are in the rack. A rack with slots for 42 servers, for example, can hold several servers that occupy two slots (2U), a server that is four units high, and one that is 8U. The rest of the slots may be empty or contain similar configurations that fill all or part of the rack.

The features that present a disadvantage for towers present an advantage for rack servers. Their modular nature results in less real estate being taken up, and cabling and other wiring is easily streamlined.

The ProLiant DL 385, a rack server, is one of HP's most popular offerings. In November 2008, the OEM released the fifth generation of the product, touting it as a particularly virtualization friendly offering. A large part of what makes the server so virtualization friendly has to do with the processor. It can contain up to two quad-core Shanghai Opteron 2300 series processors, AMD's 45 nm x86 processor built with virtual environments in mind. HP added some virtual bells and whistles of its own, including Ethernet interconnects.

Even more virtualization friendly than rack servers are blade servers. At their core, blade servers are slimmed down rack servers with streamlined componentry, making them easier to manage and maintain, and providing greater reliability. The biggest downside to blades is their lack of conformity: There is currently no compatibility among the vendors, so HP's BladeSystem sits in its own chassis and cannot integrate with IBM's BladeCenter. Much noise was made about this earlier in the decade, but blades seem to have caught on despite the need for enterprises to standardize around a single vendor.

So if blades are basically slimmed down and streamlined rack servers, what is it that makes them suitable for virtualization? Their architecture, for one thing. Because blades have fewer switches and cables to start, they can more easily adapt to virtual counterparts. They also take steps to resolve I/O issues at the hardware layer.

The vendors saw this synergy early on, and products are available to facilitate virtual machines (VM) running on a blade.

Note, however, that a VM running on a blade is not the same as a virtual blade. A VM on a blade is a VM that just happens to sit on a blade, whereas a virtual blade is virtualizing the blade as a whole. In most cases it is the software that makes the call.

If you're vacillating between racks and blades, investment protection is one factor to consider. The hardware vendors are putting more and more of their virtualization eggs in their blade baskets, so the options will increase with time. On the other hand, understand that whatever blade infrastructure you opt for will likely lock you in to that vendor for the foreseeable future. If your company is already tied to a vendor, both the issue and the selection process are moot.

One not so insignificant consideration when it comes to blades is their density. On the one hand, they can pack a powerful punch into a small amount of space. On the other hand, the power they consume and the heat they give off must be taken into account. In some cases, the increase in computing power will outweigh the additional power and cooling requirements compared to rack servers delivering equivalent computing power. This is not always the case, however, so be sure to take that into account when planning your purchase.

Table 12-1 compares the basics of towers, racks, and blades servers.

TABLE 12-1 Server Form Factor Options

	TOWER	RACK	BLADE
	Standalone	Modular	Modular
Cabling	Singular	Multiple	One per chassis
Pros	■ Inexpensive ■ Scalable ■ Minimal density ■ No vendor lock-in	■ Easy to manage ■ Generally more powerful than tower servers ■ Small footprint	■ Simpler cabling ■ More powerful computing in small footprint
Cons	■ Noisy ■ Inefficient to manage ■ Consumes more real estate than other form factors ■ Tend to not be as powerful as other form factors	■ Some degree of vendor lock-in ■ Power and cooling issues that often result in underutilization of racks ■ Less modular than towers ■ Often more expensive than tower models ■ Cabling and peripheral quickly grows in complexity	■ Denseness may result in power and cooling issues ■ Lack of standardization resulting in vendor lock-in

In addition to these three options, a fourth option is emerging, which lacks a footprint in the data center. In 2008, cloud computing began gaining acceptance. We will discuss cloud computing and how it compares to more traditional solutions in the next chapter.

BEYOND FORM FACTOR, FILLING THE FOOTPRINT

After you've decided on a given form factor, it's time to decide what you want within the box. Looking at how the full package approaches virtualization is important, but before that can be examined, it is important to understand what is going on at a component level. Currently, AMD and Intel have a lock on x86 hardware from OEMs. They have been building virtualization support into their chips since 2005, and the latest iteration from both vendors is intended for servers that will be virtualized. Thus, if the hardware on hand or being purchased was released any time after early 2007, it's safe to assume the processor will handle virtualization just fine. Slightly older hardware may be fine as well, but be sure to check its specs carefully against those that each vendor recommends, and understand that performance needs expand with time.

The chip architectures and how they approach virtualization differ. For the most part, the major OEMs have comparable offerings from both AMD and Intel, so processor choice could theoretically be a driver. However, because most enterprises make their purchases through VARs, drilling down to that level during the purchasing process may not be doable, and in many cases looking at the package as a whole versus low-level components will be a more strategic way to go.

Still, it is important to have at least a rudimentary understanding of what you are purchasing.

Intel calls its virtualization initiative Intel Virtualization Technology (or Intel VT); AMD calls its technology AMD Virtualization (or AMD-V), although it is still sometimes referred to as "Pacifica" (admittedly, not much originality in the naming).

Both Intel VT and AMD-V are considered to deliver what is called "hardware-assisted virtualization." With hardware-assisted virtualization, the hypervisor uses processor extensions to "intercept and emulate privileged operations in the guest." The key word in this description is "assisted," however. How the environment plays out is still very much reliant on the hypervisor itself, and as one AMD whitepaper notes, a hypervisor that makes use of hardware-assisted virtualization "must provide the illusion to the guest that the guest is running on physical hardware. For example, when the guest uses processor's paging support or address translation, the hypervisor must ensure that the guest observes the equivalent behavior it would observe on nonvirtualized hardware."

The company notes that AMD-V accomplished this by allowing "the hypervisor to specify how the processor should handle privileged operations in guest itself without transferring control to the hypervisor."

Intel's initiative is of a similar nature. Its x86 virtualization technology is actually a subset of Intel VT. It is known as VT-x, and was previously code named "Vanderpool." Table 12-2 offers a side-by-side comparison of how the two chip vendors approach virtualization.

TABLE 12-2 AMD Versus Intel

	AMD	INTEL
	AMD-V	Intel VT
Website	www.amd.com/us-en/0,,3715_15781_15785,00.html	www.intel.com/technology/virtualization/
Key Attributes	Because of the Direct Connect Architecture, already present in AMD's chips, system bottlenecks that occur with front side bus architectures are reduced, and AMD's HyperTransport technology enables high-speed I/O.	
	AMD's Integrated Memory Controller offers crucial low-latency, high-bandwidth memory access, which mitigates some of the memory issues virtualization brings with it.	Investment protection and flexibility with Intel Virtualization Technology FlexMigration (Intel VT FlexMigration).
	Rapid Virtualization Indexing helps improve performance of virtualized applications and reduces software virtualization overhead.	Scalable performance with decreased footprint and power demands (65 watt processor available).
		Based on 45nm Intel Core microarchitecture enabling low voltage options for ultradense de.

UNDERSTANDING CORES AND SOCKETS

Despite these differences, for the most part, the processor itself is a commodity in the x86 server selection process. Although knowing this information will better facilitate the purchasing process, it will neither make you nor break you in the big picture so long as it is present. The processor, however, is not entirely irrelevant. In fact, the most bang for the virtualized buck is achieved by taking advantage of multicore processors. Systems powered by multicore are the standard these days. In the less than five years since multicore appeared on the x86 scene, it has become all but impossible to find a single-core server. In fact, in 2008, no new single-core servers were released.

Until virtualization took center stage, new versions of processors—and to some degree the hardware in which they sat—were by and large all about Moore's Law (as defined by the website Webopedia, Intel cofounder Gordon Moore's 1965 observation that "the number of transistors per square inch on integrated circuits had doubled every year since the integrated circuit was invented" and would continue to do so). For a time it appeared that the hold of Moore's Law was slackening, and then multicore, and with that multisocket, came on the scene. This enabled chip manufacturers and OEMs (as well as VARs) to continue to wax poetic over processor power. And now they could cook up additional benchmarks to subsequently outstrip as the number of cores and processors continues to increase.

Obviously, the OEMs picked up on this, and frequently the number of cores and sockets a chip—and, hence, a server—has are used as bragging points and for increasingly faster and higher benchmarks.

Dual-core processors, which were not so long ago heralded as revolutionary, are quickly becoming passé. According to the website Webopedia, *dual core* refers to a CPU that includes two complete execution cores per physical processor. It combines two processors and their caches and cache controllers onto a single integrated circuit (silicon chip). Each execution core thus has an independent interface to the processor's front-side bus.

Multicore takes it a step further. As Webopedia notes, a single physical processor contains the core logic for these two or more processors. The processors are then packaged into a single integrated circuit known as a die. To make things even more confusing, multicore can also refer to multiple dies packaged together.

Each core has its own cache, thus theoretically providing the operating system with sufficient resources to handle compute-intensive tasks in parallel. In practical terms, multicore's chief value proposition for data centers is performance.

Each core in turn sits on a socket. A socket is the connector on the motherboard that houses a CPU and forms the electrical interface to communicate with it. Most x86 desktops and servers are at least dual-socket based at this point. Bear in mind that the relationship between the cores and the sockets is often not one-to-one. A dual-core CPU, for example, generally consumes only one socket.

The processing power by and large is there, and has been for some time. In some ways its timing couldn't have been better.

Prior to virtualization, multicore's capabilities were grossly underutilized, and if not for multicore, virtualization technologies could well have ended up a victim of its own success.

Unlike 64-bit, which was the last big processor "revolution," and which had a pretty rough go of it when it was released earlier in the decade, OEMs quickly bought into multicore technology. Enterprises responded in kind, to the degree that single-core processors are quickly becoming extinct, and multicore has found itself into myriad corners of desktops, mobile PCs, servers, and workstations. As with 64-bit, not all applications were suited for multicore; not all apps stand to benefit from running in parallel. However, its timing was fortuitous—virtualization was heating up as multicore servers began hitting the streets.

As much as multicore's success is owed to virtualization, it's not so much in actual deployments as in concept. In many respects, multicore's capabilities were grossly underutilized. To some degree, this continues to be the case. A November 2008 article posted on ieee Spectrum online, which looked at a Sandia Labs report, found that more cores do not automatically parlay into better performance. Granted, they were looking primarily at supercomputing apps, but the findings apply to situations in which virtualization is used.

The root of the problem is that "although the number of cores per processor is increasing, the number of connections from the chip to the rest of the computer is not." As a result, many cores sit idle, awaiting data.

This disparity between how fast the CPU can operate on data versus how fast it can get the data it needs is sometimes referred to as a *memory wall*, and some question whether the incremental speed and processing capabilities we're now seeing have any real-world practicality, even when virtualization is in play.

Virtualization does not mitigate this directly, but it does use the multiple cores more effectively by allocating applications and VMs to separate cores. This means multiple applications can operate at the same time (that is, in parallel) rather than sequentially, where one application must wait for another to finish.

Although this is a vast improvement, it is far from perfect, largely because the "pipe" through which the data moves within the processor is not widened. Memory and I/O constraints remain issues with which everyone is grappling—from the chip vendors themselves (for example, AMD with its IO Memory Management Unit, or IOMMU, which is part of AMD-V) to OEMs to the major virtualization companies to various software vendors. Today, most of the memory allocation is being done at the software level, and from a practical perspective what you actually have is less than the numbers say. The memory capacity numbers the vendors are touting are, as one software company CEO described them, "smoke and mirrors."

Therefore, when making your hardware purchasing decisions, bear in mind that although multicore and virtualization are well suited to each another, and a multicore architecture is the norm (and all but a requirement for a virtual infrastructure), it is not without its limitations, which we discuss further in the next section.

MITIGATING I/O AND MEMORY ISSUES

I/O and memory issues are related to one another but are not synonymous. From a technological standpoint, memory and I/O are a combination of the elephant in the room, an 800-pound gorilla, or an albatross around your neck, depending on which side you're on. Like with much of the data center, when I/O and memory are working as expected and everything is humming along and going well, no one notices. When bottlenecks become the norm, however, I/O and memory are the first to be blamed.

You could, of course, throw more memory at the problem, but this isn't effective in the long term, and it could get costly. An even more futile solution is to up the processing power. It is very likely that the processing power already outstrips what the memory can handle.

Memory management is a complicated area. Entire books can (and have been) written about it. However, just as it was important to be able to differentiate between the processors, it is important to have at least a rudimentary understanding of how memory and I/O work in a virtualized environment and why it matters. Even if you have no desire to be an expert in memory and I/O issues, you should be cognizant of the issue when purchasing new hardware so as to not be fooled by a vendor. Exploring some of the options will also help make managing the hardware less of a headache down the road.

In a perfect world, you would plan up front to ensure that this does not become an issue, and you would have a plan in place for how to treat it if it does. You would also not skimp on hardware. Unfortunately, real-world computing environments coming with budget and the hardware these budget dollars purchase rarely resemble their benchmarked counterparts. Numbers cited by even the most honorable of vendors have an element of unreliability to them. It is also easier for the more unscrupulous to spin these numbers myriad ways.

It is always smart to take any benchmark numbers with a grain of salt, and when it comes to memory management, an entire salt grinder would come in handy.

Also, be aware that this is an area where semantics are significant. Memory virtualization, for example, is completely different from virtual memory. When vendors are spooling off feeds and speeds, it is critical to know to which they are referring. The former can refer to memory pools or clustering, whereas the latter means an extension of physical or "real" memory.

In its simplest form, memory refers to a chip's capacity to hold data. A server that has N gigabytes of memory, therefore, can hold about N billion bytes (or characters) of information. For years, this design worked just fine, and adding more memory meant the server could process more data quicker.

When virtualization enters the picture, things change. What was formerly one server with one operating system may now be 16 VMs, each with its own operating system. Although 64GB of memory might have been just fine when it was functioning as a dedicated box, it now no longer suffices, and not for the reasons you might be thinking.

The virtualization vendors would like you to believe that you simply divide up the 64GB by 16 and allocate 4GB to each VM, with some customization as needed for VMs that need more. But it doesn't actually work that way.

By virtue of how OSes are designed, the hypervisor cannot actually allocate memory into each VM. Instead, it gives each OS instance a placeholder address for its memory and keeps track of its actual location. This gets dicey and complicated and results in things like I/O latency and ballooning memory. This problem is hardly a reason to not virtualize. There is no shortage of options to resolve this from the hardware level, to OEM-specific software to remedy the issue, to the hypervisor, to third-party software. Some of these solutions work in tandem.

Their main goal is to keep the pipe moving by routing traffic to remove the bottleneck. This has become known as I/O virtualization.

Vendors of all stripes have taken steps to mitigate it, and perhaps some day processors will function in such a way that it will not be an issue. The OEMs are attempting to resolve the issue by further virtualizing the hardware through software. IBM and HP, for example, offer similar solutions that virtualize the I/O processes for their blade server families. The virtualization providers seek to make changes at the hypervisor level. Meanwhile, a growing crop of independent third-party vendors, such as 3Leaf, Neterion, and Xsigo Systems, has sprouted. Virtualized I/O is becoming big business.

Although I/O is related to memory, virtualized I/O is more closely aligned to virtual switches and cabling. We will therefore examine the concepts behind it as well as some of the leading products more closely in Chapter 14, "Beyond the Box."

SUMMARY

Hardware is the foundation of your virtual environment. Skimp on hardware, and it will come back to haunt you, particularly in performance. The good news is that most x86 hardware on the market today is virtualization ready, and systems that are not are labeled accordingly. Blades are particularly well suited for virtualization because of their design, but in some cases, rack-based servers perform equally well.

Looking beyond raw form factor are processor choices. In the x86 world, these too are now being designed with virtualization in mind. Both AMD's and Intel's processors feature hardware-assisted virtualization capabilities.

This is not to say that everything is rosy. I/O and memory issues present the biggest challenge. As roles and capabilities traditionally found in hardware find their way into software, these challenges are simultaneously exacerbated and mitigated. Chapter 13, "Choosing a Vendor," discusses this further.

Choosing a Vendor

After you have a sense of what you want or need, as well as a budget, the real fun begins. If your company is committed to a particular vendor (and with the standardization and commoditization of hardware, this is happening less frequently), your options are limited. Relationships with vendors can change; therefore it is still important to have an understanding of how the various OEMs approach virtualization as well as various less-traditional options, such as cloud computing.

The choices described in the previous chapter extend across the major hardware vendors—IBM, HP, Dell, and Sun Microsystems—which we will examine in this chapter. All of them offer tower, rack, and blade server models, and all of them offer both AMD and Intel processors. In addition, they all support three main hypervisor environments (ESX, VMware, and Xen).

The differentiator is how they pull it together and package it. Here, the large OEMs of the hardware world have a clear advantage over the white box vendors because of their ability to offer an end-to-end solution. They have the resources to not only build the boxes so that they can run virtual machines (VMs) as effectively as possible, but they can also employ the resources to develop software to manage an entire stable of boxes.

This is the level at which you are no longer choosing among commodity items and want to look at what the OEMs are offering and where they see their products in the data center and beyond. Approaches differ dramatically, as do strategic focuses. Although there is no blanket right or wrong, what is most beneficial for one data center may not be ideal for others. Therefore, having a solid understanding and strategy of what your organization hopes to accomplish with the deployment of a virtual infrastructure will make it easier to evaluate which vendor is most compatible. In general, when you commit to a vendor, you are buying more than hardware; when it comes to virtualization, evaluating each component and ensuring the full package enables you to meet your big picture goals is even more important.

ALIGNING HARDWARE WITH SOFTWARE

Before we jump into looking at what each vendor has to offer, let's look at it from the other direction, the hypervisor. Giving some thought to how the hypervisors approach the hardware helps place into context how each OEM handles the ecosystem that builds up around it. Although all of the hypervisors are supported, the way the lines connect varies.

Take Hyper-V, for example. Hyper-V ships with Windows Server 2008. Thus, by default the majority of servers that ship with Windows Server 2008 are not merely compatible with Hyper-V, they already have it at no additional cost. According to IDC's quarterly server survey, Windows-based servers have been holding steady with one-third of the market. Early reports indicate that the majority of Windows shops plan to upgrade to 2008, thus giving Hyper-V a solid foothold.

VMware, realizing the tenuousness of its position as market leader, around the same time that Hyper-V went gold (and became available as part of the Windows Server 2008), released a bare-metal offshoot of its flagship ESX hypervisor that it named ESXi. Even more significant than the fact that it is free is that VMware struck deals with the OEMs to integrate ESXi into their hardware. This means enterprises have a choice of going with either a hypervisor integrated at the operating system level or at the hardware level. VMware was banking on the maturity of its offering as well as the more comprehensive ecosystem already established around it.

Table 13-1 lists the OEMs embedding ESX3i as of early 2009. Although this is, as VMware puts it, in no way exhaustive, it does represent a good starting point for which servers are available VMware-ready from the start. For those who want to run ESXi on their current hardware, VMware offers the VMware ESXi hardware compatibility guide (www.vmware.com/resources/compatibility/search.php?action=base&deviceCategory=server), a handy tool to assess whether your hardware is capable of running it.

TABLE 13-1 Servers Shipping with ESXi Preinstalled

VENDOR	SERVER
Dell	**Rack** PowerEdge 2950, R805, R900, R905, 1950, 2900 **Blade** PowerEdge M600, M605

continues

TABLE 13-1 Continued

Vendor	Server
Fujitsu-Siemens	**Rack** PRIMERGY RX330 S1, PRIMERGY RX300 S4
HP	**Tower** ProLiant ML370 G5 **Rack** ProLiant DL380 G5, DL580 G5, DL585 G2, DL385 G2 **Blade** ProLiant BL685c, BL680c, BL460c, BL465c, BL480c
IBM	**Rack** System x3850 M2 **Blade** BladeCenter HS21 XM

Source: VMware (www.vmware.com/products/esxi/uses.html)

Xen, too, has begun inking deals with the major OEMs, but its deals have not been as pervasive. In January 2009, however, Citrix, with an eye on the virtual desktop, bypassed both operating system integration and hardware embedding and went straight to the processor.

Citrix, Xen's parent company, teamed with Intel to create a version of the Xen hypervisor to facilitate the centralization of managing and administering end user devices. The aim is to develop a hypervisor that will make "built-in" client-side virtualization capabilities available to the OEMs. Dell is already on board. It is providing engineering support to aid in the design and testing of the new technology and has already agreed to certify it for its computing platforms when it is available for commercial release.

No matter how ubiquitous the hypervisors are, they do carry with them hardware requirements. It is important to be aware of them, especially if you've already made up your mind about which one you want. Alternatively, if you've made up your mind about a particular server, it is important to see which hypervisors match up to its specs. In both cases, alterations can be made (for example, memory added), but that cannot be done until the requirements are known. Table 13-2 spells out the hardware requirements for the three most popular virtual environments.

TABLE 13-2   Hardware Requirements for Major Hypervisors

	ESX	XENSERVER	HYPER-V
Memory	Minimum: 1GB	Minimum: 1GB	Minimum: 1GB
Disk	No absolutes, but all data should be on physical disks allocated to VMs and be large enough to hold disk images to be used by all the VMs	Local or Fibre Channel boot disk with 16GB of space minimum and at least 60GB recommended	At least 10GB required; at least 40GB recommended; Systems with more than 16GB of RAM will require more disk space for paging, hibernation, and dump files
Processor	At least two processors: Intel Xeon and later, or AMD Opteron (32-bit mode) 1.500 GHz Intel Xeon and later, or AMD Opteron (32-bit mode) for Virtual SMP MHz Intel Viiv or AMD A64 x2 dual-core processors Processor Speed: 1.5 GHz	Intel VT or AMD-V required within processor for support of Windows guests, 1.5 GHz minimum, Processor Speed: 2 GHz or faster multicore	Intel VT or AMD Virtualization (as well as any other x64 processor with hardware-assisted virtualization) Processor Speed: 2 GHz or faster
Networking	At least one Ethernet controller, separate Ethernet controllers for the service console and the VMs recommended	100Mb/s or faster NIC	1 network adapter required; 2 or more are recommended

continues

TABLE 13-2 Continued

	ESX	XENSERVER	HYPER-V
Other Requirements	A SCSI disk, Fibre Channel LUN, or RAID LUN with unpartitioned space	Matching CPU family and stepping required for all systems in Enterprise Edition resource pool	Active Directory highly recommended. A second system is required for remote management running: Windows Server 2008 with the Hyper-V Manager, Windows Vista SP1 with the Hyper-V Manager, Microsoft System Center Virtual Machine Manager
Compatibility Tools	www.vmware.com/ resources/compatibility/search.php?action=base&deviceCategory=server	http://hcl.xensource.com/?showall=no&subtab=systems	www.microsoft.com /downloads/details. aspx?FamilyID =67240b76-3148-4e49-943d-4d9ea7f77730 &displaylang=en
More Specs	pubs.vmware.com/vi301/install/wwhelp/wwhimpl/common/html/wwhelp.htm?context=install&file=install_requirements.4.7.html	www.citrix.com/ English/ps2/products/subfeature.asp?contentID =1681139	www.microsoft.com /servers/hyper-v-server/system-requirements.mspx

THE VENDORS

This, however, is where the similarities end and the priorities and strategies begin to diverge.

Not surprisingly, HP and IBM offer the most variety and have a very clear vision. Sun Microsystems also has a number of offerings, but its vision has not been altogether consistent, and the future of its offerings are unclear at the time of this writing. Dell, however, should not be dismissed without evaluation. Although it is a fairly new entrant to the game, and it is not aiming for innovation, its products are moderately priced and they follow industry standards.

For organizations that want to virtualize but lack the resources, a new option is rapidly emerging: cloud computing. Later in this chapter we examine cloud computing as a vendor option and evaluate which circumstances are ideal for its usage.

The following provides a rundown of each vendor's general approach and the scope of its respective offerings. However, it cannot be stressed enough that strategies change and virtualization offerings are constantly evolving. Therefore, these "snapshots" should be viewed merely as starting points; they are by no means a replacement for checking with your VAR or vendor before making a final decision.

IBM

You could argue that IBM is the granddaddy of virtualization, and you wouldn't have to labor too hard to prove your point. Go back to IBM's mainframe roots and you'll find a long relationship with virtualization, although back then it was known as partitioning. The OEM's first VM offering was released in August 1972 (www.vm. ibm.com/overview/) as VM/370. In 35-plus years, it has undergone many changes, not the least of which was its name. It has been known as VM/SP, VM/XA, VM/SP HPO, VM/IS, VM/ESA, and today goes by z/VM, which has been around since October 2000 and is now in version 5.4.

Note, however, that z/VM is based on Big Blue's 64-bit z/Architecture and thus is limited to IBM's system Z mainframes. IBM's entry in the x86 space, although more recent, is no less of a commitment, and it has been there for about a decade. IBM was one of the first OEMs to align itself with VMware, and at present much of its software, from Director to WebSphere, assumes that some degree of vitalization is in place in an infrastructure. Because IBM is also a services company, it provides a host of services centered around virtualization.

Its virtualization efforts are centered around consolidation and are closely aligned to green computing.

IBM makes it clear from the start that not all of its servers are ideal for virtualization. The x3350, for example, a single-socket 1U server available with either quad-core or dual-core Xeon chips, is described as "delivering power-optimized performance for non-virtualized application workloads" (www-03.ibm.com/ systems/x/hardware/rack/x3350/index.html). What differentiates this from, for example, the x3755, which is billed as "ultimate performance for HPC," (www-03. ibm.com/systems/x/hardware/enterprise/x3755/index.html) is fourth-generation X-Architecture, more commonly known as eX4 technology: a chipset and other advanced capabilities found in what IBM now categorizes as its enterprise servers.

IBM is constantly reorganizing and reclassifying its servers. Remember, it wasn't all that long ago that system x servers were known as xSeries.

X-Architecture, however, is designed to deliver higher throughput and greater reliability, along with scalability for processors, memory, and networking and storage I/O. It's a solution designed to get the most out of multicore systems, particularly those running 16, 32, or 64 cores. All of these attributes are critical for virtualization, thus making its positioning a logical fit. The architecture, which IBM developed in conjunction with VMware, brings virtualization front and center with its embedded hypervisor capability. Third-party virtualization software can be an enterprise-class USB flash device.

Other attributes also contribute to its virtualization friendly nature. It supports up to 16 processor sockets across four chassis. This translates into 64 cores of processing power as well as multichassis flexibility arising from 32 memory DIMMs per chassis and the capability to provide to scale up to 128 DIMMs and up to 1.0 TB of available memory. IBM is also touting it for its flexible design that features the capacity to add more PCI-Express slots to maintain consistent I/O throughput for data-intensive applications and its willingness to accept low-cost memory.

IBM is not one to be content with the status quo, and in November 2008 it announced plans to acquire Transitive, a privately held company in Los Gatos, CA, which specializes in cross-platform technologies, especially virtualization. Transitive translation technology enables applications written for one type of microprocessor and operating system to run on multiple platforms—with minimal modification. Transitive is also no stranger to IBM: Its technology is part of IBM PowerVM, software designed to help with consolidations of x86 Linux workloads onto IBM systems.

This may turn out to be a game changer down the road because its capability to seamlessly integrate multiple virtual environments could render the hypervisor even more obsolete than its current commodified status.

HP

HP's virtual journey is a bit different from IBM's. Although HP's history with virtualization is more due to acquisition than home-grown endeavors, its software portfolio is formidable and complex. HP offers a wide spectrum of virtualization products, from software to help with the early stages, to the hardware itself (both x86 and non-x86) and into the networking infrastructure itself, and then postdeployment management solutions.

For non-x86 hardware—Integrity and 9000 servers—it offers HP Virtual Server Environment (VSE). VSE facilitates the provisioning and reprovisioning of VMs. Its many standalone components center around the following:

- Control (such as HP Capacity Advisor, HP Virtualization Manager, HP Global Workload Manager, and HP-UX Workload Manager)
- Partitioning (such as Partitioning Continuum, Hard Partitions, and HP Process Resource Manager/pSets)
- Availability (such as Clustering Solutions, HP Serviceguard for High Availability and Disaster Tolerance, and HP Serviceguard Extensions for RAC)
- Utility pricing
- VSE reference Architectures

Some components, such as HP Virtualization Manager and HP Virtual Partitions, were clearly designed with virtualized environments in mind. Others, like HP Insight Dynamics-VSE, software for analyzing and optimizing resources, are designed to treat physical and virtual resources in the same manner.

But the lion's share of interest, and thus potential growth, lies in the x86 space, and here HP has stepped up to that plate as well. Its ProLiant iVirtualization initiative is all about bringing the components together for a consistent virtualization infrastructure. The "i" stands for integrated, and indeed, integration seems to be key to HP's mission.

HP also integrates server management tools into the mix, including HP Insight Control and its components (for example, HP Systems Insight Manager, which provides predictive failure alerts and active hardware management). Smart Update Manager keeps the software on the USB key current.

As part of the iVirtualization program, VMware and Citrix's products ship pre-installed on ProLiant servers. Nothing is terribly unique about that. But where HP gets creative is in management form factor: The virtualization software resides on a USB key that lives within the server, and the server boots from the key, enabling the VMs.

HP has also partnered with Citrix to deliver the Single Server Virtual, of which Xen server is a key component. The Single Server Virtual Console consists of a setup wizard and configuration tool, as well as virtualization enablement from the get go.

Where HP really aims to differentiate itself, though, is in its holistic approach to the infrastructure. HP looked beyond virtualization at the server and processor level to the network, and found that virtualization was greatly needed at the network-connection level. Enter the Virtual Connect architecture, software that aims to replicate solutions that hardware traditionally delivered.

Currently, the Virtual Connect architecture applies only to blades. This no doubt is in part because of HP's push for virtualization on blades and in part because it is blades that stand to reap the most benefit from reduced cabling and network connections.

The Virtual Connect Flex-10 Ethernet module is interconnect technology aimed squarely at virtual storage, an area that has long been believed to be on the cusp of a virtualization explosion. The module enables the dynamic allocation of the bandwidth of a 10Gb Ethernet network port across four NIC connections, thus enabling each server blade to add four more NICs without additional hardware and the bandwidth of each connection to be adjusted based on need. A similar module for Fibre Channel is available as well.

The HP BladeSystem c3000 and c7000 enclosures are used in place of conventional pass-thru or managed switch modules. They abstract and pool the server-edge connections. The software is configured to look like physical NICs and HBAs are running on the network, and the server admin can administer the network as though they are actual NICs and HBAs.

Dell

Depending on the research firm compiling the data and the quarter, Dell is the third or fourth most popular vendor. Smaller shops, which represent a large percentage of the market, skew heavily toward Dell because of its low prices and packaging. Dell is not cutting edge, nor is it an innovator, but it does deal with standard hardware and software. It tends to not adopt technology into its products until it is proven mature and customers clamor for it, as was the case with the Opteron processor and server blades.

In 2008, Dell demonstrated a commitment to virtualization. In May, it released two PowerEdge servers (the R805 and R905) with ESXi or XenServer Dell Express Edition integrated at the factory. In the fall, it released two PowerEdge blade servers and another rackmount server that it billed as "optimized for virtualization." The servers offer high availability, fully redundant I/O fabrics, eight high-speed ports, enhanced RAM capacity, the option to add more low-cost DIMMs, and an internal SD card for embedded hypervisors.

Dell has also formed a partnership with Egenera to meet the needs of customers looking for a turnkey solution. The Dell PAN system uses Egenera's PAN Manager software to consolidate and virtualize server resources so that they can be managed similar to hard drives in a SAN. Dell has been steadily growing its storage presence for several years, so it's not surprising that many of its virtual moves center around storage.

Although Dell offers the spectrum of virtualization environments and is expanding out of its traditional domain, the path of least resistance for many customers will be Hyper-V. Historically, the majority of Dell servers ship with

Microsoft Windows, and Hyper-V is a key component of Windows Server 2008. Its inclusion may well be the tipping point for cash-strapped enterprises considering virtualization. Hyper-V at this time is little more than a hypervisor, so the caveats about management software and costs remain.

Dell also plays in the storage arena and has been steadily introducing products that integrate technology from VMware, Microsoft, and Citrix to its products, as well as a partnership with PlateSpin, now a subsidiary of Novell.

Dell's enterprise-grade options are fewer than IBM's and HP's, and the path to virtualization on its equipment is more straightforward than that of Sun Microsystems. However, the options are fewer, and Dell for the most part does not offer its own software or services, although it does offer services around design, deployment, security, and management of virtualized environments, such as infrastructure consulting services for Microsoft Hyper-V deployments, site recovery manager services for VMware environments, and various life cycle management services for VMware environments.

In keeping with Dell's culture, it also offers an online tool to assess which of its servers are best suited for virtualization. To get the most out of the tool, you must know the nitty-gritty specs of your current infrastructure, including how much memory you have in your server room, how much disk space, and which processors and how many. The implications are that the data center is either small enough to be inventoried down to the last gigabyte of memory, or you have some sort of measurement tool in place, in which case Dell's Advisor tool is largely unnecessary. Still, it is worth checking out, if only to play around with which of its servers are suitable for a given scenario.

Should you opt for a virtual infrastructure based around Dell hardware, bear in mind that its business model is built around volume and commodity, which means that you might end up spending substantially more on software than you do on the box itself. There is nothing wrong with this in theory, so long as you have proper equipment, but it does change the mindset. Also bear in mind that Dell is unlikely to offer the specialized services and support that the other OEMs do.

Sun

Sun Microsystems' virtualization offerings also span a wide spectrum and touch on virtually every option. Two key drawbacks exist, however. First, a big question mark hangs over Sun with regard to its future and its product roadmap. At the time of this writing, Oracle intends to acquire the company. It is unclear what its plan is for Sun's product line and technologies.

The second drawback is Sun's virtualization strategy itself. Its virtual solutions are fairly convoluted and restrictive. Like IBM, Sun has developed hardware-assisted virtualization technology specifically for its processor (in this case the SPARC and UltraSPARC processors), and like the other major OEMs, Sun's x86 servers integrate with software for the major virtual environments. Sun has also made virtualization a key component of the most recent version of its operating system, Solaris 10. It hits on all the virtualization options or servers—VMs, OS virtualization, and hard partitioning.

Sun Logical Domains (LDoms) uses virtualization to enable the sharing of hardware resources while also maintaining a one-app-per-server deployment model. LDoms, however, are specifically for the CoolThreads server family, Sun's UltraSPARC-based product line, and thus Solaris. Their very advantage relies on the server and processor; they make it fairly straightforward to create multiple independent VMs using the hypervisor already built into every CoolThreads system. When LDoms are up and running, they dynamically reallocate resources to ensure that workloads and services are getting the resources they need.

LDoms become even more powerful when combined with Solaris. Because LDoms are exclusive to CoolThreads servers, and Solaris is the only operating system that run on the servers, the combination is a given. Sun has smartly coupled them, enabling LDoms to take the virtualization capabilities in Solaris a step further and bring other features in Solaris into the virtual realm. LDoms, for example, take advantage of ZFS cloning and snapshots to speed deployment and dramatically reduce disk capacity requirements.

If not a cornerstone of the new features in Solaris 10, Containers are a key selling point. With Containers, multiple instances of Solaris 8, 9, and 10 can run on the same box. This allows organizations to upgrade their OS (and hardware) but keep their legacy apps running without a hiccup. Note, however, that this is OS-level virtualization, and these are not independent VMs. Another factor to consider is that Containers is limited to Solaris.

Sun offers a VM ecosystem as well. xVM is an open source VM environment based on the open source version of the Xen hypervisor from Xen.org. xVM is compatible with Windows, Solaris, UNIX, and Linux, and Mac compatibility is on the road map. It runs on SPARC as well, as its name implies. xVM Ops Center is a software suite that manages both physical and virtual infrastructures. Like the hypervisor, it was designed with interoperability in mind.

Unlike the other OEMs, however, Sun has its own desktop virtualization offering. In February 2008, Sun acquired innotek, a German company that had developed a desktop virtualization software. Its product, VirtualBox (which we examined closely in Chapter 8 "VirtualBox") is an open source platform licensed under the GPL in January 2007. It enables a desktop or laptop PC to have multiple operating systems running concurrently. Sun officially integrated VirtualBox into its xVM strategy and product line as the year rolled on, and in December, it released version 2.1 of xVM VirtualBox.

NOTE

The nomenclature here is a bit confusing. Back in the days of VMware GSX, "desktop virtualization" referred to slicing and dicing a PC into several independent systems. Now, however, the term *desktop virtualization* comes closer to resembling a thin-client computing model.

The Achilles heel of these technologically advanced offerings is that they are by and large tied to Solaris. Thus, to take advantage of them you must commit not only to a virtualization ecosystem but also to an OS, and in the case of LDoms, hardware. Neither is particularly pervasive, and thus the pool of apps and management tools that work with them is limited. This, like everything else Sun involves itself with, could change, but Sun's near-decade of floundering for a strategy is hardly a confidence builder. Should you find the technology enough to proceed, consider also that virtualization is dramatically changing the role of the OS, so not only might you find yourself locked into an environment, but you might also find yourself stuck in a model that no longer applies.

In many ways, Sun has been ahead of the curve in its virtualization offerings. It introduced virtualization in Solaris 10, in the form of Containers and DTrace, a few years before the other OEMs, and its use of the technology and the final product received many kudos from analysts and users alike.

As good as Sun's technology is, it faces many obstacles, not the least of which is Sun's legacy of being mired in a muddied strategy that seems to switch focus every six months or so. For Solaris shops or data centers with a significant Solaris footprint, choosing a Sun solution is an easier choice than for others.

Comparing the Offerings

Although each vendor brings its own focus to its virtualization portfolio, there are certain commonalities in terms of the types of virtualization offered and resources available. Table 13-3 compares what the four major OEMs bring to the table. Note that this information is far from static. The vendors are constantly adding to what they offer. Still, it is a starting point and provides an overview of their respective strengths and emphasis.

TABLE 13-3 Vendor Offerings, A Side-by-Side View

	IBM	HP	SUN	DELL
x86 Server Virtualization	•	•	•	•
Non-x86 Server Virtualization	•	•	•	
Services Offerings	•	•	•	•
Assessment Tool(s)	https://www-304.ibm.com/jct0 9002c/ partnerworld/ wps/servlet/ ContentHandler/ isv/di_assess_virt /lc=en_US (Requires a PartnerWorld membership, contact IBM)	http://h71019. www7.hp. com/Active Answers/ Secure/ 595493-0-0-0-121.html http://h71019. www7.hp. com/Active Answers/us/ en/sizers/ microsoft-hyperv.html		http://adviso rs.dell.com/ AdvisorWeb/ Advisor.aspx ?advisor= c82c3ec8-c94f-4602-9a41-c2038 2db1cd0&c= us&l=en&cs =555
Storage	•	•	•	•
Desktop	•	•	•	•
Network	•	•		

continues

TABLE 13-3 Continued

	IBM	HP	SUN	DELL
Virtualization Info	http://www-03.ibm.com/systems/virtualization/	http://h71028.www7.hp.com/enterprise/cache/454414-0-0-0-121.html?jumpid=hpr_R1002_USEN http://h71028.www7.hp.com/enterprise/cache/454748-0-0-0-121.html	www.sun.com/solutions/virtualization/index.jsp	www.dell.com/virtualization

WHITE BOX

Historically, a large segment of companies, especially SMBs, did not buy their hardware from an OEM, but rather from a company that put it together based on spec or sold prepackaged options with parts from often unknown sources. Obviously, this was a way to save money. As the x86 market became increasingly commoditized, however, the price savings became negligible as the Big 3 in particular cut their price points year after year. In early 2008, IDC estimated the white box market to be about 10 percent (www.serverwatch.com/trends/article.php/3729276). With the OEMs continuing to slash prices, it's doubtful it will ever be the bright spot it once was, even with Intel and AMD chips now powering some of the servers.

If you're buying white box servers with the expectation that they will be virtualized, bear in mind that you will probably not receive any hardware support for it from the vendor. Nor will there be any hardware-specific software. Chip-level advantages will be there, assuming the chips inside are virtualization optimized.

If that is not a concern, be sure that you don't skimp on memory and the I/O throughput benchmarks in line with the recommendations of all the major hypervisors and supporting software. It's not enough for it to just be compatible with the one you're planning to use, because you don't know for certain that you won't be changing down the road. It should be compatible with the major hypervisors, and you want some level of investment protection should you chose to upgrade the software.

Beyond that, the usual caveats about reputability apply.

CLOUD COMPUTING

If you've read through this and are thinking, "That's interesting, but my budget was slashed in half and my headcount is frozen," but you still need to virtualize and don't want poor planning to bite you down the road, do not despair. There is one more option: cloud computing.

For cash-strapped enterprises for which new hardware is not possible, cloud computing may be the silver bullet. In 2008, cloud went from being an eye-rolling concept that was mostly vaporware to an initiative that a host of companies are embracing and developing revenue models around. Depending on which analyst you ask, cloud is poised to be the next paradigm shift or is a popular fad that will eventually find value in a niche. When it comes to virtualization, and desktop virtualization in particular, cloud computing may turn out to be the secret sauce for an organization that lacks the infrastructure and skill sets.

Cloud computing, it should be noted, is not a new concept. Indeed, it has gone by other more familiar names such as utility computing, clustering, and in some cases, high-performance or supercomputing. In fact, some initiatives previously labeled "software as a service" now seem to fall under the cloud heading.

Even the idea of renting out compute units isn't new. If you go back to IBM's earliest days, much of its business was built renting out use of its mainframe. More recently, IBM opened up the Deep Computing Institute in Poughkeepsie, NY. The facility launched with 512 systems in June 2003. Less than a year later it was almost out of space, running nearly 2,400 xSeries servers, Opteron-based servers, and BladeCenter systems, as well as a second Deep Computing Center in Montpellier, France. Since then, Sun and HP have launched similar initiatives with mixed success.

This is the high end of cloud. For organizations in need of supercomputing services, having access to processing units on demand puts them in a league they would likely not be able to compete in otherwise. As IBM put it, "it levels the playing field," making it possible for smaller firms in industries like pharmaceutical, animation, and gas and oil exploration to compete against their well-heeled competitors.

For a long time, that was the extent of it. Utility computing and grid computing bumbled along, but they were used primarily in specialized niches, and although their price was lower than in the supercomputer model, their merit was not so easily understood. The growing acceptance of virtualization worked in their favor, and vendors in this space started referring to their technology as reverse virtualization or virtualization, a semantic change that seemed unthinkable several years ago when they took offense at their technology being referred to as virtualization.

What really changed the picture, however, was Google—specifically, Google Apps for Domains and Google Docs. With Google Docs, the spreadsheet, word processor, or whatever tool you are using is accessed via a browser. Both the data and the application reside on Google's servers, which are a collection of commodity servers grouped together—you can think of them as virtualized or clustered. Documents can be created, edited, and shared without them ever taking up space on your desktop. The downside is that you need to be connected to it for it to work, and the server must be up and running. Backing up with regularity mitigates both of these issues, however.

Much of the first draft of this book was written using Google Docs. From an end-user perspective, the experience feels more like working on a traditional desktop PC than on the thin clients of old.

From a desktop virtualization perspective, cloud, especially a public cloud, is a slam dunk. It lowers the costs associated with it considerably, and eliminates the human "ownership" issues. With Google, Amazon, and a growing number of hosting providers making applications and resources available via clouds (which to many end users simply feels like a browser-based application), acceptance of completing tasks this way continues to grow. However, in some circumstances a public cloud will not be acceptable. In those cases, working with a managed service provider (MSP) or building your own cloud would be better courses of action. Working with MSPs is much less costly than building your own cloud, and in many cases it will meet the necessary security, privacy, and uptime requirements that the public cloud is unable to.

The rapid acceptance around netbooks will no doubt fuel cloud growth as well. Their low price point makes them attractive, but they lack the power and capacity of a full-fledged notebook or desktop. Thus, running applications on them and storing the resulting data will not be feasible. They are, however, well suited to a cloud model. If new hardware is needed on the client side, this represents an easy savings.

Another ball in cloud's court is that hardware companies are taking notice. Intel is partnering with Xen to provide PC manufacturers with "built-in" client-side virtualization capabilities on new desktop and laptop computing systems. Dell was one of the first OEMs to come on board and it is providing engineering support to aid in the design and testing of the new technology.

Although the desktop is the clear winner when it comes to cloud computing synergy, virtual storage is also poised to gain big from the cloud. Here, security remains the biggest challenge and concern. Storage is an ever growing area, both literally and metaphorically. As more data accumulates, it must be stored and managed and remain retrievable. Putting it up on a cloud is an efficient way to deal with this, so long as security and regulatory issues are handled appropriately.

To meet these requirements, an internal or private cloud is preferable to a public cloud. In some cases that may not only be feasible, but may also make the most sense; in other cases, it may not be anywhere near cost effective. Here, going with an MSP may make the most sense, assuming service levels are up to snuff, and proper security is put in place. Although it will cost more than using a public cloud, it will be a fraction of the cost of building your own.

We will take a deeper dive into storage in the next chapter as we examine virtualization options beyond the box.

SUMMARY

Although all the OEMs have fully embraced virtualization, each has taken an approach unique to the company's history and customer base. IBM, for example, has a wide array of non-x86 solutions, HP has chosen to emphasize the network, and Dell's offerings adhere to industry standards with an eye on the SMB space. Organizations should be aware of these differences when purchasing hardware for their virtual infrastructure.

Cash-strapped enterprises that do not have the hardware suitable for virtualization on hand but still want to move forward with virtualization should consider using a cloud computing model to meet their needs, particularly if they're planning a desktop virtualization initiative.

## CHAPTER 14

Beyond the Box

As complex as server virtualization is, if that was all server admins had to worry about, life would be relatively simple—relative to the big picture as it stands, anyway. There is, of course, no rule that says you have to virtualize your entire data center. What you choose to virtualize depends on your objectives. We looked at various objectives in Chapter 1, "To Virtualize or Not to Virtualize?"; we will reexamine them in relation to their respective deployment strategies in Chapter 15, "Laying the Foundation: The Planning Stage."

Server virtualization is easily defined. Sure, there are multiple ways to go about it and several environments and hypervisors from which to choose, but by and large it's confined to the box. To get the most bang from your buck, and to build a virtual infrastructure in contrast to a virtual machine (VM) or virtual server, you must go beyond the box and onto the network. An entire complementary universe of virtualized network and server-related products has sprouted in recent years.

A word of caution, however. As the virtualization hype heated up, attaching the word "virtual" to an offering became a fairly common occurrence (much like trend of attaching ".com" to a company name a decade ago). In some cases, the offerings were legitimately optimized to deal with virtual environments. In other cases, particularly in storage, the word "virtual" was used to describe technology that was neither new nor modified but had characteristics quite similar to those now used to describe virtual environments.

Further complicating the picture is the reality that many of these companies exist with the goal of being acquired. As one CEO told us, when explaining that his company doesn't compete with BMC and CA, "Hopefully one of these days, one of those guys are going to acquire us." Many of the large companies that deal in the physical realm are slowly making their way into the virtual through both their own development and acquisition. One downside is that many of their solutions are not as tailor-made to a given facet of virtualization. The downside of going with a smaller (usually start-up) vendor is that you don't know if they'll remain a going concern for the duration of your needs for the product. You're also building a solution piecemeal, which complicates support needs. We will discuss these pros and cons from a general perspective in Chapter 15.

Chapter 4, "VMware ESXi," stepped through the process of setting up a virtual private network and virtual LAN and discussed what goes into creating a virtual SAN. This chapter returns to those topics, but we will look at it from an ecosystem perspective and discuss the various available options for pulling together your virtual infrastructure. Chapter 13, "Choosing a Vendor," ended with a discussion of I/O. We look closer at the products in this space.

We also discuss server-related virtualization options to help you assess whether such technologies are appropriate for your organization at this time. In some cases, the functionality inherent in the hardware of virtualization environments, or even in the infrastructure management tool within your organization, will suffice.

In the interest of clarity, we have divided this chapter into three areas: storage virtualization, network virtualization, and I/O virtualization. Not all enterprises require all these product types, and overlap exists between categories. Xsigo's I/O Director, for example, facilitates I/O management, as its name implies, but also contains a rack-mounted switch that replaces Ethernet NICs and Fibre Channel HBAs. Moreover, it is focused on meeting the needs of the storage space. This is not uncommon. Many of the I/O and network virtualization offerings were designed with storage in mind, even though they will provide many benefits to virtual servers.

This convergence will no doubt continue as this space evolves further.

STORAGE VIRTUALIZATION

Storage in general seems to speak its own language, and storage virtualization (or virtual storage) is no exception. When it comes to storage and virtualization, the biggest challenge is reading through semantic differences to determine what is real and what really matters. The word cited most frequently to describe storage virtualization? Murky.

From its beginnings, storage virtualization has been a touchy subject. Go back three years and the party line was that virtualizing storage would be pretty much a slam dunk because the technologies that drive storage aren't all that different from the technologies behind virtualization itself. Activity has indeed been strong in some areas, but some today believe that much of what is labeled as storage virtualization really is not.

Then there is the debate about what storage virtualization actually is. Not surprisingly, many of the definitions around storage virtualization are somewhat contradictory. Wikkipedia, for example, refers to it as "the process of abstracting logical storage from physical storage," noting that the abstraction can take place at any layer in the storage software or hardware stack. The most commonly cited layers are file and block.

Webopedia, on the other hand, defines storage virtualization as "the amalgamation of multiple network storage devices into what appears to be a single storage unit." Here the aim is to make storage-related tasks such as archiving, backup, and recovery easier and faster.

Back when the virtualization zeitgeist first began, the analysts all seemed in agreement that storage virtualization would be a much easier sell than general-purpose servers. This was largely attributable to storage's underpinnings—RAID, SANs, NAS, interconnects—whose very structure is similar to a virtualized environment. For storage technologies related to backup, virtualization has been described as a natural fit, and indeed, virtualization products related to backup have taken off.

So semantics and definitions vary, and the fact remains that virtualized activity around the actual storage space has not lived up to the hype of several years ago. That is not to say, however, that virtualization has not had an impact on storage. Nor would it be prudent to not factor it in for storage when sculpting a virtualization strategy.

Virtualization has, in fact, had a tremendous impact on storage, albeit not in the way the vendors and pundits anticipated. By their inherent dynamic nature, VMs increase storage needs. A great deal of activity centers around storage as it relates to virtualization, but it has come from the increased storage needs of the servers now containing multiple VMs. These servers hold more data and apps than dedicated servers do, and as a result they have greater availability and disaster recovery needs. Hence, a greater need exists for storage resources—in particular, backup. In fact, backing up and protecting VMs is by far the biggest storage virtualization issue.

Beyond that is where much of the heavy murkiness kicks in. Two terms that get tossed around a lot are block-level virtualization and file-level virtualization. The easiest way to think of them is that block-level virtualization applies to storage area networks (SANs), and file-level virtualization applies to network attached storage (NAS). The abstraction layers are applied where the names imply. SAN virtualization is pretty straightforward. For the most part even a traditional SAN functions similarly to a virtualized environment, so simply relabeling its feature set as "virtualization" doesn't so much change the functionality as give it some bling.

It could be argued that many of the common storage management functions are being liberally peppered with the "virtualization" label. Is heterogeneous management virtualization? Pooled storage? Sure, virtualizing the physical storage is important, but that pretty much sums up a SAN. At its simplest, a SAN is a subnetwork of shared storage devices. This theoretically makes it well suited for clustering and virtualizing. A virtual SAN generally refers to a section of a SAN that has been broken into logical sections or partitions.

There's also file or NAS virtualization, which at one point was the hottest thing since sliced bread but has since gone stale. NAS virtualization remains an option, chiefly because dealing with files is pretty much unavoidable—even SANs need file systems on top of them. Although file-level virtualization was thought to be a very hot market for a while, at this time it is used primarily for data migration. Block-level virtualization is considered higher performing and more scalable than its file counterpart, and it is a key reason why Fibre Channel SANs are the standard.

Nevertheless, file-level virtualization does remain an option. Whether your primary storage needs are data migration or you feel you must be able to abstract at the file level, a variety of solutions exist, even if the market never took off. F5's ARX product line and EMC's Rainfinity are two options to consider. NetApp, Brocade, and Cisco also offer solutions, as do a number of smaller independent vendors.

The bits and pieces of what the grand plan of storage virtualization set out to do—migrate data, increase utilization, and centralize management—are by and large available either as standalone products or products operating under different names. Strip away the optional virtualization label but keep the definition, and a great many technologies may fall under the storage virtualization label.

Perhaps because of this, unlike other segments of the virtualization market, many of the vendors who play in the storage virtualization space did not get their start in virtualization. Rather, they are traditional storage vendors that saw the potential impact of virtualization, but their primary point of view is how to provide storage for a virtualized environment. Many of these vendors are not immune to slapping on a label that has a bit more glamour to it.

Consider, for example, Commvault, whose flagship product, Simpana, started out as a "back up" product but is now described as a "data management solution." Various modules make up the offering, including Backup and Recovery, Archive, and Resource Management. When Simpana released version 8 of its backup and recovery software in January 2009, it looked not at storage virtualization, but at the storage needs of companies with a virtualized infrastructure. It found that as companies add more VMs and grow their virtual infrastructure, their storage needs also increase. They need more deduping (that is, the elimination of redundant data so that only a single copy is backed up), for example, which often means adding more hardware to keep throughput where it needs to be.

To mitigate this, the new release offers the capability to dedupe to tape at the block or appliance level. Virtual server protection has also been added in this version, along with advances in recovery management, data reduction, and content organization.

Commvault is not unusual in its fence-straddling tactics. Traditional storage management vendors make up most of the storage virtualization landscape. In addition to Commvault, DataCore, Emulex, FalconStor, and Pillar all offer products aimed at the storage virtualization market.

Partnering and integrating aside, VMware and the other vendors have largely stayed out of the storage space. Although this presents more choice to the enterprise, it also means additional components to integrate as well as to determine their necessity.

While Commvault is seeing an uptick in virtual deployments, and a growing percentage of Simpana deployments are in virtualized environments, a typical use case is for backup archived environments and multiple sites. It just so happens that these sites are virtualizing and as a result need technology that takes it into account.

In other cases, the "virtualness" isn't so clear. Falconstor, for example, touts its Network Storage Server (NSS) as a holistic solution, claiming NSS integrates storage virtualization and provisioning across multiple disk arrays and connection protocols to deliver a scalable SAN solution. This sounds especially impressive when you look at Falconstor's partnerships with VMware and Virtual Iron to integrate storage-centric technology into their offerings. FalconStor even offers a virtual appliance version of software that runs on a virtual SAN on a VMware ESX Server.

The heart of Falconstor's offering, however, is virtual tape. Despite the "virtual" moniker, virtual tape has nothing whatsoever to do with virtualization. Rather, it makes disks appear like tape to backup software so the legacy system can remain in use.

Something else to bear in mind when evaluating virtual storage management products is that much functionality overlap occurs between storage and the network. In addition to backup, various connectivity applications and devices often accomplish the same ends within the virtual environments being created.

If you're attempting to determine whether to virtualize the storage infrastructure as a whole, including data and apps, the answer is probably not. If, on the other hand, you're looking to virtualize various parts of the storage process, virtual solutions abound, and in many cases will be available from a vendor with which you may already be working.

It is also pretty much a given that you will need to modify your storage strategy to accommodate the backup needs of your VMs. A good starting point is to look at what sort of virtualization offerings your current storage provider offers. Assuming you're satisfied with what's already deployed, adding a module to better facilitate the storage needs of your VMs will, with few exceptions, be the most cost-effective and efficient way to go.

Relative to storage virtualization, server virtualization is a relatively straightforward undertaking. The complexities of storage management carry over from the physical to the virtual, and the stakes are exponentially higher.

NETWORK VIRTUALIZATION

In the early days of virtualization, there was little thought beyond the actual boxes. Then someone saw the similarities between clustering (or grid, or high performance computing —there are slight differences beyond the semantic) and virtualization. In many ways it was basically reverse virtualization. In simplest terms, rather than one box being divided into several, several boxes are pooled together as one.

This model quickly became far more popular with storage than with general-purpose servers because of the inherent nature of SANs. It also presented a variety of challenges to enterprises and opportunities for vendors.

In a traditional network, a variety of connectivity components that make the network a network must be managed. From HBAs and NICs on the servers to switches and routers and, eventually, cabling, each of these represents a potential point of failure.

Chapter 11, "Network and Storage Virtualization in Action," stepped through setting up a VPN and a VLAN. In this section, we again cast our eyes on the network, only this time we look at some of the intricacies of managing a network consisting of VMs.

In a virtual environment, the hypervisor establishes something akin to a "virtual interface" for VMs that are in actuality no more real than anything else to which the guest thinks it's talking. Nevertheless, they have an inherent capability to be able reach out and communicate or screw up stuff for the host. Management software—specifically, virtual network components—is one way to manage this relationship and mitigate potential problems.

Virtualization in this mix has come to be known as "the softwarization of hardware" and thus makes it possible for software to perform functions hardware has traditionally performed. This makes the VMs and the network more secure, but it is more taxing for I/O. It also does not reduce overall complexity, but merely shifts it from the hardware to the software. Chief among these are switches and HBAs, which the next two subsections will address.

In addition, in recent months, the term "infrastructure orchestration" has come to the fore to describe these products. The term has been gaining in acceptance, if not in penetration. The products in this space are varied, and for the most part the functionality is found in various products that seem to change capabilities with the same regularity with which they change version numbers. We also look at how these products are pulling it all together.

Switches

Of all of the infrastructure orchestration solution and connectivity offerings, virtual switches are perhaps the most critical. Just like a physical server needs a physical switch to connect to the network, for a VM to connect to have network access, it must have a virtual network switch. Fortunately, many options exist for dealing with switches, and solutions come from vendors ranging from OEMs to the virtualization vendors to the physical switch vendors. Each takes a different approach to the situation, and in most cases the solutions work in tandem.

When we think of switches, our thoughts usually turn first to Cisco, which has been in the connectivity space since its founding in 1984. Cisco has been steadily increasing its focus on virtualization this decade, and it is far ahead of its competitors. Recognizing that VMs now have a permanent place on the network, the company's latest focus is on bringing to them the functionality and benefits that it brings to physical machines. Enter the virtual switch, VN-link, which Cisco first introduced in September 2008.

The underpinnings of VN-link aim to mitigate this issue. The technology seeks to virtualize the network domain and subsequently to abstract the physical infrastructure of the network, whether it's on the LAN side or the SAN side. This enables it to transport data, apps, and so on to VMs as one unified fabric.

The first products to include VN-link technology were in the high-end Nexus family: the Nexus 1000V and Nexus 5000. The Nexus 5000 is a physical switch. Aside from its strong performance benchmarks, it is not an unusual offering for Cisco. The Nexus 1000V, on the other hand, takes Cisco into new territory. The switch is a pure-software play designed to handle VM traffic. It resides on a server and integrates with the VMware ESX.

It is also but one part of the Cisco "unified computing" strategy, which is driving many of the company's decisions, in particular its entry into the blade space in early 2009. Unified Computing seeks to link data center resources (computing, storage, networking, and virtualization) together under a common architecture. In the Cisco data center of the future, as Cisco CTO Padmasree Warrior explained in a blog post outlining the strategy, the compute and storage platform is architecturally "unified" with the network and the virtualization platform.

Like the physical switch space, where Cisco dominates handily, in the virtual switch space it has little company. The competition it faces does not, in fact, come from its traditional competitors. As of early 2009, neither Juniper nor Alcatel-Lucent have carved out a presence, and with Nortel in bankruptcy and liquidating divisions, it is unlikely to be much of a threat.

Competition is found on the softwarization front, however. VMware does offer a virtual switch, the vNetwork Distributed switch framework, but it too integrates with the Cisco Nexus 1000V switch.

VMware's vNetwork Distributed Switch is closely aligned with the Nexus 1000V. It, too, abstracts the configuration of individual virtual switches and enables centralized provisioning, administration, and monitoring through VMware vCenter Server. VMware vNetwork Distributed Switch maintains network runtime state for VMs as they move across multiple hosts, enabling inline monitoring and centralized firewall services. It provides a framework for monitoring and maintaining the security of VMs as they bounce around from physical server to physical server and enables the use of third-party virtual switches, including the Nexus 1000v, to extend familiar physical network features and controls to virtual networks.

The hardware vendors themselves are also bringing hardware capabilities to software, not just the virtualization vendors. HP, for example, is offering virtual switches from within its Integrity line.

No matter how virtualized your systems are, you will always need a physical switch. There are pros and cons to consolidating physical onto multiple software-based switches. The pros and cons are typical for the softwarization of hardware: easier management, but the more you consolidate, the bigger the performance hit. By placing switching responsibilities within your system, you're adding another app with potentially high performance needs and a potential for bottleneck.

HBAs and Other Network Connectivity

Virtualization brings with it connectivity needs that go beyond switches. Network connectivity, although critical, is a commodity market with few players. Emulex and QLogic together own the lion's share of the market, and Emulex has made great strides to bring its functionality, in particular its host bus adaptor functionality, to VMs.

For the most part, Emulex sells directly to OEMs, which then rebrand its HBAs for use in storage devices. By and large, user enterprises are unaware they are purchasing an Emulex solution. Emulex has partnered with the virtualization vendors to ensure compatibility between the offerings.

Emulex's LightPulse Virtual adapter technology, for example, is designed to better enable VM network connectivity, particularly as it relates to storage. LightPulse Virtual adapter technology can be found on Emulex's 4Gb/s and 8Gb/s Fibre Channel HBAs and Fibre Channel over Ethernet converged network adapters (CNAs), which are then rolled into hardware sold by a host of OEMs, from the major ones such as HP, IBM, and Dell, to the less major, like Bull, LSI, and NetApp. Emulex has made its solutions, and thus technology, so pervasive that when all is working well, those who manage the data center are largely unaware of what's pulling the strings.

The underpinnings of LightPulse Virtual adapter technology are N_Port ID Virtualization and Virtual Fabric. N_Port ID Virtualization enables users to "virtualize" Fibre Channel adapter functionality so each VM shares a pool of adapters while maintaining independent access to its own protected storage. Virtual Fabric divides a single SAN into many logical SANs, each with its own set of fabric services. This facilitates the consolidation of multiple SAN islands onto one large physical SAN, while still maintaining the same logical topologies as prior to consolidation. Figure 14-1 illustrates how N_Port ID Virtualization facilitates this distribution.

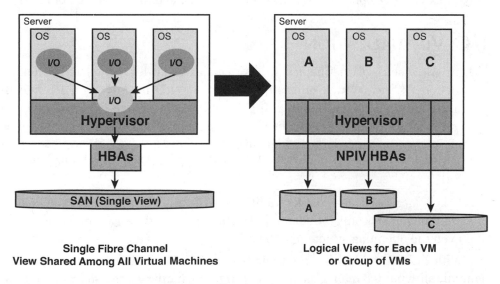

Single Fibre Channel
View Shared Among All Virtual Machines

Logical Views for Each VM
or Group of VMs

FIGURE 14-1   N_Port ID Virtualization (Source: Emulex).

When to Consider Infrastructure Orchestration

Developing trends often generate buzzwords, and the up and coming buzzword here is "infrastructure orchestration." The meaning of the term is still very much in flux. The technology that comes under its umbrella has yet to be decided, and in some cases the buzz is stronger than the concept's soundness. Time will tell how much merit is in technology like virtual NICs or virtual cabling. Even virtual HBAs don't have the same market relevance they had in previous years, and you don't hear nearly as much about the other two as back then.

Note, however, that (switches excepted) despite the proliferation of vendors, much like with storage space, enterprises have for the most part not jumped into infrastructure orchestration software with the same zeal that they have taken to server virtualization. Part of this is no doubt attributable to it being a fairly nascent market, which lacks true understanding of the need for such products, and part is perhaps attributable to the products not having found a niche. Another possibility is that virtualization, although widely accepted and deployed, has not achieved deep acceptance within very many enterprises. Thus, the need for such products is not yet there. A final possibility is that admins are skeptical about adding several additional infrastructure management tools to the mix, bringing layers of integration complexity that may negate the gains.

Also, like with storage, for enterprises already using these products to manage their physical infrastructure, adding the virtual component is logical and prudent. As a virtual infrastructure becomes an inherent part of a physical infrastructure, expect much of this technology to find its way into infrastructure management (or orchestration) tools via development, OEM-like relationships, and full-on acquisition.

I/O VIRTUALIZATION

I/O, as we discussed in Chapter 13, is a major issue for virtual environments. Internet.com's ServerWatch offers this metaphor: "I/O on VMs is a lot like the plumbing in an apartment building. If everyone flushes at once, there's sure to be a mess. It's the job of the hypervisor or the virtual I/O handler to ensure those flushes happen in an orderly fashion so nothing gets overloaded, and everything goes through in a timely manner" (www.serverwatch.com/virtualization/article.php/3792201).

This is largely because unlike traditional I/O, which is directly related to memory and thus impacts only the server, I/O virtualization also drags storage, networks, and even the operating system into the mix.

With that in mind, there are a number of ways to handle I/O management. In general, minimal I/O management is built into the hardware and software, and that may be adequate for a test and dev environment, as well an initial virtualization deployment. However, it's one thing to take a chance on back-office apps running slowly; it's quite another when your mission-critical applications or customer-facing applications hit a bottleneck.

The OEMs and virtualization vendors are well aware of its criticality and are addressing the issue in various ways. Dell, for example, has partnered with Xsigo to offer Xsigo I/O Director with its PowerEdge servers and storage solutions. This enables users to manage I/O resources from multiple vendors from a single console, as opposed to cherry picking from each vendor. The other major OEMs also integrate varying levels of I/O and virtual I/O management into their offerings, as noted in Chapter 13.

The virtual environments themselves also address I/O. Their approaches differ significantly. VMware ESX uses what it calls the "direct driver model." It certifies and hardens I/O drivers to work with the ESX hypervisor, in some cases, modifying some of their capabilities (such as CPU scheduling and directing memory resource) to more efficiently process I/O loads from multiple VMs.

In contrast, Citrix XenServer and Hyper-V, which have similar architectures, use standard device drivers in their management partitions. They route all VM I/O to generic drivers installed at the operating-system level (whether Linux or Windows) that is open in the hypervisor's management partition.

Hyper-V includes a Windows Server Virtualization feature known as Enlightened I/O. Enlightened I/O, according to Microsoft (msdn.microsoft.com/en-us/library/cc768520.aspx) is a specialized virtualization-aware implementation of high-level communication protocols (for example, SCSI) using VMBus—a channel-based communication mechanism that facilitates inter-partition communication and device enumeration on systems with multiple active virtualized partitions—to bypass the device emulation layer. This speeds up communication, but for it to work, the "enlightened" guest must be both hypervisor and VMBus aware. Hyper-V enlightened I/O and a hypervisor-aware kernel are provided via installation of Hyper-V integration services. Integration components, which include virtual server client (VSC) drivers, are also available for other client operating systems.

Citrix's XenServer is known for having better disk I/O than VMware (hence its popularity with cloud vendors), but VMware still dominates in the majority of deployments. Figure 14-2 illustrates the differences between the ESXi architecture and those of Hyper-V and Xen.

Supplemental Products

As virtual infrastructures expand and VMs become more dense, the built-in I/O management may not be enough. A growing market of third-party solutions has cropped up to alleviate this perceived need. Many of these products come from companies that deal purely with I/O management, and in some cases they are the flagship product of a company focusing on virtualized I/O management.

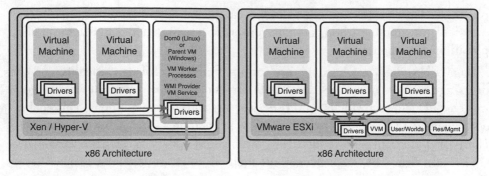

FIGURE 14-2 ESXi versus Hyper-V and Xen (Source: VMware).

Another thing to keep in mind is that despite I/O being related to memory, virtualized I/O, particularly as it relates to these third-party offerings, is closely aligned to switches and cabling. This makes it a bit less surprising that, unlike in the network and even storage virtualization space, where third-party products tend to focus on the softwarization of hardware, most I/O virtualization solutions actually add hardware.

Enterprises that are virtualizing are generally looking to consolidate, not add, hardware. However, to improve I/O, adding may not be a bad thing. Think about it: The heart of I/O is keeping movement going through the pipes. Add software to move it along, and you're basically masking the problem by introducing more of everything into the equation. Your total capacity will not increase, but you will be consuming more disk space and RAM. You're probably even rerouting. Performance may not suffer noticeably, but it likely will not improve as dramatically as it could otherwise.

Three prominent vendors in this space are Neterion, NextIO, and Xsigo Systems. By and large, these vendors deal with the OEMs, which in turn rebrand their products. This makes it a bit tricky to discern what is actually being purchased, but as with server components, it's important to know what's out there.

Neterion

Neterion takes on virtual I/O with its V-NIC family. The V-NIC family consists of a series of 10Gb Ethernet adapters souped up for I/O virtualization (www.neterion. com/products/overview.html). They are found inside Fujitsu PRIMEQUEST servers (under the name 10GBASE-SR LAN Card), Hitachi (as PCI-X 10 Gigabit Ethernet Adapter), IBM servers (as IBM 10 Gigabit Ethernet SR Server Adapter in System x servers and IBM 10 Gigabit Ethernet PCI-X 2.0 DDR Adapter, SR & LR, in System p & i), HP servers (HP 10 Gigabit Ethernet PCI-X 2.0 DDR Adapter), and various others.

Xframe V-NIC augments some of the capabilities of the virtualization vendors offer. "Passthru," for example, is an emerging model providing much better support for high-speed I/O virtualization. It requires hardware to pick up the features being removed from the operating system. Xframe V-NIC brings the interchannel communication inside the ASIC. This, according to Neterion, improves performance while providing true hardware separation and better protection between channels.

The Xframe V-NIC family supports IPv4 and IPv6 as well as drivers for all major operating systems, including Windows, Linux, and Solaris. Stateless offloads, which maintain the integrity of TCP/IP implementations without "breaking the I/O stack," are supported too.

NextIO

NextIO also starts with the physical, but it describes itself as sitting at the opposite side of Neterion. Like Neterion, however, NextIO also deals directly with the OEMs; its biggest partner is IBM.

However, rather than latching between the hardware and the network, NextIO makes chips and software that transform physical-to-physical connections into a pool of virtualized I/O resources that servers can dynamically share. Its Adaptive Connect platform is based around the PCI Express protocol, making it compatible with pretty much all I/O connectivity options—Ethernet, Fibre Channel, T1/E1, and InfiniBand—as well as the remaining infrastructure, including software. In addition, NextIO's architecture separates the CPU from the I/O in the server. This enables each to be added or upgraded as needed.

Xsigo Systems

Xsigo Systems is fast becoming one of the best-known of I/O virtualization vendors. This is perhaps because of the deal it scored with Dell in February 2009 to offer the Xsigo I/O Director with its PowerEdge servers and storage solutions.

Xsigo takes yet another approach to I/O management with its I/O Director offering. I/O Director consolidates the I/O infrastructure and replaces physical network and storage interfaces (NICs and HBAs) with virtual equivalents. Thus, instead of multiple I/O cards and cables attached to every server, servers are connected with a single cable and can be deployed on-the-fly. Users can create, migrate, and allocate virtual connectivity, virtual NICs, and virtual HBAs without physical recabling.

SUMMARY

When evaluating what components to include in your virtual infrastructure, you must think beyond your servers. Storage, I/O, and the network itself are all potential components of an effective virtualized infrastructure. In some cases, the inherent capabilities of the virtual environment and the hardware on which it is installed will be enough. In most instances, it will not be. With technology from these three areas converging, it is important to identify weak spots and determine which technology is truly in order.

The further you get in the planning process, the more critical it is to know your infrastructure well enough to determine which components are best to virtualize. The next chapter will discuss this further as we look at what goes into planning an effective virtual deployment.

Part IV

From Development to Production: Managing the Virtual Infrastructure

Laying the Foundation: The Planning Stage

The previous chapters looked at virtualization from both a conceptual and technical perspective. We explained many of the options and components that go into a virtualized infrastructure.

In Part 4, we switch to a slightly different perspective. We will look at the process of taking a virtualized infrastructure off the drawing board and into the data center. Many of the virtualization vendors brag that it takes only 15 to 45 minutes to completely install a virtual server, and while this is indeed true, it is but a small part of the process. Chapter 2, "Comparing Virtualization Technologies," touched on the importance of building the VM host with virtualization in mind. A sound virtualization strategy takes this even further. The best way to achieve a sound virtualization strategy is through careful planning. Plan, plan, analyze, and plan some more. Test, deploy, assess, and revise the plan.

Part 4 looks at the deployment process from planning to the deployment itself to important postdeployment steps. We approach this from a management and strategy angle. Although we discuss pros and cons of various management products, we will not drill down to that level with the virtualization products themselves because that has already been done. Although it is not necessary to have settled on an environment prior to coming up with a strategy, it is a separate process, and one that has been examined in previous chapters.

Planning thoroughly, without falling into paralysis by analysis, and then following the plan through implementation and beyond is, of course, easier said than done. The payoff of a well-planned deployment is a more easily managed infrastructure. Postdeployment, management becomes the key to the infrastructure's standing. Proper planning goes a long way toward making this possible.

We speak with a wide spectrum of virtualization vendors, and increasingly in recent months nearly all of them confirm a lack of planning from many of the enterprises they work with. Planning may not seem glamorous, and it may be tedious, but it will save you a lot of money and headaches down the road. Not only does a lack of planning have the potential to set you down the wrong path (resulting in unnecessary expenses for both the present and future), but it also opens you up to security vulnerabilities, server failures due to overload, and additional human error.

SELLING SENIOR MANAGEMENT ON VIRTUALIZATION

You may have sipped the virtualization Kool-Aid and been sold beyond your wildest dreams by what you saw in test and development. Perhaps you're envisioning virtualizing your enterprise from the receptionist's desktop through the most mission-critical server.

Slow down, take a breath, and think carefully.

Remember that this needs to be sold to the CTO or CIO and after that, most likely to the CFO. You probably understand the fundamentals of what's involved, why it's important, and how it will help you do your job better. Although the CIO probably does (or at least should) understand the technology, it's doubtful the CFO does—or to some degree cares. Thus, the merits of virtualization will need to be explained in terms of how it will bring value to the company.

In today's economic climate, saving money is a key driver. Virtualization will save money in both the short and long term, but only if it is implemented properly, and that means thinking about more than whether you're going to take advantage of Hyper-V on your boxes running Windows Server 2008 or download a free copy of ESXi from VMware.

In other words: What will it cost? How much will it save the company? And how long before a return on investment (ROI) is realized? Presenting ROI is always tricky; at best it's an estimate and often little more than a guess with some prediction. The more you know, however, the more accurate your numbers will be.

Table 15-1 lists examples of potential costs and savings for a virtualization endeavor. We've left room to jot down the amounts. To determine the ROI, divide the amount saved by the amount spent.

TABLE 15-1   ROI—Costs and Savings to Consider

COST	AMOUNT SPENT
New equipment	
Training	

TABLE 15-1   Continued

Cost	Amount Spent
Software (including the virtualization environment itself, autodiscovery tools, and management tools)	
Savings	**Amount Saved**
Power	
Licensing costs	
Real estate	

Note that reduced headcount and security are not listed as areas of potential savings. Virtualization will not save you in those areas. Fewer boxes in this case does not mean less to manage. Nor does it mean you get a pass on security. Security, as noted previously, becomes even more important.

In the end, the final cost may not bear any resemblance to the initial projections, but having a sense of what it will cost and what it will save in an ideal situation will get it on the table and give everyone numbers to begin working with to figure out how to maximize ROI.

As appealing as it would be to present virtualization as pure savings, in most cases this would be disingenuous. Sure, you could slap Hyper-V on that Compaq server that's been sitting around since before Compaq was part of HP, and it may be tempting, but don't. That hardware wasn't designed for a virtualized infrastructure, and it probably cannot handle most of today's workloads or the software to run it.

So when calculating costs, if the hardware on which you're planning to virtualize is more than three years old, do yourself a huge favor and budget for new hardware. This may make for a tougher sell (and make for a far lower ROI), but you have a better chance of getting the results you're after, and in the end it will deliver a better return. Also bear in mind that although there is no way to work it into the ROI numbers, you will theoretically be buying fewer servers with higher utilization rates, which means in the long run your spending will be less.

Another approach to a virtualization strategy is to approach it from the opposite side: If your organization is in the process of a hardware refresh, tacking virtualization on will likely require only a light touch. Much of the hardware released in the past year has been designed to be virtualized, and anything multicore is worthy of more careful review.

If new hardware is being purchased, it's best to piggyback virtualization strategy onto that to ensure the hardware and software will be in synch. Because Part 3 examined hardware closely, we will not factor it into the planning process here but will instead assume multicore, x86-based systems running Windows or Linux with sufficient processing power, disk capacity, and memory to support any of the three major hypervisor environments that are either on hand or being purchased.

VIRTUALIZATION BENEFITS BEYOND COST SAVINGS

Let's assume you're one step closer to making your virtualization dreams a reality: The CFO has begrudgingly bought in, and the CIO is excited at the prospect of freeing up some boxes and clearing some space in the data center. Going virtual is either one component of a hardware refresh or an initiative in its own right with some hardware being purchased. Again, don't even think about downloading ESXi, popping a few corks, and going home, especially without some sort of buy in from senior management.

Before attempting to decide what to virtualize, consider your goals: consolidation, disaster recovery, efficiency, or a combination. Yes, cost savings is a goal, and in many cases a tremendous benefit, and it probably is what got you the sign-off in the first place. Focus too much on it, however, and it could mean that you will not receive the additional support necessary for a successful deployment (such as new hardware or management tools) down the road. "Green computing" has been in the spotlight lately, but even the most eco-conscious enterprise is cost conscious, so environmental soundness will not win on its own virtue. If you can tie green to cost savings (and over the long term, the savings does indeed bear out), then it makes sense.

Also bear in mind that even if saving money is what earns you senior management buy-in, from an IT perspective, it should not be looked upon as the only driver. Some level of spending will also be necessary in any strategy for it to be sound. As we've been saying from the beginning and can't emphasize enough: Don't assume that just because Hyper-V is free that you can load up underutilized servers—or worse, servers sitting around since the last boom—and instantly have a virtual infrastructure. You will incur software costs, and the larger the deployment, the higher they will be.

If your organization is tightfisted to the degree that "saving money" is the only way to get sign-off, consult Chapter 1, "To Virtualize or Not to Virtualize?" for a concise rundown of ways in which virtualization will save money. When preparing the all-important official proposal for senior management, be sure to highlight benefits that are quantifiable in terms of money saved and pinpoint technological goals. Examples include the following:

- Fewer boxes consume less real estate, which means the data center requires less square footage, thus freeing up X% of space.

- Consolidating workloads X% will result in a power savings of Y% (your data center's power reduction will vary).
- Disaster recovery cost savings.
- Shorter maintenance windows with little to no planned downtime.
- Hardware savings (applies primarily to situations where hardware is expected to be purchased).

As tempting as it is to consider headcount or security as areas in which to save money: *don't*. Fewer boxes do not mean less to secure or manage. Yes, there is less hardware to secure, but the cost of tagging and tracking and ensuring your box doesn't walk out of the data center is marginally reduced, and that reduction is offset by the complexities of monitoring and securing multiple virtual servers. Headcount is a similar animal. You can automate, and you can make it so establishing and provisioning a server takes fewer man-hours, but you still need people to manage and track what's going on and prevent the dreaded "virtual server sprawl," which we will discuss more thoroughly in Chapter 16, "Deployment," and Chapter 17, "Postproduction: Wrapping It Up."

Note that selling virtualization on the merits of cost cutting will not work if you're looking to virtualize the desktop (cloud computing via a public cloud being the exception, as noted in Chapter 13, "Choosing a Vendor"). Although desktop virtualization will likely deliver a savings over time, in the short run, it requires a much higher investment. The lengthier ROI is not likely to earn it additional fans. If, for whatever reason, you chose to make desktop virtualization a top priority and cost is a key driver, consider using a managed service provider (MSP) or public cloud.

Assuming appropriate hardware is on hand, or a purchase order is approved or pending, and the powers that be have been sold on the benefits, it is time to move forward in building a strategy. The first step in coming up with a virtualization strategy has nothing to do with virtualization and little to do with technology. It is about developing a cross-functional understanding of the business: processes, priorities, and people issues.

CROSS-FUNCTIONAL TEAMS

If the process has not already been formalized, now is the time to do so. The next consideration is what to virtualize. Even if the long-term plan is to go completely virtual, you have to start somewhere, and that's where things can get tricky.

You can pick something that seems to make sense from an IT perspective, but from a business perspective, it may not be the best choice. The easiest way to get an understanding of that is to speak with users throughout the enterprise. Ideally, you want to build a cross-functional team. If that is not possible, processes should be documented along with any potential issues and concerns.

Here, too, a strategy comes into play. Moving back-office functions to a virtualized environment is unlikely to deliver the same ROI as operations, but it is a much safer move (and it's been well documented that Microsoft Exchange is a fine candidate for virtualization). If improved disaster recovery is your goal, you probably don't want to start with an application that is frequently down, unless you're able to isolate what is causing it to fail. Similarly, if your goal is consolidation, moving several low throughput apps used by different departments onto the same box is probably a safe move.

Myriad tools to assess workload compatibility are available to assist in the virtualization process. These should also be brought into play. Some are standalone and some are part of larger suites. Some are designed primarily for the deployment process; others step you through that and then can be used for automation. As useful as the tools are, however, by their very nature the view they present is literal. Yes, there is tremendous value in this, and we will talk more about such tools later in this chapter. To get a holistic view of what goes on as well as to gain an understanding of what's behind the workflow, you must look to the various organizations involved. At the very least, accounting, sales, operations, human resources, IT, facilities, and legal should weigh in with information that includes the following:

- Peak periods
- Critical periods (those where they absolutely cannot risk being down)
- Compliance issues
- Potential conflicts

The human factor can present as much, if not more, of a bottleneck. Do not underestimate or gloss over it. Accounting, for example, may insist on a dedicated box for its tasks. In some cases, such as for regulatory or compliance reasons, it may make sense. Other times, it may simply be an issue of ownership or lack of trust that the location of data or apps will have no bearing on the ability of department members to get their work done uninterrupted. By keeping the line of communication open, you can build trust and alleviate many worries.

Only you know the culture of your organization best, but for most enterprises, a virtualization project will be a success if the environment that end users see and work in postdeployment is no different from what they are used to, and if it works at least as efficiently. Seamlessness, therefore, must be emphasized, as well as proper allocation of resources so that neither performance nor security suffers.

This is where discovery tools come into play.

THE RIGHT TOOL FOR THE RIGHT JOB

As valuable as talking to reps from the various lines of business can be, it carries limitations and biases. This is where tools come in. The next, or perhaps simultaneous, step is to review resource needs. These tools evaluate apps and resources to ensure that technological conflicts do not take place. A number of software companies sell products that scan the data center, determine what's running where, and what is most compatible with what. Unless your server room is really a server closet (that is, fewer than ten servers) some sort of equipment (and possibly real estate) inventorying should be done. It never hurts to know what IT assets you have on hand.

In many ways it is far easier to autodiscover how your servers, network topology, workloads, and workflows hum than it is to grapple with the human element. Tools, after all, are unbiased in their assessment. Performance compatibility boils down to applications and workflows, not office politics or job security issues. A retailer with a fast-moving inventory, for example, would not want to have its inventory software and billing application running on the same box. Back-office applications may or may not be compatible: payroll and personnel apps don't inherently conflict, but the way each is used within the organization may or may not make this desirable. Similarly, placing multiple mission-critical apps on the same machine as high-throughput apps would basically be playing system outage Russian Roulette. Assessment tools will flag these issues.

You can use a plethora of tools currently available on the market to help facilitate the planning stage. Some are a small component of a larger solution, and some are products that deal with specific aspects of the virtualization or server management in general, with some applicability to virtualization. The majority of stand-alone tools are from single-offering vendors, many of which are small, and some of which may not be around in the long term because of acquisition or insolvency. Only you can decide the desirable level of risk for your organization, but bear in mind the pros and cons.

Although the larger vendors (IBM with Tivoli, CA with CA Advanced Systems Management, or Symantec with its Endpoint Virtualization Suite and Veritas Virtual Infrastructure) will likely charge more, they offer an end-to-end solution, a deep knowledge pool, and some sort of guarantee of service level. You also gain a sense of security that the company is not going anywhere, and you will not need to ensure that the products all interoperate with one another because they are all coming from the same source and the vendors ensure that. The downsides are that customization is limited to the available modules and the price tends to be high.

Many of the larger infrastructure solutions, in particular those from BMC, CA, HP, Symantec, Oracle, and IBM, are designed as whole-enterprise solutions. If your enterprise is a sizable one, chances are you already have at least one of these vendors' solutions in place. They were developed and have been enterprise fixtures long before virtualization was mainstream. In recent years, modules designed for virtualization have been added. CA's Advanced Systems Management, for example, integrates with VMware VirtualCenter and also supports Sun's Logical Domains. If such tools are in place in your organization, you may be able to get the data you need by picking up a new module rather than investing in specialty tools. In many cases, simply adding the appropriate module will be the most cost-effective and holistic way to go.

If you can't find a module that meets your needs but would prefer a standalone specialty tool, note that many of them hook into the more comprehensive solutions to retrieve the data. You can also pick up a standalone solution, where appropriate, along the way to plug specific functional holes.

For smaller organizations and those that have been managing their infrastructure without a comprehensive tool, opting for a piecemeal strategy may be preferable. By going with a collection of standalone offerings, you get exactly what you want, and possibly an optimal solution for each stage. You may save a bit of money on each individual piece, but by the time it's strung together the cost savings will likely be negligible. Another downside is that you're putting the solution together yourself, so the onus of it working falls on you. You'll be stringing together a series of independent solutions that may or may not be compatible and that may or may not interoperate. Each connection point presents an additional potential security vulnerability. Should you hit a snag (and you will, it's inevitable), you'll likely find yourself ping-ponging between vendors. There is also a somewhat increased risk that a vendor will go out of business, thus leaving you with unsupported software.

Going with a value-added reseller is a middle of the road approach, and one that works particularly well if a company is also buying hardware. Oftentimes, VARs certify solutions and have done the heavy lifting to confirm compatibility and interoperability, and the VAR provides first-line support. The downside is that you're limited by what the VAR has to offer.

TYPES OF PLANNING TOOLS

If only it were a case of all discovery tools setting out to discover the same thing. That would, of course, make it easier to compare one to the other, but many discovery tools are out there. For the most part, available tools provide the following:

- Infrastructure assessment
- Process assessment
- Network assessment

In some cases, the capabilities overlap.

Two companies in this space worthy of note are CiRBA and Reflex Systems. Both ISVs have been in this space for a while and offer assessment solutions. CiRBA was founded in 1999, with the aim of easing the pain associated with consolidation, the constant solution of server sprawl, which was so rampant at that time. This makes it especially well suited for virtualization endeavors, even those not necessarily planned around consolidation.

Its Advanced Analytics Engine is designed to be used before the consolidation gets under way. It pulls in audited server room workload data from any agent or agentless source. Figure 15-1 provides an example of how the data is presented. After the needed information is imported, the software runs a host of algorithms to analyze the information and determine possible configuration conflicts based on everything from operating system and platform incompatibilities, workload patterns (for example, CPU utilization, and network and disk I/O) and business constraints (geography, business service, or maintenance windows). It then makes recommendations for virtualization and other consolidation endeavors.

What's particularly unique about CiRBA's solution is how it presents the data. The results are displayed, color-coded, on grids and are given scores indicating which servers are compatible with which based on the potential conflicts it has assessed. The maps can then be broken out based on the type of constraint and then overlaid for a cumulative picture. They can also be modified and reevaluated to illustrate possible changes. This enables you to see which workloads would be in varying degrees of conflict and which consolidate nicely.

Perhaps the biggest downside of Advanced Analytics Engine is that it is purely a reporting tool. So you are on your own for the rollout. The software is meant to be used throughout the life cycle of a deployment, so you can run it as often as you see fit to determine that no new inherent conflicts might be brewing.

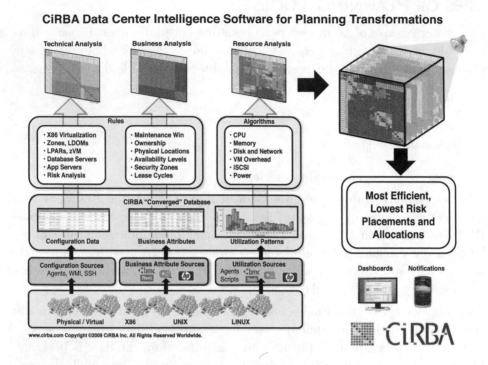

CiRBA Data Center Intelligence Software for Planning Transformations

FIGURE 15-1 CiRBA's Advanced Analytics Engine (Source: CiRBA).

Another product worthy of consideration is Reflex Systems' Virtualization Management Center. Although Virtualization Management Center is a more expansive offering than Advanced Analytics Engine, it is nevertheless worth looking at, if only to contrast its approach. The virtual infrastructure planning software discovers and maps the entire infrastructure, both physical and virtual. Reflex believes that the infrastructure management vendors like CA, BMC, and their ilk, do not provide products that go beyond the physical infrastructure to meet the needs of a virtualized infrastructure. However, although Virtualization Management Center is capable of tracking both the physical and virtual, most customers are using it alongside a traditional infrastructure offering, and it is designed to be complementary.

A variety of components make up Virtualization Management Center, but the most relevant one to planning is "Virtual Infrastructure Discovery and Mapping." The discovery and mapping capabilities present a logical visual representation of the virtual environment, which enables the admin to correlate events and see how they impact performance.

Granted, if you're just getting started with virtualization, you won't have anything virtual to track, but you will be starting off with a product that assesses what you have and its capabilities, and down the line will be able to fold the virtual into that. This is especially handy for SMBs that up until now have found infrastructure management suites completely out of their price range.

Whether you choose a product like Advanced Analytics Engine or Virtualization management, or opt instead to go with a tool already in-house, it is critical to have an understanding of where all your servers reside and what they are running. Ideally, if you're using a tool designed with only a physical infrastructure in mind, you are running a complementary virtualization tool along with it or some sort of autodiscovery tool.

TESTING THE DEPLOYMENT

After you've determined which apps will be virtualized and on which server, you can go ahead and begin rolling them out. However, a more prudent next step would be to test things out in a simulated environment that a lab management tool offers.

Here, the choice of virtualization environment will be a driver. You can't use VMware vCenter Lab Manager with Xen or Hyer-V, but VMLogix' LabManager works with ESX, Hyper-V, and Xen. The other player in this relatively uncrowded space is Surgient, which offers a variety of lab management systems. For the most part, however, VMware and VMLogix dominate.

Lab manager tools offer the capability to create a test environment that encapsulates the entire server environment on a few boxes, thus enabling you to take your virtual infrastructure out for a spin before ever putting a single actual server into production.

VMware's Lab Manager's "sandbox" environment enables users to design, simulate, and test various system and network configurations needed to support multi-tiered apps. The software offers a host of features, such as graphical configuration diagrams and a network fencing feature that enables users to work in parallel by deploying multiple instances of those configurations simultaneously.

Enterprises opting for an end-to-end VMware environment will find much to like about Lab Manager. VMLogix' Lab Manager solution is not without its own bells and whistles. First and foremost, it automates the building of production-like environments with end-to-end configuration of operating systems and applications. It also provides the capability to automate the build and test execution process by leveraging advanced configuration of software, tools, scripts, and data at the guest OS level, as well as the capability to capture and share "live" multi-machine configurations from the configuration library.

As valuable an addition as Lab Manager is, it does carry with it a high price tag. If you're looking to cut costs somewhere, and your virtual infrastructure is simple and not likely to change often, this is one area that can be labeled nonessential.

LOOKING AHEAD TO THE LONG TERM

As critical as it is to set goals and plan the deployment, it is equally important to think about what will happen after the virtual infrastructure goes live. It is all too quick and easy for an admin to set up a VM; without policies in place, you'll soon see virtual server sprawl that is more complex and more difficult to clean up than any physical sprawl ever encountered. Add to that the fact that human error is responsible for the vast majority of unplanned downtime, and it becomes even more critical to put policies in place sooner rather than later. Remember, a well-planned deployment is far easier to manage.

Now is the time to begin thinking about the following. Note that there are no right or wrong answers, but the appropriate path is the one that fits best with your organization's culture.

- **Who has the authority to establish a VM (from both an operations and IT perspective)**—Can any project manager request that a VM be set up, or does sign-off need to come from the director level or higher? There will also need to be an approval process from IT side to determine what makes sense from a technical perspective.
- **What circumstances merit a VM being set up**—Will each project or temporary undertaking be allowed its own VM, or will VMs be restricted to long-term or permanent projects?

- **What happens when a VM exceeds a certain size**—Will it be automatically resized or moved, or will IT need to manually approve its expansion? If it is not expanded, what sort of storage strategy will be implemented?

- **How long should the VM be allowed to exist, and what are exceptions to this**—Will there be a default time frame, or will it be set to the estimated time frame of the project? In general, it is preferable to have an end point for the VM, because that ensures a review that the resources allocated to it are in line with its needs.

- **What happens to the VM after the expiration date, if it is still in use**—Will the VM be kept live indefinitely or given an automatic extension, or will IT or operations be required to set a new time frame?

- **What happens to VMs laying dormant after a given amount of time**—Will it automatically be locked? Where will the contents of VM be moved to? Will the server be reprovisioned? Will IT or operations be warned of its impending shut off? If so, how far in advance will a warning be issued, and how many times?

It is especially important to think about how you would like to handle the retirement of VMs, because abandoned VMs present a management and resource challenge as well as a gaping security hole.

It is also important to evaluate management tools at this time. Without management tools, it will be difficult, if not impossible, to manage the environment after it is live. Now is also a good time to consider adding automation tools to the mix, especially if such tools were part of the autodiscovery or planning process and thus are already part of the infrastructure. We will talk more about specific tools in Chapter 16 and Chapter 17.

SUMMARY

Getting your virtual infrastructure up and running can be broken down into three steps: planning, deployment, and maintenance. Although all three stages are important, the planning stage is arguably the most important because it establishes the foundation for how the infrastructure will function.

To get most out of the planning stage and be most assured of a successful deployment, you must determine what the goal of virtualizing is. It is also critical to inventory both your hardware and software and determine which workloads are most compatible.

Coming up with return on investment projections is also helpful at this time, because it will make for an easier sell to senior management and give you a clearer target with which to work.

The planning stage is also the ideal time to begin thinking about policies and tools to put in place after the deployment rolls out.

## CHAPTER 16

Deployment

We often joke that a well-planned virtual deployment follows four basic steps: Install software, configure software, provision virtual machines (VM), and go home. Theoretically, if you planned properly and determined which technology is best suited to meet your objectives, the actual deployment is fairly simple. It is a matter of following the instructions laid out in Part 2 for your virtualization environment of choice on live servers, provisioning the physical servers into VMs, and migrating data and apps to the VMs.

It is in fact that easy. What is not that easy is deploying well.

However, if you planned properly, your path to a virtual infrastructure will be far smoother than that of an organization that did not. That does not mean issues won't crop up as your virtualization infrastructure moves off of the drawing board and into the data center. Nor does it mean that when you're done, you're well and truly done. Very few deployments are done in one fell swoop, which means you'll be back to the deployment phase time and again. It's not unreasonable to assume a full-scale virtual deployment in a large enterprise could take years before it is considered complete.

Chapter 15, "Laying the Foundation: The Planning Stage," focused on planning your virtual infrastructure; this chapter focuses on the nitty-gritty that comes with the actual rollout and flipping the switch. It discusses the deployment itself and the decisions that must be made. It assumes, however, that objectives have been set, hardware is appropriate, and people issues (ownership and others) have been worked out as best as they can be. We also assume that the virtual environment has been selected, and a test and development (frequently referred to as test and dev) environment is in place.

This chapter covers decisions you must make during the VM deployment process: autodiscovery tools, incorporating automation, and understanding and planning for security. We will not, however, be reviewing the installation of the virtualization software itself. That was done meticulously in Part 1, and it should be consulted should the technical specifics be needed when looking at the big picture.

CHOOSING WHICH APPLICATIONS TO VIRTUALIZE

You've set your objectives for virtualization, gotten everyone (not just IT) on board, or at least made them aware of what's going on, planned out your virtual infrastructure, set it up in a test environment, and given thought to postdeployment processes.

Even if you plan to virtualize your entire infrastructure, you still must start somewhere. Although every organization has somewhat different needs, some applications are better suited for an initial deployment than others. It would be foolish, for example, to move your mission-critical customer-facing applications to a VM in an initial rollout.

An early 2009 Forrester survey of 124 clients about their x86 virtualization deployments sheds some light on typical successful virtualization deployments. Among the characteristics it looked at was what is most frequently virtualized. Granted, this is a somewhat self-selected group, but the most frequently virtualized applications at that time were web servers or web app servers (81 percent of environments), off-the-shelf apps (65 percent of environments), and infrastructure servers (65 percent). In-house developed/custom applications (60 percent) and Microsoft SQL Server (53 percent) were also popular.

Despite the claim that Microsoft Exchange is very well suited to run in a virtual environment, it was used in less than one-third of deployments. No doubt those numbers will increase as Windows Server 2008 increases its traction.

Oracle was also popular, both for applications and its database. This is interesting in the light of Oracle's moves in the virtualization space.

Despite the willingness of enterprises to move their database apps into virtual environment, vendors and analysts alike do not see mission-critical apps moving onto VMs presently.

Forrester left these categories quite broad in the published study, however. Drilling down to a more granular level, apps frequently cited as ideal slam-dunks for virtualization are DHCP and DNS servers. Network services in general are a good place to start, as are back-office apps, particularly those running on underutilized servers.

It's interesting to note that the pattern of applications migrating to virtual environments is not unlike the migration pattern to Linux that began almost a decade ago. First came the edge applications (mainly web servers), then database and those supporting back office apps, and eventually mission-critical customer-facing apps.

Virtualization is being accepted at a much faster rate, no doubt because it is not butting up against the legacy baggage that Linux faced. Nor does it appear to have the same learning curve or lack of support. And while it does bring its own issues (for example, reliability and ownership) it also offers the promise of savings with little effort, which makes it an even more appealing sell in the current economic climate.

Unfortunately, this also creates many false assumptions that may end up being very costly down the road for many enterprises.

Knowing What You Have: Autodiscovery Tools

We've made it abundantly clear that flipping the switch is easy and efficient. Bear in mind, however, that although provisioning may seem to go down from weeks to hours, the bulk of time that goes into provisioning is outside of the virtualization process.

For the initial deployment, the manual part of the process—getting the necessary sign-offs for the purchase order, ensuring license requirements will be met, readying the hardware, and so on—remains. Provisioning occurs at the end of this.

Thus, the process before the provisioning must be fixed or it will be impacted. Automation tools are one way to mitigate this issue, and we will talk about them later in this chapter.

Before you can automate processes, however, you must know what you're working with. We touched on autodiscovery tools in the previous chapter. Most large organizations have some sort of autodiscovery functionality in place, either as an individual tool or as part of a larger suite.

Autodiscovery tools are important in any infrastructure, but they are particularly critical in a virtual infrastructure where the lines are less clear. Prior to deployment, they tell you what you have and where it is. After the initial deployment, they tell you where everything is. One of the value propositions of a virtual infrastructure is being able to move apps and data from box to box, often on-the-fly. Autodiscovery tools enable you to know exactly where your apps are at any given time.

Webopedia defines autodiscovery tools as software that "collects data on a network and records any changes made to the network assets." This typically means not just servers, but also switches, routers, NICs, storage devices, and in some cases anything that has an IP address. Some autodiscovery tools can also track changes made to memory, software versions, and storage, as well as any new or deleted files and equipment added or removed.

Some autodiscovery tools have traditionally focused on devices themselves. Many of these vendors have recognized the winds of change and added VM recognition and other capabilities they think will benefit a virtual environment.

If this sounds familiar, it's because it is. Autodiscovery tools are by and large the same products that were sold as "infrastructure monitoring tools" earlier in the decade.

Thus, many enterprises, particularly large enterprises, have tools already in place that can assess the infrastructure. If you're going with what you have in place, be sure the inventory and tracking capabilities extend to VMs and are capable of tracking VM migrations.

You can probably get away without an autodiscovery or monitoring tool if all of the following apply:

- Your deployment is small (however, fewer than ten servers and your returns on virtualization may be negligible).
- You can locate every single piece of equipment in your data center.
- You have no intention of migrating apps and data from one server to another.

In other words, nearly all deployments require some sort of autodiscovery tool, and those that don't may not deliver the ROI that makes a virtualization deployment worthwhile.

You can choose from many autodiscovery tools. Both VMware and Citrix offer autodiscovery options: VMware vCenter Server offers autodiscovery among its many management options (as well as provisioning, automation, and management capabilities) as does Citrix Essentials for XenServer, although it focuses more on automation than on autodiscovery. For simpler or limited deployments, using the built-in functionality will likely suffice, and indeed many midsize deployments get by with it.

For large-scale deployments, the heavy hitters are on hand to offer, in most cases, autodiscovery software that is frequently a module in an infrastructure orchestration or life cycle management suite. These products are becoming increasingly attuned to virtualization needs, and in many cases assume they are going into an environment that is at least partially virtualized.

Table 16-1 provides a sample of the most popular products on the market. For companies looking for an autodiscovery tool, particularly one that is part of a more comprehensive solution suite, it is a good starting point. However, it is by no means a complete list.

TABLE 16-1   Popular Autodiscovery Tool Options

Vendor	Tool	Product Family
BMC	BMC Performance Manager for Virtual Servers	BMC Performance Manager (Formerly PATROL)
HP	HP Discovery and Dependency Mapping software	HP Data Center Automation Center
IBM	Tivoli Monitoring	Tivoli Monitoring
Symantec		Altiris Server Management Suite
EMC	Smarts Discovery Manager	Smarts family

If your organization is using one of these product suites (and for the vast majority of midsize enterprises and above, one will likely be in place), confirm that the autodiscovery module is installed and running, and that it is a recent enough version to detect VMs. If not, you need to upgrade or install the appropriate module.

Not all organizations are willing to commit to an end-to-end life cycle solutions suite management suite. Price, vendor lock-in, lack of internal resources (including staff with the appropriate skill sets) are all reasons, valid or not, that organizations have for not investing in these solutions.

Thus, do not panic if an infrastructure management suite is not in place or if an autodiscovery module is not present or suitable for a virtualized environment. Alternatives exist.

A number of autodiscovery tools focus on the virtual. Embotics (V-Scout), Hyperic (System Information Gatherer), ToutVirtual (VirtualIQ Pro), and Novell (PlateSpin Recon), as well as a host of others, sell products with autodiscovery capabilities. In some cases, these products are also part of a modular-like suite. Some also hook into the infrastructure tools from larger vendors; still others offer autodiscovery and automation within the same product. This is a space that is changing fast, because of acquisitions and the entrance of new players. PlateSpin Recon, for example, came to Novell via acquisition.

Note also that in many cases the "unique" capabilities touted in the sales pitch will become less unique with time as enterprises come to expect this level of functionality.

Incorporating Automation (Before and After Your Virtual Machines Go Live)

Closely related to autodiscovery tools are automation tools. The lines between the two categories are somewhat fuzzy, especially among the independent vendors whose main emphasis is on virtualization. So long as the capabilities meet your needs on both fronts, nothing is wrong with using a product capable of pulling double duty, especially because a virtualization deployment is never really "done."

For purposes of clarification, let's assume automation kicks in after some sort of autodiscovery mechanism is in place, and ESX, Hyper-V, XenServer, or whatever environment you have selected is in installed on at least one box, although in real life it would likely be more. Provisioning one server into four or eight or even 12 VMs is generally quite manageable, but provisioning 20 or 40 into four or eight or 12 VMs gets unwieldy real fast.

When looked at from a visual perspective, as illustrated in Figure 16-1, the difference between one and two servers being provisioned into multiple VMs becomes even clearer.

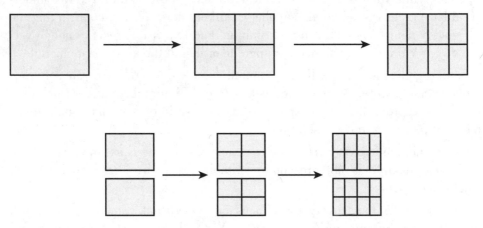

FIGURE 16-1 Exponential VM growth.

Now multiply that by a hundred and add in the ability to move these thousands of provisioned VMs on-the-fly, as needed, using VMotion or other similar technology. Not only is it a Sisyphean task to figure out what you have, but it's also equally, if not more, difficult to locate where a given app or data is.

Choosing an Automation Tool

Automation tools mitigate this inherent complexity by offering two key benefits to a virtualized infrastructure: They minimize the human involvement in process, and they enable admins to know exactly where a VM is and what it is doing.

The former function is a universal advantage of automation tools. As we stated previously, much of the time spent in the provisioning process is not the actual provisioning, but rather the human processes and inherent time lags around it. Similarly, many of the errors that come into play stem from human errors during this process. Whereas assigning a VM as a "new" server is much simpler than adding a new box to the data center, this simplicity brings with its own set of issues, which automation goes a long way toward solving.

Consider the process that goes hand in hand with getting a new box: request for hardware, approval, formal purchase order, purchase, waiting for the box, box arrives, box is delivered to the data center, box likely sits in data center for several days waiting for IT staffer with corresponding skill set to install and configure software. Depending on the organization, this could take several weeks or even months.

Now contrast this with deploying a VM: Sign-offs are achieved, the autodiscovery software scans servers to determine its optimal location, and with a few mouse clicks, a server is up and running.

There are only three points where the process can be held up, and automation tools can facilitate the process to minimize each of the three potential bottlenecks. Depending on the function, the tool can prompt for the sign-off, alert you about trouble, or automatically undertake a function previously handled manually. It can also ensure due process is followed and alert you when it is not.

The flipside to this is that it is all too easy to create VMs. The metaphors that abound around provisioning VMs say it best, likening VMs to "breeding them like rabbits" and provisioning to being "the drug of choice for IT admins."

This is obviously not an ideal situation, and, indeed, the lack of proper processes in place to provision VMs results in what has come to be known as "virtual server sprawl" or simply "virtual sprawl." VM sprawl is much like the server sprawl issue of the previous decade, except, in this case it is VMs, not physical servers. VM sprawl presents resource allocation, licensing, and security issues, and it can easily transform a virtualization endeavor from a streamlining effort into a management nightmare.

Automation software can facilitate a solution to this, but ultimately it is the humans who are in the driver's seat. Again, it boils down to setting up the processes; exploration, if not implementation, of such policies should be done during the planning stage, before the first VM is rolled out. The previous chapter noted six key processes within the VM life cycle, all of which bear repeating:

- Who has the authority to establish a VM (from both an operations and IT perspective)?
- What circumstances merit a VM being set up?
- What happens when a VM exceeds a certain size?

- How long should the VM be allowed to exist, and what are exceptions to this?
- What happens to the VM after the expiration date, if it is still in use?
- What happens to VMs laying dormant after a given amount of time?

In addition, the following permissions and policies should be determined early on:

- Who has the authority to override the processes in place, and under what circumstances?
- Which actions require sign-offs to proceed, and which can be done automatically?
- Who receives alerts and how?
- What requires an immediate response, and what gets default resolution with notification?
- How will patches be rolled out?
- How will exploits and vulnerabilities be handled?

Parameters for all of these can and should be set within the automation tool. But bear in mind that managing people to manage the servers properly is as critical as the tools themselves. Therefore roles, responsibilities, and permissions must be assigned with great care. Too much access is a security risk, but not enough creates huge bottlenecks. This applies not just to VMs, but to the infrastructure as a whole.

Automation Vendors and Products

The vendors in the automation space are a mixed bag. Like in the autodiscovery space, many of the traditional infrastructure management vendors offer products that either recognize VMs or are designed specifically for them. A good number of players come not from the server management space, but from the storage space. Some, such as Commvault with Simpana Software Suite, focus on compliance. Others, such as Embotics, home in on security.

At first, the automation space appears to be a similar, although more kinetic environment than the autodiscovery space. A closer look reveals that when it comes to virtualization, it is also a more mature space. As virtualization has grown in popularity, the playing field has gotten narrower because of consolidation, with many of the established infrastructure tools vendors picking up the independent players.

In the past two years, HP acquired Opsware, which was once considered the leading independent vendor for virtualized deployments. BMC acquired BladeLogic; CA acquired Optinuity; Novell acquired Platespin; Quest Software acquired Embotics; and the list could go on and on. A few independent automation vendors remain, including Opalis, which is deeply partnered with CA and at one point was considered an acquisition play; ClearCube, whose Sentral offering is centered around the virtual desktop; ToutVirtual with ProvisionIQ, which is part of its VirtualIQ Suite; and nlytc from Global Data Center Management, better known as GDCM.

Here, perhaps more than at any other process point, the decision of whether to go with a smaller independent vendor carries with it the very real possibility that a vendor could be acquired, and you could end up working not with a BladeLogic or Opsware, but BMC or HP, respectively, and thus in a vendor relationship you may have been trying to avoid in the first place. This is not to say that independent vendors should be avoided at all costs, but it should be part of the consideration process and more than lip service should be paid to the possibility.

For the truly gun-shy, another option remains. Both Citrix and VMware offer automation and management capabilities centered around their tools. From Citrix comes Essentials, both for XenServer and Hyper-V, and from VMware is vCenter Server. Both of these are modular solutions, and both focus strictly on the automation of VMs and the processes around them. They will help with the provisioning, and if a VM goes down they can be set to fail over to another VM, but they will not be able to tell that a NIC is down or a server has crashed.

For that you need an end-to-end automation solution, and these will come up short. However, these tools, like their autodiscovery counterparts, will suffice in smaller deployments, especially in smaller data centers. They are also complementary to and well integrated with the more comprehensive suites without the upfront vendor lock-in.

SECURING YOUR VMS

Despite dire predictions from analysts and warnings from vendors, there has yet to be a major security breach attributable to a VM. Vulnerabilities have been found, publicized, and patched within VMware's products, but exploitation has yet to occur on any mass scale.

This is a good thing, so long as it doesn't lead to complacency.

Security is an ongoing concern and must be taken into consideration. It does not stop after the initial deployment; nor can you first start thinking about security after the VMs start rolling out. A virtual infrastructure is inherently more vulnerable to attack than a traditional one because each VM is a server and thus an entry point to the network. Should a hacker get into the hypervisor layer, the entire machine, and subsequently the network, is vulnerable as well.

Each instance of the operating system must be kept up to date, and patched where appropriate. Automation software makes patching VMs a straightforward endeavor. In some cases, it may be best to keep the VM isolated, and assign privileges and permissions on a per-virtual-machine basis.

Think of it as having more eggs in fewer baskets. It's critical that the baskets be even more cushioned and locked down because 16 servers, not one, must be protected. These principles apply to disaster recovery, which we will discuss in the next chapter, as well.

Unfortunately, the selection of security-related products is nowhere near as varied as that of automation or even autodiscovery software. It is also very appliance-centric.

VMware, has by and large taken the lead here with VMware VMsafe, a security technology designed specifically for virtualized environments. Because it originates from VMware, it hooks into VMware Infrastructure, and provides a direct look at VMotion and other VMware offerings. Although VMsafe technology will be delivered in future versions of VMware Virtual Infrastructure product, it is currently available to VMware partners in the form of an application program interface (API) that the vendor has made available to them, and with which they can develop their own tools and appliances. VMware itself also offers a number of security-related appliances that it claims "defend against viruses, spyware, spam, hackers and network intrusions."

The traditional security vendors also have products designed for the virtual: McAfee offers Total Protection for Virtualization, a security suite designed to run within VMs, and Symantec has Symantec Security Virtual Machine, an appliance that runs as a guest operating system on the box being protected.

Independent vendors include Reflex Systems with Virtual Security Appliance and Embotics' V-Commander (which focuses more on prevention and control than security, per se).

Because of this Spartan selection, and because security is pervasive, the best tactic for securing your VMs and your infrastructure is to ensure that the policies around your VMs are as stringent as those around your physical infrastructure. This will go a long way toward protecting your data center.

SUMMARY

Deploying a virtual infrastructure is more than merely pushing some buttons. To sum up this chapter we offer the following as a rudimentary best practices "cheat sheet" of steps to be taken. Some enterprises will skip some steps, and some will spend more time on some steps than others. Like any set of best practices, there are no absolutes or one-size-fits-all scenarios.

1. Use cross-functional teams to plan out the ideal virtual infrastructure.

2. Inventory and assess hardware, and purchase if needed.

3. Examine processes and applications to determine which are better suited for virtualization and decide which virtualization environment to use.

4. Send likely candidates to a test and dev environment for evaluation.

5. Install VM-friendly autodiscovery tools and select production hardware.

6. Install and configure automation and security software.

7. Install virtualization software on the live machine, and push VMs from test and dev to the live server via lab management software.

8. Use automation tools to begin facilitating the management of the virtual environment.

You're on your way to a virtualized infrastructure. Next, we will look at the post-deployment environment.

## CHAPTER 17

Postproduction: Wrapping It Up

As the deployment rolls out, the real day of reckoning arrives. The decisions made during the planning process will come back to haunt or help you when you go live. Theoretically, if you planned correctly, this stage is all about maintaining. Unfortunately, theory sometimes has little to do with reality, however.

The good news is that nothing is permanent. Policies can be changed, new hardware can be purchased or swapped, even virtualization environments can be changed. The bad side is that none of these things come cheap, in both monetary and other resources, and the more changes you have to make, the greater the chances for mistakes. After you're live, mistakes become costly and could result in lost revenue, if, for example, a server goes down in the integration process.

For purposes of this chapter, we'll assume a successful initial deployment in a production environment. As we said previously, however, a virtualization deployment is never truly complete in the same sense that an Exchange or SAP rollout is complete. It is highly unusual for an enterprise to virtualize its entire data center overnight, and some analysts go so far as to estimate that an end-to-end virtual infrastructure could take as long as seven years to build and roll out.

Further complicating the picture is that virtualization is rarely a straight-line endeavor. This makes determining the how and when to implement a particular tool fairly subjective, especially if one phase bleeds into another. Some of the tasks that must be done are not unique to this phase, and organizations should not wait until after the metaphorical switch has been flipped to accomplish them. The earlier in the process you begin thinking about which tools you will use and start integrating them, the smoother your deployment will be and the more effectively your infrastructure will operate.

This chapter discusses automation, autodiscovery, and security from the perspective of a virtualized environment. We also look at reprovisioning and moving VMs on-the-fly; monitoring tools, which are similar to but not synonymous with autodiscovery tools; and the importance of having in place a disaster recovery plan tailored to a virtual infrastructure.

We also address two key business concerns that were always present, but now come to the forefront: budgeting and long-term benefits, after the dramatic gains have been met. Our previous mention of monetary cost was in Chapter 15, "Laying the Foundation: The Planning Stage," where we discussed projected return on investment in relation to putting together a RFP to get the ball rolling. This chapter will again look at costs, only this time it will be in the context of budgeting.

Up and Running, Keep Things Humming

Just as discovery is critical to laying the foundation, having a monitoring system for your infrastructure is paramount. Policies should be reevaluated constantly to make sure they're still relevant and accomplishing what they set out to do. If bottlenecks are occurring somewhere in the decision-making process, the process may need revamping. The need for automation software does not go away, but its focus changes a bit. Monitoring tools, which to some degree overlap with discovery tools (and in some cases automation tools), come into play at this stage.

Dynamic Movement

One of the biggest challenges in managing the day-to-day aspects of a virtual infrastructure is knowing where everything is. Dynamic migration (the capability to move workloads from one virtual machine [VM] to another and to move VMs from one server to another) is a key selling point for virtualization. VMware calls its capability VMotion, and Microsoft and Citrix call theirs Live Migration.

It is part of what keeps a virtual infrastructure agile, and it is a key selling point, especially for organizations that have peak workload periods requiring a great deal of compute power sometimes and not so much at others. A dedicated server that meets these needs would be underutilized much of the time. Being able to move workloads from one machine to another makes for easier upgrades and hardware maintenance. It also simplifies disaster recovery efforts.

VMotion and similar programs make VM migration fairly effortless on the admin's part. The software identifies the optimal placement for a VM in seconds with a migration wizard providing real-time availability information. It can migrate multiple machines simultaneously, regardless of operating system or type of hardware and storage, including Fibre Channel SAN, NAS and iSCSI SAN, so long as VMware ESX supports it.

The inherent ease of virtualizing also complicates the picture. Chapter 16 "Deployment," talked about how easy it is to flip the switch. That ease of use does not go away and results in an infrastructure that gets more complex with time. Imagine three servers, A, B, and C. Server A is provisioned and eight VMs are running on it. Server B is provisioned into four VMs and is underutilized. Server C has not yet been provisioned. One of the VMs on Server A needs more space, which is not available on that machine. VMotion determines whether Server B or Server C is the best place for the VM. If it is Server C, it is then provisioned, the VM is migrated over, and Server A is reprovisioned because it is now running only three VMs. If Server B is more efficient, it is reprovisioned and the VM moved to there, and Server A is reprovisioned.

All this is done in the background, without requiring intervention from the administrator and without the end user seeing any sort of dip in service. This makes software upgrades much easier to schedule; it reduces planned downtime to near nil; and it minimizes unplanned downtime if systems are set to automatically failover (more on that later in this chapter).

It is not without a downside, however. Such flexibility makes it difficult for admins to know exactly where a particular application is being processed, or what is impacted if a server must be taken offline for some reason. Automation tools do an adequate job of stepping through the paces, making sure everything moves along as it should and alerting when things aren't working where they should. Where they often fall down, however, is in identifying and determining the connectedness of infrastructure components.

Monitoring Tools

This is where monitoring tools come in. Unlike autodiscovery tools, which search out what you have, monitoring tools determine that everything is working as it should. They let you know which apps are running where. Often, monitoring tools work in coordination with automation tools, and in some cases the functionality overlaps. Semantics also come into play, as capabilities that one product attributes to monitoring fall under autodiscovery or automation in another vendor's wares. It is not surprising, therefore, that the leading monitoring tools are actually modules in larger software suites. In the vast majority of cases, they were not designed specifically for virtualization infrastructures, yet that functionality has been added in recent versions. BMC's Performance Manager Suite, HP's Data Center Automation

Center, and IBM's Tivoli Monitoring suite all offer end-to-end solutions. Independent players in the mix include Uptime Software and Vizioncore.

Monitoring tools keep an eye on three basic functions: server operations, server traffic, and the results of server use (for example, keeping logs, statistics, and analysis). Drilling down further, monitoring tools make sure the physical hardware is operating as it should (temperature, power supply and components); server performance (CPU usage, available disk space, memory availability, and in some cases VMs) is as intended; services (DNS, POP3, and TCP) are operational; and network functions are operating how they are supposed to.

Not surprisingly, all the major OEMs offer monitoring tools. Although these tools by and large are comprehensive, they are limited to the OEM's hardware. Therefore, an enterprise with a heterogonous data center (which is to say pretty much any data center) will find itself somewhat constrained by these offerings, and is more likely to need to come up with a patchwork of solutions.

There are myriad tools out there, and not every tool covers every task. As in the automation and autodiscovery space, if you have a suite that meets your needs, the most cost-effective strategy will be to see if a monitoring module is in place and confirm that it has VM monitoring capabilities. If not, an updated module should be purchased. If no management suite is in place or the virtualization capabilities are not up to snuff for your needs, consider standalone products that hook into your management suite.

The chief advantage of adding a monitoring tool to the mix is that it can cut to the heart of the problem, instead of addressing the symptoms. For example, if a cable is unplugged in the data center, an automation tool is likely to flag that a data transfer was unable to be completed, whereas a monitoring tool will either flag a server as down or alert the admin that the cable is down.

Organizations on a tight budget may find themselves forced to choose between autodiscovery, automation, and monitoring tools. In many cases, the monitoring tool is the most critical, because at least minimal autodiscovery and automation functionality can be found in the virtualization environment itself. Even the small data centers that can get by without automation and have a solid understanding of their resources need to know when a server or other device in the data center goes down.

Which brings us to the next postdeployment issue: disaster recovery.

DISASTER RECOVERY

Improved disaster recovery is an oft-cited reason for virtualizing. From a big picture perspective, it makes sense: A VM goes down and the application and data fails over to another VM, either on the same box or to another server on the network. In fact, having a VM fail over to another VM is a perfectly acceptable solution and is the tip of the iceberg as far as options (and advantages) go. In addition to VM to VM failover, there is physical to virtual failover (a box goes down and the entire box fails over to a VM on another server) and virtual to physical (a VM goes down and fails over to a dedicated box).

This is a fairly easy way to achieve the high availability that network managers crave and for the most part require. However, to really reap the advantages and to have the sought-after reliability, bear two things in mind. First, the same redundancy that is in place for physical servers must also be in place for VMs, and second, if you opt to fail over to another box, that box must be the same caliber as the original.

The latter is particularly critical in situations where the hardware goes down. Although virtualization does not alter the inherent principles of disaster recovery, it does place more eggs in fewer baskets, so an effective strategy means the baskets must be more cushioned and locked down. Suppose, for example, a NIC fails on a server running 16 VMs. Now, instead of one server being down, the equivalent of 16 servers have gone down. When drawing up your disaster recovery plans, you must think in terms of protecting 16 servers, not one, which means the box that you plan to fail over to must be as capable of handling each of the 16 VMs as the one that went down.

Thus, when you reach the point that important, if not mission-critical, applications are running on VMs, it is vital to consider each VM the equivalent of a dedicated box for disaster recovery purposes.

Disaster recovery touches on a number of areas previously covered, mainly related to storage. Backup, automation, and monitoring all play into your disaster recovery plan. These tools will by and large determine the plan that is put in place, so it is important to be somewhat cognizant of the plan you ultimately want when you are picking these tools. How redundant your systems are or how retrievable your backup is makes a difference in your uptime.

At this point, nearly every standard disaster recovery tool accommodates virtualization, but it is important to ensure you are also getting the end-to-end protection you need, and a number of vendors have stepped in to fill the gap between what the traditional storage and security vendors offer and the unique needs of VMs. Those differences are primarily their portability (that is, VMotion's capability to move a VM from one box to another) and inherent sprawl, which can make backing up each VM somewhat inefficient.

A number of solutions have sprouted up to mitigate this issue. "Snapshotting" appears to be evolving into the technology of choice. Snapshotting technology does exactly what its name implies—it takes a snapshot of a data set at a particular point in time that can be used, if needed to restore it down the road. It is replication-based technology that consumes minimal overhead regardless of whether it is performed at the hardware, application, or system level.

Snapshotting is available within all three environments, but without some sort of intelligent agent, using it is by and large a manual process. For a simple deployment with minimal VM movement, it may suffice, but for most enterprises, it will not be enough.

For enterprises that cannot afford downtime, the pool of solutions is growing, albeit not as quickly as resolutions for other pain points. Among the more sophisticated solutions is Symantec's NetBackup, which incorporates snapshotting and goes one step further. NetBackup uses Symantec's Granular Recovery Technology on a single snapshot. An admin involved in a recovery can then peek inside the snapshot to find the needed file or directly pull out the missing piece.

Double-Take Software is another vendor offering a disaster recovery solution for a virtual environment. Its products focus on workload optimization to move workloads more easily between the physical and the virtual. Double-Take for Virtual Systems is designed specifically with VMs in mind. It uses shapshotting to provide continuous data protection. It can fail VMs over to another physical host within minutes. Protection is available from the host operating system, thus covering all the virtual systems on a server, or the guest operating systems, and protecting each as though it were a physical server. Another Double-Take offering, DoubleTake Move, helps facilitate the initial migration into the virtual from physical, as well as moves from the virtual to physical. The goal is easier back up and recovery, higher workload availability, and the capability to more flexibly run workloads.

Snapshotting is not the only disaster recovery option. Marathon Technologies has taken a completely different approach with its solution. everRun VM is integrated with XenServer Enterprise Edition and Hyper-V. The application itself functions transparently. It uses automation to ensure availability during the setup and configuration stages, including automating fault tolerance and policy management. It also provides availability protection for each VM as appropriate and application independence so that Windows applications are supported without requiring modification.

Related to disaster recovery is security. We discussed security in the previous chapter, but it bears repeating that just as you must think of a VM as the equivalent of a server for disaster recovery purposes, so too must you think of it that way for security purposes.

BUDGETING

With enterprises increasingly cost conscious, money is typically the first thing that springs to mind when the word "budget" enters the conversation. Chapter 15 looked at the importance of ROI to win over senior management. Thinking about costs does not end there, however. It is just as important to have an understanding of the ongoing costs associated with virtualization as it is to know the upfront ones. In addition, although many of the heavy upfront costs that come with virtualizing are a one-time occurrence, for the most part, the big gains that come from picking the low-hanging fruits can be harvested only once.

The ongoing costs of virtualization are typical IT costs (for example power and cooling, and licensing). Unfortunately, because of the nature of virtualization, attributing these costs to a department gets dicey. Short of measuring compute units in very small time increments, there are few options at this time to directly attribute them. VMware's recently released vCenter Chargeback is a major step toward resolving this thorny issue. Chargeback uses an algorithm that takes into account multiple factors, such as cost-based models and fixed costs, and maps them to data center resources, which it then applies across cost centers. For IT shops committed to vCenter and a VMware infrastructure it is a viable option. In general, however, these are not identifiable costs that can be segregated to a department or cost center. The clearest and most effective way to break them down is to treat them as centralized overhead (also known as an indirect cost) of the business.

A new and separate cost center within the general IT budget should be created to house all virtualization costs incurred. We'll refer to it here as Virtual Cost Center. Part of the costs should be capitalized and depreciated over the life of the servers (generally a five year time frame, although equipment often is kept in use far longer), whereas other costs should be expensed. As these expenses are incurred, they would be expensed directly in the Virtual Cost Center.

Costs associated with the Virtual Cost Center can then be pushed down to individual departments through a weighted average based on compute usage. High-volume storage areas, like finance, should receive a heavier weight than a manufacturing plant, for example.

One cost to keep an eye on is that of licenses. With the exception of virtual appliances, none of the ISVs seem to have come up with a way to price their wares. For the most part, pricing remains per-node or per-CPU. As VMs become more and more prevalent, you can expect that to change. In fact, Microsoft Windows and Red Hat Enterprise Linux already have pricing specific to virtualized environments. For cost allocation purposes, this will make things easier.

The accounting department, particularly the budgeting group, should be brought into the conversation to have an understanding of how the calculations are being set and to ensure the methodology conforms to current regulations and accounting bylaws.

In terms of billing and allocating human resource costs, you can either bill all activity to the Virtual Cost Center and allocate from within, or require employees to keep time sheets on what they are working on and bill departments directly, with tasks not related to specific departments being billed to Virtual Cost Center.

FINAL THOUGHTS

Although much has been written about the long-term benefits of virtualization, little is actually known. Although virtualization has a long history in concept, x86 virtualization is relatively new on the scene, and despite what the vendors claim, deep production deployments remain the exception.

At this point, the majority of long-term benefits fall either into the soft benefits category—a more agile enterprise—or the difficult, if not impossible to quantify— longer hardware life cycles, shorter maintenance windows, and improved disaster recovery and high availability (assuming everything is put into place properly).

Virtualization has been labeled a "disruptive" technology, which gives it a double burden to bear: The inherent nature of its disruptiveness means an overhauled infrastructure—never an easy sell—but at the same time, because it is changing the model, no one actually knows what the future holds. Is cloud computing the next face of virtualization? Where will wireless devices come into play? Will anyone care about the operating system five years from now, or will we be building data centers based around hypervisor choice—or will the hypervisor cease to matter as well?

Even the best-planned infrastructure will need to grapple with the answers to these questions as they unfold. It is important, therefore, that enterprises remain flexible and willing to adapt to changing trends to best meet end user and ultimately customer needs.

At the time of this writing, there has also yet to be a serious breach. With more and more enterprises virtualizing for the initial cost savings, we're due to hear of some headaches. It's only a matter of time before the inappropriate use of hardware or the incorrect applications virtualized comes home to roost. VM sprawl is an issue for even the best planned deployment. Now consider a not-so-well planned one, and the threat is even bigger.

As we've noted repeatedly, proper planning and management remains the antidote to this. Multiple tools are available to facilitate this. Although making use of them will facilitate a sound infrastructure, ultimately, it is people behind the processes setting, tweaking, and retweaking that enable the desired result.

Virtual Machine Installation

Each of the virtualization technology overview chapters in Part I recommended that you "Refer to Appendix." This is where those chapters continue—with the virtual machine (VM) installation. The appendix refers to the installation of Debian 4, a specific Linux distribution; it is generic and refers to the installation of any operating system.

We're including this appendix to demonstrate that after you've created your VM, the installation of the operating system into that VM is no different from installing an operating system onto a physical machine. The only notable difference is that some operating systems are "smart" enough to detect that the disk they're using is virtual (as you'll see in Figure A-10).

PREINSTALLATION CONSIDERATIONS

Chapters 3 through 8 explain how to use an ISO image or CD/DVD disk to boot a new VM and begin installation. Thus, if you haven't already done so, set up your VM to boot to an ISO image or from a CD/DVD, and power on the VM.

From here, getting started is fairly straightforward.

1. Figure A-1 shows the initial Debian 4 boot screen. To get the installation started, you simply press the Enter key.
2. You'll then see the screen depicted in Figure A-2, which is the language prompt for installing and using the Debian distribution. Select your preferred language, and press Enter to continue.
3. You are asked to select your location, as shown in Figure A-3. Use the keyboard's arrow keys and press Enter to continue.

FIGURE A-1 The Debian 4 ISO initial boot screen.

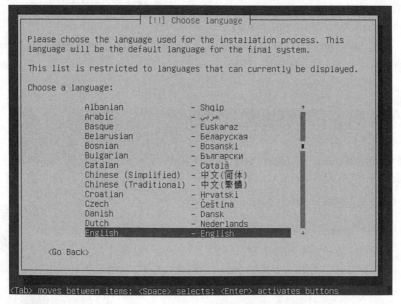

FIGURE A-2 Selecting your preferred language.

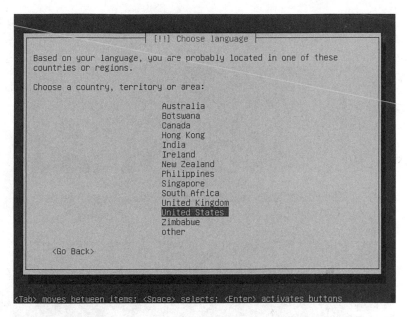

FIGURE A-3   Selecting your location.

4. Select your keyboard layout, as shown in Figure A-4, and press Enter.

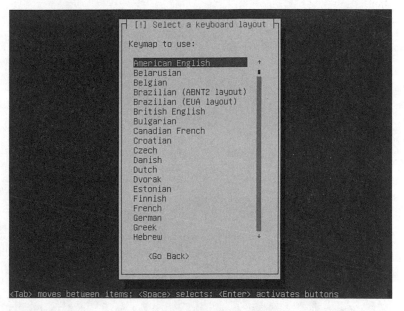

FIGURE A-4   Selecting a keyboard layout.

5. The installation begins with the screen shown in Figure A-5 followed by the screen shown in Figure A-6.

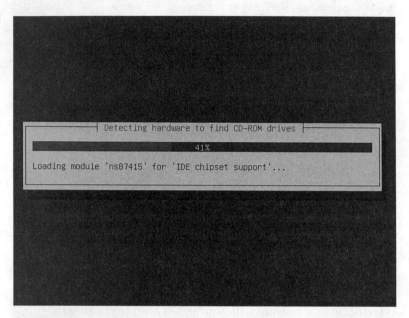

FIGURE A-5   The detecting hardware screen.

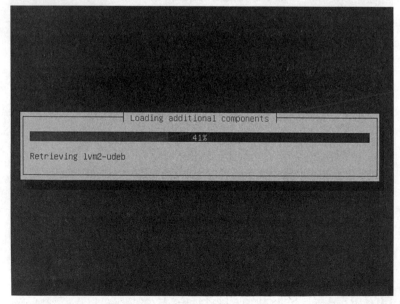

FIGURE A-6   Preparing for installation.

6. You will be taken to the screen shown in Figure A-7. Input the computer (host) name. Press Enter to continue.

7. The Debian installer attempts to detect your domain from DNS. If successful, you'll see it and need to confirm it in the screen shown in Figure A-8. Press Enter to continue.

```
┌─────────────────┤ [!] Configure the network ├─────────────────┐
│                                                                │
│ Please enter the hostname for this system.                     │
│                                                                │
│ The hostname is a single word that identifies your system to the │
│ network. If you don't know what your hostname should be, consult your │
│ network administrator. If you are setting up your own home network, │
│ you can make something up here.                                │
│                                                                │
│ Hostname:                                                      │
│                                                                │
│ debian                                                         │
│                                                                │
│     <Go Back>                                      <Continue>  │
│                                                                │
└────────────────────────────────────────────────────────────────┘

<Tab> moves between items; <Space> selects; <Enter> activates buttons
```

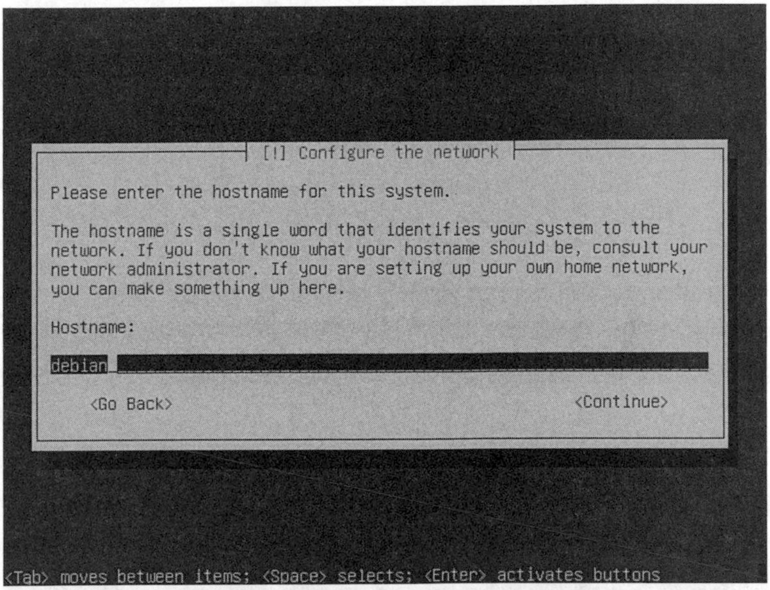

FIGURE A-7   Entering the hostname.

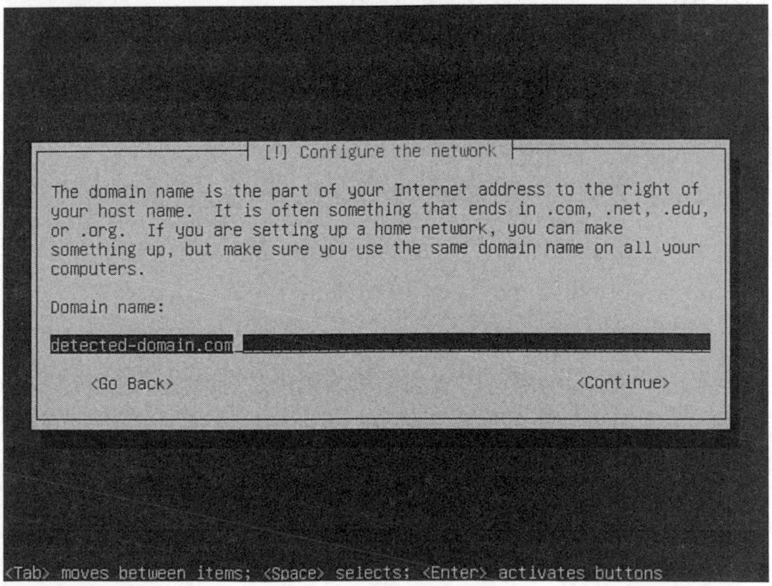

```
┌─────────────────┤ [!] Configure the network ├─────────────────┐
│                                                                │
│ The domain name is the part of your Internet address to the right of │
│ your host name.  It is often something that ends in .com, .net, .edu, │
│ or .org.  If you are setting up a home network, you can make    │
│ something up, but make sure you use the same domain name on all your │
│ computers.                                                     │
│                                                                │
│ Domain name:                                                   │
│                                                                │
│ detected-domain.com                                            │
│                                                                │
│     <Go Back>                                      <Continue>  │
│                                                                │
└────────────────────────────────────────────────────────────────┘

<Tab> moves between items; <Space> selects; <Enter> activates buttons
```

FIGURE A-8   Entering the computer's domain name.

PREPARING TO INSTALL YOUR VMS

Now you're almost ready to install your VMs. The next few screens involve setting up the VM's disk drive for installation. Figure A-9 shows the first of these. This screen offers multiple options. Use the arrow keys to select an option and press Enter to continue.

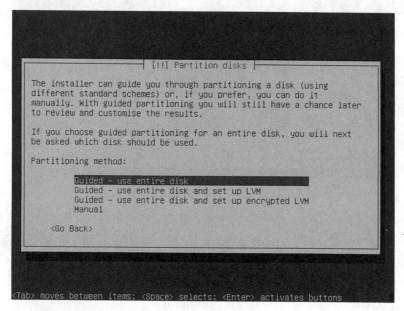

FIGURE A-9   Setting up the VM's disk.

1. Select the disk(s), as shown in Figure A-10, on which to install Debian, and press Enter.

2. Select the disk's filesystem layout on the screen shown in Figure A-11.

3. You'll be prompted to continue with your disk and filesystem choices or to go back and edit them, as Figure A-12 shows. Press Enter to continue with the currently displayed configuration.

4. The final screen (Figure A-13) in this disk and filesystem series prompts you to confirm the permanent changes about to be made to the disk. Select Yes and press Enter to continue. Note that the installer has added a swap partition; its size is determined by the amount of RAM allocated to the VM.

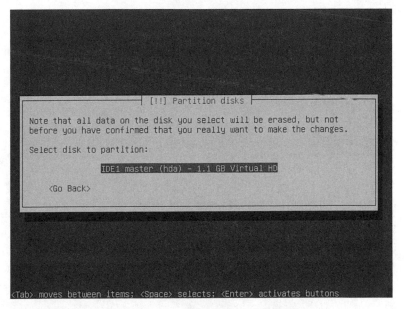

FIGURE A-10   Selecting disks for the new VM.

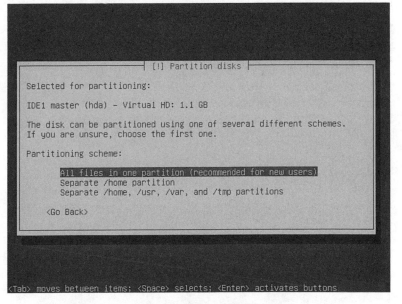

FIGURE A-11   Selecting the filesystem layout.

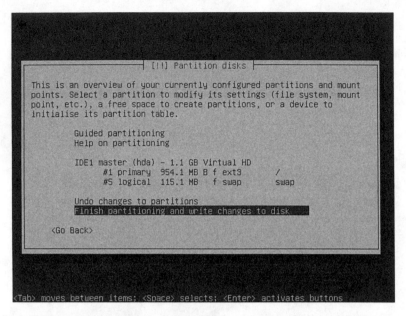

FIGURE A-12 Proceeding with the current disk and filesystem layout.

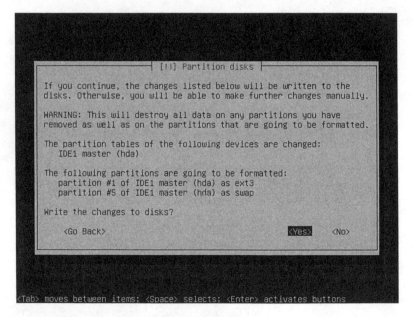

FIGURE A-13 Confirming changes.

5. Use your arrow keys to select your VM's time zone, as shown in Figure A-14, and press Enter to continue.

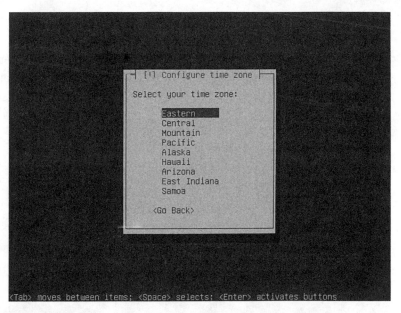

FIGURE A-14   Selecting the time zone.

SETTING A PASSWORD

Now it's time to set up a password.

1. Input the root (Administrator) password for your VM and press Enter to continue (see Figure A-15).

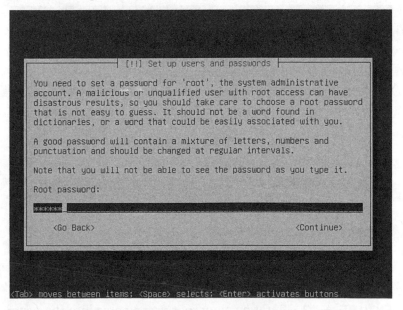

FIGURE A-15   Entering the root password.

2. Input the root password again (Figure A-16) to confirm that you've typed it correctly. Press Enter to continue.

3. The next screen, as shown in Figure A-17, prompts you to enter a nonroot user's proper name into the system. Enter the user's full name and press Enter when finished.

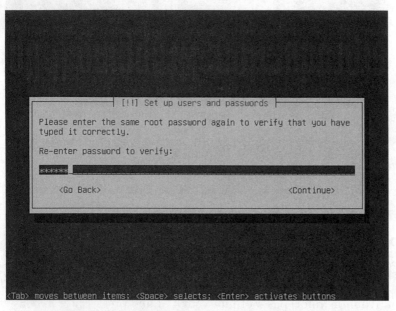

FIGURE A-16   Reentering the root password.

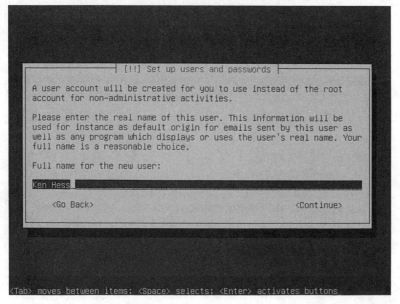

FIGURE A-17   Entering a nonroot user's name into the system.

4. Enter the new user's username into the system. This is the name that the user enters when connecting to the new system via SSH or at the console to login. See Figure A-18.

5. Enter a password for the new user, as shown in Figure A-19, and press Enter to continue.

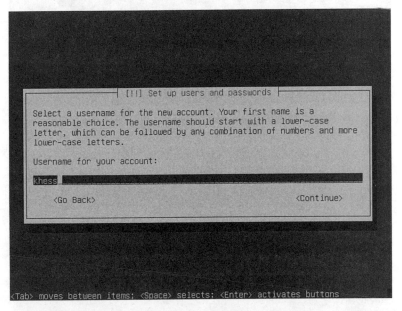

FIGURE A-18   Entering the new user's username.

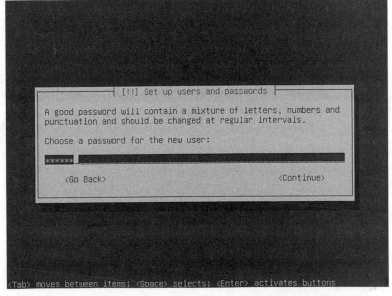

FIGURE A-19   Entering a password for the new user.

6. Enter the user's password again to verify it (see Figure A-20). Press Enter when it's complete.

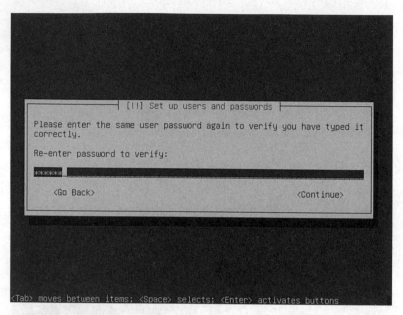

FIGURE A-20 Reentering the user's password for verification.

OPERATING SYSTEM INSTALLATION

Next up is the installation of the operating system, the beginning of which is depicted in Figure A-21. This procedure will take from several minutes to more than an hour, depending on the hardware and the VM's properties.

1. The installation prompts you (Figure A-22) to use a network mirror for updating your system during and after installation. Always choose Yes to this, unless your system isn't connected to a network during installation.

2. Select the country from which you'd like to use a mirror (see Figure A-23) and press Enter.

3. Select the mirror you'd like to use for your updates, as shown in Figure A-24, using your arrow keys. Press Enter to continue.

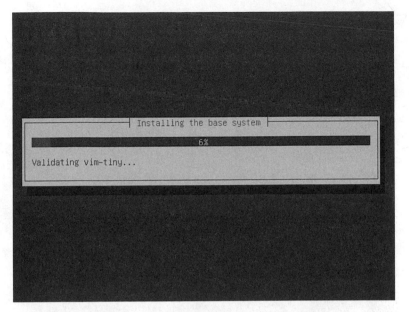

FIGURE A-21   Installation begins for the new VM.

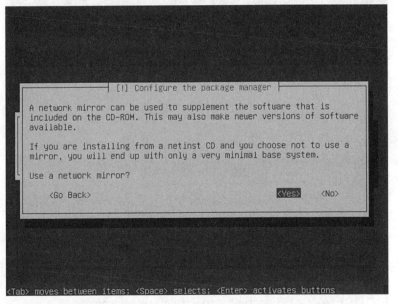

FIGURE A-22   Confirming the choice to use a network mirror.

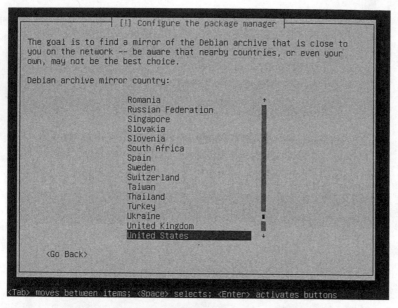

FIGURE A-23 Selecting a network mirror source country.

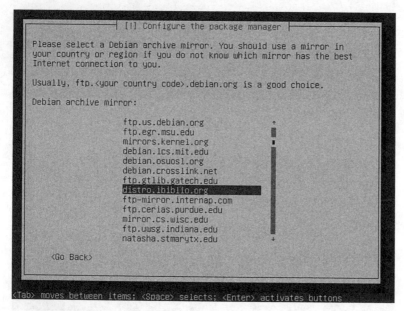

FIGURE A-24 Selecting a specific network mirror.

4. As shown in Figure A-25, enter a HTTP proxy, if any, that you'll need to connect from your VM to the Internet for updates. Press Enter.

5. Figure A-26 shows a prompt to participate in a Debian distribution survey. Select Yes or No, and then press Enter to continue.

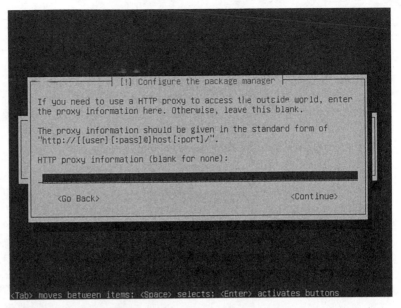

FIGURE A-25   Entering HTTP proxy information.

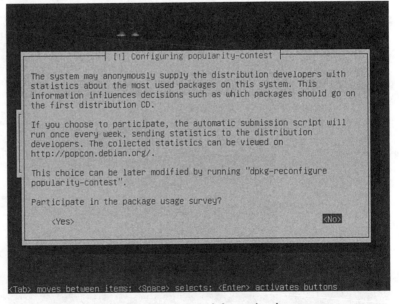

FIGURE A-26   Selecting to participate in the usage survey.

6. Select the type of system you want to configure, as shown in Figure A-27, and press Enter to continue. Use the arrow keys and space bar to select.

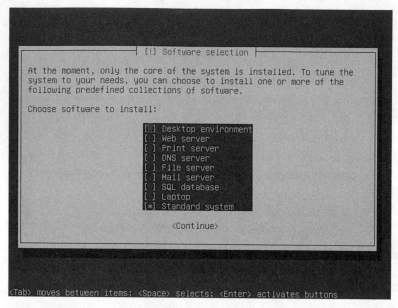

FIGURE A-27   Selecting the type of system to install.

7. The installation proceeds to completion, which might take from a few minutes to an hour or more. The progress bar will move as the installation progresses, as shown in Figure A-28.

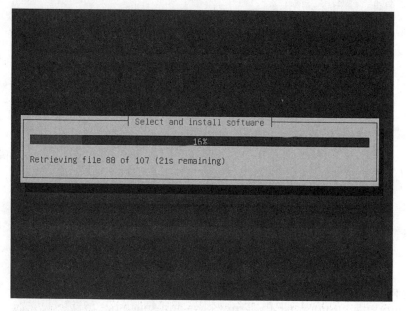

FIGURE A-28   Installing the operating system.

8. When the installation completes, you will be asked whether you want to install GRUB (the bootloader) to the Master Boot Record on the virtual disk (see Figure A-29). Select Yes and press Enter to continue.

9. You are then taken to the final screen (shown in Figure A-30) prior to a system reboot and subsequent login prompt. Press Enter to continue.

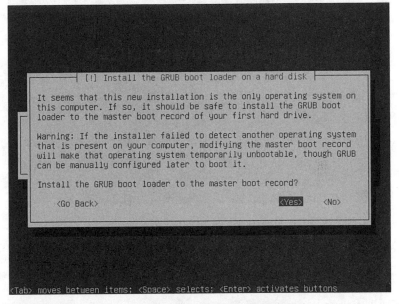

FIGURE A-29   Installing the GRUB boot loader.

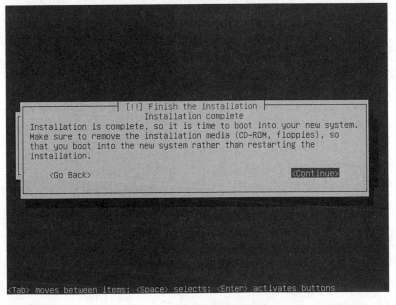

FIGURE A-30   Finishing the installation.

10. Your new Debian VM is ready for you to login as shown in Figure A-31.

The VM is now fully installed and operational.

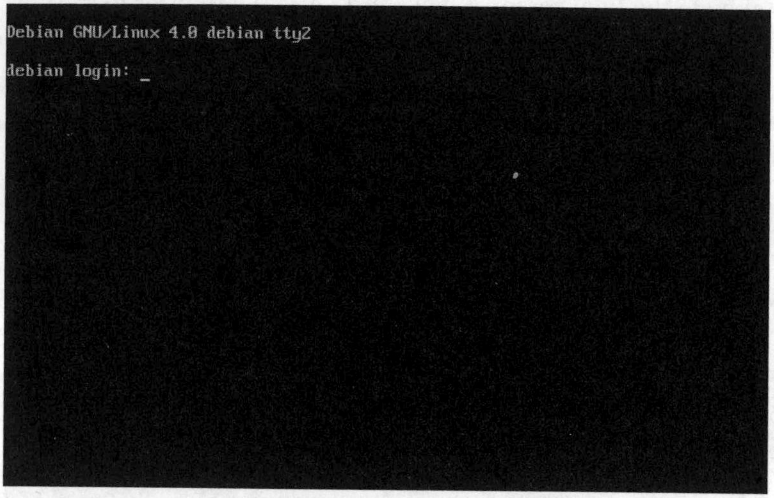

```
Debian GNU/Linux 4.0 debian tty2

debian login: _
```

FIGURE A-31   The new VM prompting for login.

Index

Also Available in the Negus Software Solutions Series

Google Apps Deciphered
Compute in the Cloud to Streamline Your Desktop
Scott Granneman | 0137004702 | ©2008

The First Comprehensive Guide to Deploying, Customizing, Securing, and Extending Google Apps in Any Organization!

Say goodbye to old-fashioned "shrinkwrapped" software—use Google Apps and save a fortune! *Google Apps Deciphered* covers gmail, IM, Calendar, Chat, Contacts, Google Docs office productivity software, and much more. Scott Granneman brings together brand-new information on successfully implementing Google Apps—as well as information currently scattered across the Internet in hundreds of locations.

This book covers everything organizations and individuals need to use Google Apps to the fullest. Granneman begins by describing how Google Apps work and the growing advantages of using them. Next, he offers start-to-finish guidance on getting started with Google Apps and making them work for you. Granneman covers today's most valuable Google Apps services, from Gmail through the Google Docs office suite. He offers advanced tips and tricks for using these tools and collaborating with them; extending them; safeguarding the security of your data; migrating from other email providers and software; customizing your organization's Start Page; and much more.

The Official Damn Small® Linux® Book
The Tiny Adaptable Linux That Runs on Anything
Robert Shingledecker, John Andrews, Christopher Negus | 0132338696 | ©2008

Make the Most of Today's Smallest, Fastest Linux Distribution—Damn Small Linux!

Damn Small Linux (DSL) is a super-efficient platform for everything from custom desktops to professional servers. Now, DSL's creator and lead developer have written the first definitive, practical guide to this remarkable system. *The Official Damn Small® Linux® Book* brings together everything you need to put DSL to work in just minutes. Simply learn a few essentials, boot the live CD, and master the rest...one step at a time, hands-on.

If you're new to Linux, you can quickly discover how to use DSL to take your data on the road, safely running your programs and personal environment on nearly any computer. Easily adapt DSL to run on anything from an alternative device (Internet appliance, hand-held, diskless PC, or mini-ITX system) to an older PC that might otherwise be headed for a landfill.

Ajax Construction Kit
Building Plug-and-Play Ajax Applications
Michael Morrison | 0132350084 | ©2008

Supercharge Your Sites with Ajax Right Now...No Scripting Expertise Needed!

You've heard how great Ajax is—how it can help make your Web sites more usable, more interactive, more responsive, more successful. *Ajax Construction Kit* lets you put Ajax to work right now, even if you've never written a script! Just learn a few essentials, check out a few examples, and then run the live CD and discover all the plug-and-play code you need to hit the ground running.

Ajax Construction Kit's built-in applications work right out of the box. And with easy guidance from Michael Morrison, you'll gradually deepen your understanding—learn how to customize, extend, and reuse these applications—and even build skills for creating new ones. Walk away an expert.

Practical PHP and MySQL®
Building Eight Dynamic Web Applications
Jono Bacon | 0132239973 | ©2007

Build Dynamic Web Sites Fast, with PHP and MySQL...Learn from Eight Ready-to-Run Applications!

Suddenly, it's easy to build commercial-quality Web applications using free and open source software. With this book, you learn from eight ready-to-run, real-world applications—all backed by clear diagrams and screenshots, well-documented code, and simple, practical explanations.

Leading open source author Jono Bacon teaches the core skills you need to build virtually any application. You discover how to connect with databases, upload content, perform cascading deletes, edit records, validate registrations, specify user security, create reusable components, use PEAR extensions, and even build Ajax applications.

PRENTICE HALL

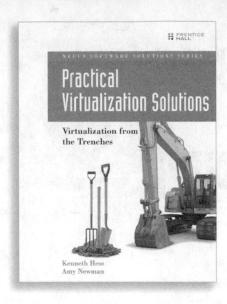

FREE Online Edition

Your purchase of *Practical Virtualization Solutions* includes access to a free online edition for 45 days through the Safari Books Online subscription service. Nearly every Prentice Hall book is available online through Safari Books Online, along with more than 5,000 other technical books and videos from publishers such as Addison-Wesley Professional, Cisco Press, Exam Cram, IBM Press, O'Reilly, Que, and Sams.

SAFARI BOOKS ONLINE allows you to search for a specific answer, cut and paste code, download chapters, and stay current with emerging technologies.

Activate your FREE Online Edition at
www.informit.com/safarifree

> **STEP 1:** Enter the coupon code: BFTXZAA.

> **STEP 2:** New Safari users, complete the brief registration form.
> Safari subscribers, just log in.

If you have difficulty registering on Safari or accessing the online edition, please e-mail customer-service@safaribooksonline.com